HIS FINEST HOURS

HIS FINEST HOURS

THE WAR SPEECHES OF
WINSTON CHURCHILL

GRAHAM STEWART

Quercus

Contents

INTRODUCTION

'In wartime', suggested Winston Churchill in one of his most famous world broadcasts, 'there is a lot to be said for the motto: "Deeds, not words."' Well did he recognize the limited punch of poetic allusion in the age of blitzkrieg and mass atrocity. No facility with words would save him – or what remained of the free world – without the physical means to back the sentiments up with action. If listeners believed his eloquence was merely the product of verbosity enhanced by long years of reading they would have dismissed it as windy rhetoric removed from reality and unworthy of their attention. They did not do so. In part, it was because the future Nobel Laureate for Literature meant what he said. Churchill, the man, really was as good as his word.

For all his privileged background, he had never flinched from hardship or danger. In the Sudan, in 1898, at the Battle of Omdurman, he had ridden in the last major cavalry charge of the British Army. The following year in South Africa he had been taken prisoner by the Boers. Rather than sit out his captivity, he escaped. Later, in the middle of the First World War, he dealt with the disappointment of his political demotion by risking all, serving in the trenches with the Royal Scots Fusiliers. His subsequent career in public life was marked by sharp reversals of fortune. Seemingly riding high in the 1920s, he was confined to the political wilderness in the 1930s. During this last decade he had been reduced to fighting with words alone. He argued the case for rearmament against the mounting dangers from Hitler's Reich. Not enough people had listened to him then. With the outbreak of the Second World War and the fear that Britain was ill-matched for the struggle, he won the right to a wider audience.

The enormity of the struggle between 1939 and 1945 underlined the seriousness of Churchill's message. But the enduring appeal of his speeches rests not just on the circumstances in which they were delivered. After all, Britain had been in danger before. But few today can recite lengthy passages of what previous prime ministers said in moments of peril. William Pitt the Younger's oratory on the eve of the Battle of Trafalgar or Lord Liverpool's observations after Napoleon escaped from Elba intrigue only the most dogged historians. Nothing the lucid mind of Herbert Asquith could come up with in 1914 is reeled out to reassure us now. More surprisingly, the same can be said of his successor, David Lloyd George, who energetically led Britain in some of the most desperate but ultimately victorious moments of the First World War. He was a brilliant and gifted orator, but his words have subsequently lost their sting. Only his somewhat hollow promise of a postwar future in which there would be homes 'fit for heroes' finds any echo in the popular consciousness.

In one respect, at least, Churchill had an advantage over some of his predecessors. The amplifications of radio broadcasting and newsreels lifted his language beyond the printed page and the live audience. This technology gave a vividness and immediacy to an anxious nation and the world beyond. There were 9 million radio wirelesses licensed in Britain in 1939, ensuring that the vast majority of the population had access to the radio directly or via friends and neighbours. By such means Churchill could reach his wider audience directly. But this was not the only reason he was listened to then or remembered subsequently. After all, microphones have not made most other politicians' words memorable.

Why, then, have Churchill's wartime exhortations so outlived their moment so that they continue to inspire today? Partly it is because their appeal resides at several levels. He tapped into a deep well of patriotic feeling. Like Shakespeare's English kings – in whose language he was steeped – Churchill delivered oratory that seemed to come from the thick of the action. His sense of history and his belief that his nation was playing a part worthy of the heroic deeds of past generations reassured anxious minds at the time and stir British hearts still. But Churchill was no narrow nationalist, no divider, no English Hitler. Except when directing his contempt against the principal fascist leaders, his speeches are noticeably devoid of hate. For the most part, his themes are expansive. As such, they retain their uplifting quality. His sympathy for Poland, his love for France and his belief that its best traditions would ultimately triumph over the dark acts of the defeatists and collaborators shine through.

He particularly felt that strong bonds held together the 'English-speaking peoples'. Already in his 27th year when Queen Victoria died in 1901, he retained a romantic belief in the unity of the British Empire and the brotherhood of its Dominions. Their wartime exertions moved him deeply. But he appealed also to the 'Great Republic' of the United States of America. In 1940 and 1941, the prospect of that country supplying and eventually coming to Britain's assistance remained the one lifeline of hope. When Churchill broadcast, he weighed how his words would be received across the Atlantic. This was no cynical exercise. With a mother who hailed from New York, he had always admired the energy of the New World. He perceived its natural inclination for freedom, democracy and individual liberty. It was because his themes were essentially generous and progressive that they struck such a chord in America.

Most of all, Churchill spoke from the heart and consequently his audience believed what he said. Although his delivery was somewhat old-fashioned it was resolute in manner and he was rarely afraid to be frank. This was important in a period otherwise marked by propaganda and restriction of information. It is true that he knew the task was to inspire and reassure as well as to warn, and he was not above putting the most optimistic spin on the news. Yet, his speeches – particularly the lengthier ones delivered first to Parliament – are noticeably rich in substance as well as style. Churchill's orations generated hope because he inspired trust. Unlike later public performers, he needed no speech writers. According to John Colville, his assistant private secretary during the war years, 'he never to my knowledge spoke words not his own in a political speech delivered as prime minister'.

It is impossible to calculate the contribution Churchill's speeches made to the Second World War. Moral authority and psychological effect cannot be weighed. But there is ample testimony from those who read or heard them at the time that they played a vital part in stiffening morale on the home front and enhancing Britain's – and ultimately the Allies – cause before the wider world. Indeed, those who lived through that war seldom forget the effect his speeches had, and millions of those born afterwards have difficulty conjuring the period without his more stirring phrases coming to mind. Ultimately, it is hard to improve upon Edward R. Murrow's verdict that Churchill 'mobilized the English language and sent it into battle'.

'A hush over all Europe'

Broadcast to the American people, 8 August 1939

On the likelihood of war

When Winston Churchill came to the microphone on 8 August 1939 to warn the American people that the coming holiday season might be the moment Europe was plunged into war he could not be certain of an appreciative audience. True, he had – long ago – been a major figure in British governments. He had been First Lord of the Admiralty during the First World War until forced out after he backed the misconceived campaign against the Turks in the Dardanelles. Surviving a spell serving in the Western Front's trenches, he had bounced back, rising to the post of chancellor of the exchequer between 1924 and 1929. But by the summer of 1939 he had not held office for a decade.

During these long 'wilderness years', he sat on the backbenches as a Conservative Member of Parliament. From there, he frequently voiced eloquent but impotent criticism of his own party in government for its inadequate spending on defence and its appeasement of Adolf Hitler. It was a frustrating time for him. In the two and a half years leading up to the outbreak of war in September 1939, Churchill was able only to make radio broadcasts on foreign policy to the American public. At home, the BBC – which then enjoyed a monopoly of the airwaves – failed to offer him a microphone at any stage during this critical period. Britons had to make do with what they read in the newspapers.

Yet, for all his isolation, Churchill did have a claim on the public's attention. Hitler had begun to make his prophesies come horrifyingly true. Initially, there had always been excuses for the German Führer's aggressive methods. Against the terms of the Treaty of Versailles, he had remilitarized the Rhineland, but he could protest he was only moving soldiers into a part of his own country. He had unified Austria with Germany, and many Austrians appeared content with the change. In September 1938, Hitler's determination to bring the German-speaking areas of Czechoslovakia into his Reich had almost led to a European war. But at Munich he had convinced the British and French governments to let him proceed on the understanding he would be reasonable in future. Neville Chamberlain, the British prime minister, had declared that the resulting Anglo-German understanding meant 'peace for our time'. Six months later, in March 1939, it was clear Chamberlain had been duped when Germany invaded the rest of Czechoslovakia. Scrambling to retrieve the situation, Britain issued a hasty pledge to defend Poland if Germany attacked her. With the onset of summer, just such a possibility seemed imminent.

On 2 August, Neville Chamberlain used his huge majority in the House of Commons to reject Churchill's appeal that Parliament

ON THIS DAY
8 AUGUST 1939

• Germany sabre-rattles against Poland in their fractious dispute over the Free City of Danzig and the so-called 'Polish Corridor' of land that separates East Prussia from the rest of Germany.

• Italy's fascist leader Benito Mussolini and his foreign minister continue their attempts to dissuade Hitler from attacking Poland, as a wider war would then become inevitable.

• A *New York Times* headline claims that the 'Japanese Emperor Will Oppose Any Attempt at War with Britain'.

should not – as proposed – disband for the summer recess until October. One Cabinet minister, Sir Thomas Inskip, who had until recently been minister for defence coordination, even went so far as to assure his fellow legislators, 'War today is not only not inevitable but is unlikely. The government have good reason for saying that.'

In need of a break, Chamberlain departed for the peace and quiet introspection of his favourite pastime, taking his fishing rods to the banks of a Scottish river. Churchill, however, was not in holiday mood. The week after he broadcast his warning to the United States, he accepted the invitation of the French General Staff to tour its fortifications along the Maginot Line. After lunch with General Gamelin, he was driven to the border with Germany. Behind him, on the French side, a great hoarding faced Germany with the motto *Liberté, Egalité, Fraternité*. It was answered from the German side with another banner proclaiming *Ein Volk! Ein Reich! Ein Führer!*

As for the Führer himself, he was surveying the Bavarian countryside below from his retreat, the Berghof, dramatically positioned high on the mountainside of the Obersalzberg. Churchill's fears were well founded. Hitler was indeed intending to invade Poland. But he was also planning a quick diplomatic triumph first, something that would astonish the world.

Holiday time, ladies and gentlemen! Holiday time, my friends across the Atlantic! Holiday time, when the summer calls the toilers of all countries for an all-too-brief spell from the offices and mills and stiff routine of daily life and bread-winning, and sends them to seek if not rest at least change in new surroundings, to return refreshed and keep the myriad wheels of civilized society on the move.

Let me look back, let me see. How did we spend our summer holidays twenty-five years ago? Why, those were the very days when the German advance guards were breaking into Belgium and trampling down its people on their march towards Paris! Those were the days when Prussian militarism was – to quote its own phrase – 'hacking its way through the small, weak, neighbour country' whose neutrality and independence they had sworn not merely to respect but to defend.

'Such is history as it is taught in topsy-turvydom'

But perhaps we are wrong. Perhaps our memory deceives us. Dr Goebbels and his propaganda machine have their own version of what happened twenty-five years ago. To hear them talk, you would suppose that it was Belgium that invaded Germany! There they were, these peaceful Prussians, gathering in their harvests, when this wicked Belgium – set on by England and the Jews – fell upon them; and would no doubt have taken Berlin, if Corporal Adolf Hitler had not come to the rescue and turned the tables. Indeed the tale goes farther. After four years of war by land and sea, when Germany was about to win an overwhelming victory, the Jews got at them again, this time from the rear. Armed with President Wilson's Fourteen Points they stabbed, we are told, the German armies in the back, and induced them to ask for an armistice, and even persuaded them, in an unguarded moment, to sign a paper saying that it was they and not the Belgians who had been the ones to begin the war. Such is history as it is taught in topsy-turvydom.

'There is a hush over all Europe'

And now it is holiday again, and where are we now? Or as you sometimes ask in the United States – where do we go from here? There is a hush over all Europe, nay, over all the world, broken only by the dull thud of Japanese bombs falling on Chinese cities, on Chinese universities or near British and American ships. But then China is a long way off, so why worry? The Chinese are fighting for what the founders of the American Constitution in their stately language called: 'Life, liberty, and the pursuit of happiness'. And they seem to be fighting very well. Many good judges think they are going to win. Anyhow, let's wish them luck! Let's give them a wave of encouragement – like your president did last week, when he gave notice about ending the commercial treaty. After all, the suffering Chinese are fighting our battle – the battle of democracy. They are defending the soil, the good earth, that has been theirs since the dawn of time against cruel and unprovoked aggression. Give them a cheer across the ocean – no one knows whose turn it may be next. If this habit of military dictatorships' breaking into other people's lands with bomb and shell and bullet, stealing the property and killing the proprietors, spreads too widely, we may none of us be able to think of summer holidays for quite a while.

But to come back to the hush I said was hanging over Europe. What kind of a hush is it? Alas! it is the hush of suspense, and in many lands it is the hush of fear. Listen! No, listen carefully; I think I hear something – yes, there it was quite clear. Don't you hear it? It is the tramp of armies crunching the gravel of the parade-grounds, splashing through rain-soaked fields, the tramp of 2,000,000 German soldiers and more than 1,000,000 Italians 'going on manoeuvres', yes, only on manoeuvres! Of course it's only manoeuvres – just like last year. After all, the dictators must train their soldiers. They could scarcely do less in common prudence, when the Danes, the Dutch, the Swiss, the Albanians – and of course the Jews – may leap out upon them at any moment and rob them of their living-space, and make them sign another paper to say who began it. Besides these German and Italian armies may have another work of liberation to perform. It was only last year they liberated Austria from the horrors of self-government. It was only in March they freed the Czechoslovak Republic from the misery of independent existence. It is only two years ago that Signor Mussolini gave the ancient kingdom of Abyssinia its Magna Charta. It is only two months ago that little Albania got its writ of Habeas Corpus, and Mussolini sent in his Bill of Rights for King Zog to pay. Why even at this moment, the mountaineers of the Tyrol, a German-speaking population who have dwelt in their beautiful valleys for a thousand years, are being liberated, that is to say, uprooted, from the land they love, from the soil which Andreas Hofer died to defend. No wonder the armies are tramping on when there is so much liberation to be done, and no wonder there is a hush among all the neighbours of Germany and Italy while they are wondering which one is going to be 'liberated' next.

The Nazis say that they are being encircled. They have encircled themselves with a ring of neighbours who have to keep on guessing who will be struck down next. This kind of guesswork is a very tiring game. Countries, especially small countries, have long ceased to find it amusing. Can you wonder that the neighbours of Germany, both great and small, have begun to think of stopping the game, by simply saying to the Nazis on the principle of the Covenant of the League of Nations: 'He who attacks any, attacks all. He who attacks the weakest will find he has attacked the strongest.' That is how we are spending our holiday over here, in poor weather, in a lot of clouds. We hope it is better with you.

'In Germany, on a mountain peak, there sits one man, who in a single day . . . can plunge all that we have and are into a volcano of smoke and flame'

One thing that has struck me as very strange, and that is the resurgence of the one-man power after all these centuries of experience and progress. It is curious how the English-speaking peoples have always had this horror of one-man power. They are quite ready to follow a leader for a time, as long as he is serviceable to them, but the idea of handing themselves over, lock, stock and barrel, body and soul, to one man, and worshipping him as if he were an idol; that has always been odious to the whole theme and nature of our civilization. The architects of the American constitution were as careful as those who shaped the British constitution, to guard against the whole life and fortunes, and all the laws and freedom of the nation, being placed in the hands of a tyrant. Checks and counter-checks in the body politic, large devolutions of state government, instruments and processes of free debate, frequent recurrence to first principles, the right of opposition to the most powerful governments, and above all ceaseless vigilance, have preserved, and will preserve, the broad characteristics of British and American institutions. But in Germany, on a mountain peak, there sits one man, who in a single day can release the world from the fear which now oppresses it; or, in a single day can plunge all that we have and are into a volcano of smoke and flame.

'If Herr Hitler does not make war, there will be no war'

If Herr Hitler does not make war, there will be no war. No one else is going to make war. Britain and France are determined to shed no blood except in self-defence or in defence of their allies. No one has ever dreamed of attacking Germany. If Germany desires to be reassured against attack by her neighbours, she has only to say the word and we will give her the fullest guarantees in accordance with the principles of the Covenant of the League. We have said repeatedly we ask nothing for ourselves in the way of security that we are not willing freely to share with the German people. Therefore if war should come there can be no doubt upon whose head the blood-guiltiness will fall. Thus lies the great issue at this moment, and none can tell how it will be settled.

It is not, believe me, my American friends, from any ignoble shrinking from pain and death that the British and French peoples pray for peace. It is not because we have any doubts how a struggle between Nazi Germany and the civilized world would ultimately end, that we pray tonight and every night for peace. But whether it be peace or war; peace with its broadening and brightening prosperity, now within our reach; or war with its measureless carnage and destruction, we must strive to frame some system of human relations in the future, which will bring to an end this prolonged hideous uncertainty, which will let the working and creative forces of the world get on with their job, and which will no longer leave the whole life of mankind dependent upon the virtues, the caprice, or the wickedness of a single man.

**'Our consciences
are at rest'**

House of Commons, London, 3 September 1939

On entering the fight against
Nazi 'pestilence'

On 24 August 1939, Hitler pulled off the diplomatic initiative the rest of the world least expected. Disregarding the ideological differences between fascism and communism and all the bitter invectives traded between them, the Nazi foreign minister, Joachim von Ribbentrop, signed a treaty in Moscow with his Soviet counterpart, Vyacheslav Molotov. This cynical non-aggression pact boded ill for Poland, the country wedged uncomfortably inbetween. In a secret clause, Germany and the Soviet Union agreed to carve her up between themselves.

The government in Warsaw did not have long to wait for the first blow to fall. On 1 September, Germany launched a full-scale invasion. During the course of the next two days, while the Poles offered desperate resistance, the clamour mounted in London for Neville Chamberlain's government to honour its pledge to stand by Poland if she were attacked. When Germany refused appeals to withdraw, and facing a major Parliamentary rebellion if he prevaricated further, Chamberlain sadly bowed to the inevitable and ended his long toil for appeasement. At 11.15am, on 3 September, Britain declared war on Germany. France followed suit at 5pm.

One of Chamberlain's first actions was to create a new War Cabinet. The clearest signal that Britain was finally in earnest was the appointment of Churchill to this body with the post of First Lord of the Admiralty. As had been the case at the outbreak of the First World War 25 years earlier, Churchill would again have responsibility for Britain's guard and lifeline, the Royal Navy. He was 64 years old, but appeared to have all the necessary stamina for the challenge.

> ## ON THIS DAY
> ### 3 SEPTEMBER 1939
>
> • Thousands of British children from cities at risk of aerial attack are on the move, being evacuated to regional towns before dispersal to rural destinations. Pregnant women and mothers of babies and toddlers leave too.
>
> • A French plane sighted south of London accidentally provokes the first British air-raid warning of the war.
>
> • Anthony Eden, also a firm opponent of appeasement, joins the War Cabinet with Churchill, as Secretary of the Dominions.

'Our consciences are at rest'

In this solemn hour it is a consolation to recall and to dwell upon our repeated efforts for peace. All have been ill-starred, but all have been faithful and sincere. This is of the highest moral value – and not only moral value, but practical value – at the present time, because the wholehearted concurrence of scores of millions of men and women, whose cooperation is indispensable and whose comradeship and brotherhood are indispensable, is the only foundation upon which the trial and tribulation of modern war can be endured and surmounted. This moral conviction alone affords that ever-fresh resilience which renews the strength and energy of people in long, doubtful and dark days. Outside, the storms of war may blow and the lands may be lashed with the fury of its gales, but in our own hearts this Sunday morning there is peace. Our hands may be active, but our consciences are at rest.

We must not underrate the gravity of the task which lies before us or the temerity of the ordeal, to which we shall not be found unequal. We must expect many disappointments, and many unpleasant surprises, but we may be sure that the task which we have freely accepted is one not beyond the compass and the strength of the British Empire and the French Republic. The prime minister said it was a sad day, and that is indeed true, but at the present time there is another note which may be present, and that is a feeling of thankfulness that, if these great trials were to come upon our island, there is a generation of Britons here now ready to prove itself not unworthy of the days of yore and not unworthy of those great men, the fathers of our land, who laid the foundations of our laws and shaped the greatness of our country.

'We are fighting to save the whole world from the pestilence of Nazi tyranny'

This is not a question of fighting for Danzig or fighting for Poland. We are fighting to save the whole world from the pestilence of Nazi tyranny and in defence of all that is most sacred to man. This is no war of domination or imperial aggrandisement or material gain; no war to shut any country out of its sunlight and means of progress. It is a war, viewed in its inherent quality, to establish, on impregnable rocks, the rights of the individual, and it is a war to establish and revive the stature of man. Perhaps it might seem a paradox that a war undertaken in the name of liberty and right should require, as a necessary part of its processes, the surrender for the time being of so many of the dearly valued liberties and rights. In these last few days the House of Commons has been voting dozens of Bills which hand over to the executive our most dearly valued traditional liberties. We are sure that these liberties will be in hands which will not abuse them, which will use them for no class or party interests, which will cherish and guard them, and we look forward to the day, surely and confidently we look forward to the day, when our liberties and rights will be restored to us, and when we shall be able to share them with the peoples to whom such blessings are unknown.

'A riddle wrapped in a mystery inside an enigma'

World broadcast, 1 October 1939

Poland could not look to her eastern neighbour for salvation from the German onslaught. On 17 September, she was also invaded by the Soviet Union, Stalin having agreed to partition her with Hitler. Now attacked on both sides, Poland's hopes of successful resistance crumbled.

Even without this stab in the back, Poland would not have received much help from her British and French allies. The concentration of German forces against the Poles meant that on the Western Front 85 French divisions faced only 34 German ones, and of the latter 20 were reserves. But, if this was an opportunity to strike into the lightly defended industrial heartland of the Reich, it was not exploited. The French effort to relieve pressure on her doomed ally was restricted to a minor and short-lived incursion into the Saarland. It was a meaningless tiptoe across the German border that fooled nobody. Britain and France had gone to war on Poland's behalf. But they had not worked out an offensive strategy for saving her. Before the month was out, she had fallen.

There were no plans for marching deep into Germany. Having hoped to avoid a major continental commitment, Britain had concentrated on building up the strength of an air force, the RAF, capable of defending the British Isles rather than an army strong enough to fight its way across Europe. By the end of September, just four British divisions had been committed to France. It was hardly surprising that many in the French Republic wondered if Britain intended to fight to the last Frenchman.

It was the War Cabinet's assumption that the war could last three years. Plans were drawn up accordingly. Indeed, the strategy was to play for time, using the Royal Navy on the one hand to protect the gathering of the British Empire's vast natural resources and on the other to stop supplies reaching Germany, a country heavily dependent upon imported raw materials. 'It won't be by defeat in the field,' Neville Chamberlain assured his sister Ida, two months into the war, 'but by German realization that they can't win and that it isn't worth their while to go on getting thinner and poorer.' He liked to imagine that such hardship would make Hitler vulnerable to an internal coup. This was why in the first days of the war, the RAF showered the citizens of Hamburg, Bremen and the Ruhr with nothing more incendiary than propaganda leaflets.

Here was a gigantic leap of wishful thinking in which the war could be won without massive bloodshed. It was naturally appealing to Chamberlain, a prime minister who shrank from the horrors and evil degradations that the ideology of 'total war' involved. But it was based on a faulty assumption that Britain had the means to strangle the Third Reich by denying it the resources to continue. This took no account

ON THIS DAY
1 OCTOBER 1939

• The last fighting units of the Polish armed forces surrender, at Hel naval base.

• Germany, worried at the possibility of Allied naval blockade (as happened in the First World War) extends its system of rationing.

• Polish code-breakers, aided by British Intelligence, escape to Paris with two Enigma machines, whose secrets, once revealed, will prove invaluable to the Allies.

of an alternative option available to Germany – that of invading neighbours and appropriating their resources. In wartime as in peacetime, the leaders of Britain and France continued to underestimate the sheer scale of Hitler's ambitions and appetite. They also failed to appreciate the will of the Germans to stay loyal to him through thick and thin.

The British Empire and the French Republic have been at war with Nazi Germany for a month tonight. We have not yet come at all to the severity of fighting which is to be expected; but three important things have happened.

First, Poland has been again overrun by two of the great Powers which held her in bondage for 150 years, but were unable to quench the spirit of the Polish nation. The heroic defence of Warsaw shows that the soul of Poland is indestructible, and that she will rise again like a rock, which may for a spell be submerged by a tidal wave, but which remains a rock.

What is the second event of this first month? It is, of course, the assertion of the power of Russia. Russia has pursued a cold policy of self-interest. We could have wished that the Russian armies should be standing on their present line as the friends and allies of Poland instead of as invaders. But that the Russian armies should stand on this line, was clearly necessary for the safety of Russia against the Nazi menace. At any rate, the line is there, and an eastern front has been created which Nazi Germany does not dare assail. When Herr von Ribbentrop was summoned to Moscow last week, it was to learn the fact, and to accept the fact, that the Nazi designs upon the Baltic states and upon the Ukraine must come to a dead stop.

'Russia . . . a riddle wrapped in a mystery inside an enigma'

I cannot forecast to you the action of Russia. It is a riddle wrapped in a mystery inside an enigma: but perhaps there is a key. That key is Russian national interest. It cannot be in accordance with the interest or the safety of Russia that Germany should plant itself upon the shores of the Black Sea, or that it should overrun the Balkan states and subjugate the Slavonic peoples of southeastern Europe. That would be contrary to the historic life-interests of Russia.

But in this quarter of the world, the southeast of Europe, these interests of Russia fall into the same channel as the interests of Britain and France. None of these three Powers can afford to see Romania, Yugoslavia, Bulgaria, and above all Turkey, put under the German heel. Through the fog of confusion and uncertainty we may discern quite plainly the community of interests which exists between England, France and Russia – a community of interests to prevent the Nazis carrying the flames of war into the Balkans and Turkey. Thus, my friends, at some risk of being proved wrong by events, I will proclaim tonight my conviction that the second great fact of the first month of the war is that Hitler, and all that Hitler stands for, have been and are being warned off the east and the southeast of Europe.

What is the third event? Here I speak as First Lord of the Admiralty, with especial caution.

It would seem that the U-boat attack upon the life of the British Isles has not so far proved successful. It is true that when they sprang out upon us and we were going about our ordinary business, with 2000 ships in constant movement every day upon the seas, they managed to do some serious damage. But the Royal Navy has immediately attacked the U-boats, and is hunting them night and day – I will not say without mercy, because God forbid we should ever part company with that, but at any rate with zeal and not altogether without relish. And it looks tonight very much as if it is the U-boats who are feeling the weather, and not the Royal Navy or the worldwide commerce of Britain. A week has passed since a British ship, alone or in convoy, has been sunk or even molested by a U-boat on the high seas; and during the first month of the war we have captured by our efficient contraband control 150,000 tons more German merchandise – food, oil, minerals and other commodities – for our own benefit than we have lost by all the U-boat sinkings put together. In fact, up to date – please observe I make no promises (we must deal in performance and not in promises) – up to date we have actually got 150,000 tons of very desirable supplies into this island more than we should have got if war had not been declared, and if no U-boat had ever cast sailormen to their fate upon the stormy seas. This seems to be a very solid, tangible fact which has emerged from the first month of the war against Nazidom.

'Hitler and his group of wicked men, whose hands are stained with blood and soiled with corruption'

… Directions have been given by the government to prepare for a war of at least three years. That does not mean that victory may not be gained in a shorter time. How soon it will be gained depends upon how long Herr Hitler and his group of wicked men, whose hands are stained with blood and soiled with corruption, can keep their grip upon the docile, unhappy German people. It was for Hitler to say when the war would begin; but it is not for him or for his successors to say when it will end. It began when he wanted it, and it will end only when we are convinced that he has had enough.

The prime minister has stated our war aims in terms which cannot be bettered, and which cannot be too often repeated. These are his words: 'To redeem Europe from the perpetual and recurring fear of German aggression, and enable the peoples of Europe to preserve their independence and their liberties'.

That is what the British and French nations are fighting for. How often have we been told that we are the effete democracies whose day is done, and who must now be replaced by various forms of virile dictatorships and totalitarian despotism? No doubt at the beginning we shall have to suffer, because of having too long wished to lead a peaceful life. Our reluctance to fight was mocked at as cowardice. Our desire to see an unarmed world was proclaimed as the proof of our decay. Now we have begun. Now we are going on. Now, with the help of God, and with the conviction that we are the defenders of civilization and freedom, we are going to persevere to the end.

'We have other resources. We have the oceans'

After all, Great Britain and France together are 85,000,000, even in their homelands alone. They are united in their cause; they are convinced of their duty. Nazidom, with all its tyrannical power, controls no more than that. They, too, have 85,000,000; but of these at least 16,000,000 are newly conquered Czechs, Slovakians and Austrians, who are writhing under their cruel yoke and have to be held down by main force. We have other resources. We have the oceans, and with the oceans the assurance that we can bring the vast latent power of the British and French empires to bear upon the decisive points. We have the freely-given ardent support of the 20,000,000 of British citizens in the self-governing Dominions of Canada, Australia, New Zealand and South Africa. We have, I believe, the heart and the moral conviction of India on our side. We believe we are entitled to the respect and good-will of the world, and particularly of the United States.

Here I am in the same post as I was twenty-five years ago. Rough times lie ahead; but how different is the scene from that of October 1914! Then the French front, with its British Army fighting in the line, seemed to be about to break under the terrible impact of German imperialism. Then Russia had been laid low at Tannenberg; then the whole might of the Austro-Hungarian Empire was in battle against us; then the brave, warlike Turks were about to join our enemies. Then we had to be ready night and day to fight a decisive sea battle with a formidable German Fleet almost, in many respects, the equal of our own. We faced those adverse conditions then; we have nothing worse to face tonight.

In those days of 1914 also, Italy was neutral; but we did not know the reason for her neutrality. It was only later on that we learned that by a secret clause in the original Treaty of the Triple Alliance, Italy had expressly reserved to herself the right to stand aside from any war which brought her into conflict with Great Britain. Much has happened since then. Misunderstandings and disputes have arisen, but all the more do we appreciate in England the reason why this great and friendly nation of Italy, with whom we have never been at war, has not seen fit to enter the struggle.

'Of all the wars that men have fought in their hard pilgrimage, none was more noble than the great Civil War in America nearly eighty years ago'

I do not underrate what lies before us, but I must say this: I cannot doubt we have the strength to carry a good cause forward, and to break down the barriers which stand between the wage-earning masses of every land and that free and more abundant daily life which science is ready to afford. That is my conviction, and I look back upon the history of the past to find many sources of encouragement. Of all the wars that men have fought in their hard pilgrimage, none was more noble than the great Civil War in America nearly eighty years ago. Both sides fought with high conviction, and the war was long and hard. All the heroism of the South could not redeem their cause from the stain of slavery, just as all the courage and skill which the Germans always show in war will not free them from the reproach of Nazism, with its intolerance and its brutality. We may take good heart from what happened in America in those famous days of the 19th century. We may be sure that the world will roll forward into broader destinies. We may remember the words of old John Bright after the American Civil War was over, when he said to an audience of English working folk: 'At last after the smoke of the battlefield had cleared away, the horrid shape which had cast its shadow over the whole continent had vanished and was gone forever.'

'The first ten weeks'

World broadcast, 12 November 1939

On the reasons to be optimistic

Poland was lost, but Britain never had a coherent plan for saving her beyond declaring war on her German oppressor. Yet, nearer to home, the conflict was not going as badly as many doom-mongers had prophesied.

First and foremost, Britain's cities were not subject to immediate obliteration from the skies. In the first days of the war, almost 1.5 million schoolchildren and toddlers had been tagged and sent out on trains that carried them away from the cities to the countryside, where it was assumed they would be safe from the saturation bombing expected to rain down on the urban centres. It was the greatest population migration of its kind in British history.

Such jumpiness was hardly surprising. The German invasion of Poland had been accompanied by the Luftwaffe's bombing of Warsaw. The pulverization of Guernica during the Spanish Civil War testified to what was possible. The belief that the 'bomber will always get through' was rarely questioned and estimates forecast Britain would suffer 600,000 fatalities in the first fortnight of air assault. In the event, the entire war claimed 60,000 British civilians. The other great expectation that Hitler would deploy poisonous gas also failed to materialize. During these early months, with no sign of the Luftwaffe, the main cause of civilian fatalities was the spiralling number of car accidents caused by the nightly blackout of urban lighting.

Just as absent as German airmen over Britain were German soldiers advancing towards France. Six days after the declaration of war, the British Expeditionary Force had been ferried across the English Channel to France without incident. But of an enemy to engage there was no sign. Was the war simply going to peter out? Some wags began referring to it as the 'bore war'.

ON THIS DAY
12 NOVEMBER 1939

• The Entertainment National Service Association (ENSA) gives its first morale-boosting show, for men of the British Expeditionary Force in France. The singer Gracie Fields tops the bill.

• The sovereign of Romania, King Carol, offers to be a peace-broker between the European antagonists. The fearful monarchs of neutral Belgium and the Netherlands rebuff Allied overtures while frantically attempting peace negotiations too.

• In Germany, mass arrests continue following the bomb that exploded in a Munich Bierkeller (8 November) shortly after the Führer had given a speech and left the building.

With little to fight about in the air or on the land, it fell to the Royal Navy to take the fire to the enemy. Churchill wished to use the senior service to the full and was frustrated to find his plans for tightening the blockade of German trade by mining Norwegian territorial waters repeatedly postponed. Meanwhile, the German Navy lost no opportunity to sink British merchant shipping. A terrible humiliation befell the Royal Navy when a U-boat penetrated the entrance to the base at Scapa Flow and sank HMS Royal Oak, drowning 800 sailors. Alongside the U-boats, magnetic mines proved a particularly troublesome hazard in the North Sea until a means of combating them by demagnetizing ships was devised shortly before Christmas.

Yet, as Churchill was not slow to point out, Britain was losing far less shipping in the opening months of the war in 1939 than it had done in 1914. And in December, the Royal Navy was finally able to celebrate a victory. Three cruisers chased the German pocket battleship *Admiral Graf Spee* – which had been a serious menace to shipping in the South Atlantic – into the River Plate, off Uruguay. There, its captain assessed his options and scuttled the ship. The first major naval battle had gone Britain's way.

'The first ten weeks'

I thought it would be a good thing for me to tell you now how well the war has turned for the Allies during the first ten weeks.

It is quite plain that the power of the British Empire and the French Republic to restore and revive the life of the Polish, Czech and Slovak peoples, as well as do a few other things which I will mention later, has been growing every day. Peaceful parliamentary countries, which aim at freedom for the individual and abundance for the mass, start with a heavy handicap against a dictatorship whose sole theme has been war, the preparation for war, and the grinding up of everything and everybody into its military machine. In our island particularly we are very easy going in time of peace. We should like to share the blessings of peace with every nation; and to go on enjoying them ourselves. It is only after many vain attempts to remain at peace that we have been at last forced to go to war. We tried again and again to prevent this war, and for the sake of peace we put up with a lot of things happening which ought not to have happened. But now we are at war, and we are going to make war, and persevere in making war, until the other side have had enough of it. We are going to persevere as far as we can to the best of our ability; which is not small and is always growing.

'Mr Chamberlain . . . is going to fight as obstinately for victory as he did for peace'

You know I have not always agreed with Mr Chamberlain; though we have always been personal friends. But he is a man of very tough fibre, and I can tell you that he is going to fight as obstinately for victory as he did for peace. You may take it absolutely for certain that either all that Britain and France stand for in the modern world will go down, or that Hitler, the Nazi regime and the recurring German or Prussian menace to Europe will be broken and destroyed. That is the way the matter lies and everybody had better make up their minds to that solid, sombre fact . . .

Churchill boasted that with each week Britain's armed forces were getting stronger, contrasting the fact that 'Nearly all the German ocean-going ships are in hiding and rusting in neutral harbours, while our worldwide trade steadily proceeds in 4000 vessels of which 2500 are constantly at sea.'

'The bestial atrocities . . . committed in Poland'

I do not doubt myself that time is on our side. I go so far as to say that if we come through the winter without any large or important event occurring we shall in fact have gained the first campaign of the war: and we shall be able to set about our task in the spring far stronger, better organized and better armed than ever before. Let us therefore bear discomfort and many minor – and even perhaps needless – vexations with comprehending patience, because we are all the time moving forward towards greater war strength, and because Germany is all the time, under the grip of our economic warfare, falling back in oil and other essential war supplies.

It may be, of course, that at any time violent and dire events will open. If so, we shall confront them with resolution. If not, we shall profit to the full by the time at our disposal. But Field-Marshal Goering – who is one of the few Germans who has been having a pretty good time for the last few years – says that we have been spared so far because Nazi Germany is so humane. They cannot bear to do anything to hurt anybody. All they ask for is the right to live and to be let alone to conquer and kill the weak. Their humanity forbids them to apply severities to the strong. It may be true: but when we remember the bestial atrocities they have committed in Poland, we do not feel we wish to ask for any favours to be shown us. We shall do our duty as long as we have life and strength …

I shall not attempt to prophesy whether the frenzy of a cornered maniac will drive Herr Hitler into the worst of all his crimes; but this I will say without a doubt, that the fate of Holland and Belgium, like that of Poland, Czechoslovakia and Austria, will be decided by the victory of the British Empire and the French Republic. If we are conquered, all will be enslaved, and the United States will be left single-handed to guard the rights of man. If we are not destroyed, all these countries will be rescued and restored to life and freedom.

'The whole world is against Hitler and Hitlerism'

It is indeed a solemn moment when I speak to you on this tenth Sunday after the outbreak of war. But it is also a moment sustained by resolve and hope. I am in the singular position of having lived through the early months of the last German war upon Europe in the same position, in charge of the British Admiralty, as I am now. I am therefore very careful not to say anything of an over-confident or unduly sanguine nature. I am sure we have very rough weather ahead; but I have this feeling, that the Germany which assaults us all today is a far less strongly built and solidly founded organism than that which the Allies and the United States forced to beg for armistice twenty-one years ago. I have the sensation and also the conviction that that evil man over there and his cluster of confederates are not sure of themselves, as we are sure of ourselves; that they are harassed in their guilty souls by the thought and by the fear of an ever-approaching retribution for their crimes, and for the orgy of destruction in which they have plunged us all. As they look out tonight from their blatant, panoplied, clattering Nazi Germany, they cannot find one single friendly eye in the whole circumference of the globe. Not one! Russia returns them a flinty stare; Italy averts her gaze; Japan is puzzled and thinks herself betrayed. Turkey and the whole of Islam have ranged themselves instinctively but decisively on the side of progress. The hundreds of millions of people in India and in China, whatever their other feelings, would regard with undisguised dread a Nazi triumph, well knowing what their fate would soon be. The great English-speaking republic across the Atlantic Ocean makes no secret of its sympathies or of its self-questionings, and translates these sentiments into actions of a character which anyone may judge for himself. The whole world is against Hitler and Hitlerism. Men of every race and clime feel that this monstrous apparition stands between them and the forward move which is their due, and for which the age is ripe. Even in Germany itself there are millions who stand aloof from the seething mass of criminality and corruption constituted by the Nazi Party machine. Let them take courage amid perplexities and perils, for it may well be that the final extinction of a baleful domination will pave the way to a broader solidarity of all the men in all the lands than we could ever have planned if we had not marched together through the fire.

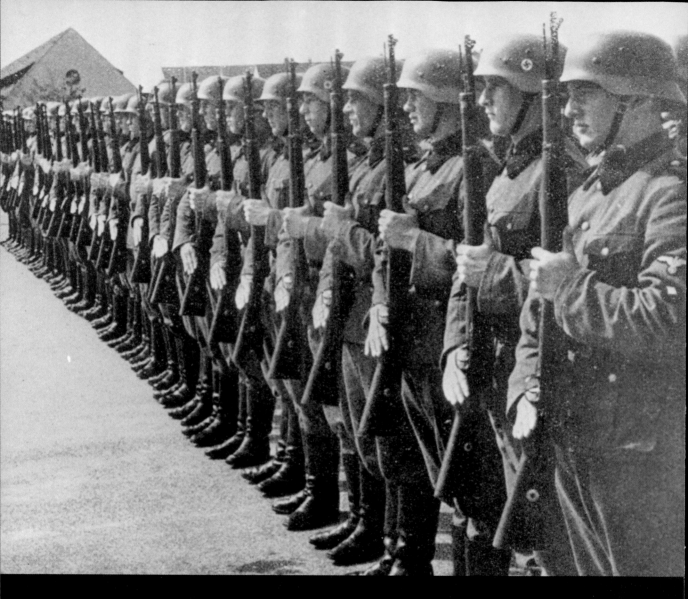

'A hideous state of alarm and menace'

World broadcast, 30 March 1940

On the perils of neutrality

On 30 November, Russia invaded Finland. It was the second neighbour Stalin had attacked in a little over two months. In London, the War Cabinet resisted the temptation to double Britain's number of enemies. But there was little attempt to hide a growing sense of admiration for the Finns who, against the odds, proceeded to win a series of impressive victories against the Red Army in what became known as the 'Winter War'. The poor performance of the Soviet military was noted especially in Berlin.

Within days of assuming control at the Admiralty, Churchill had been arguing in the War Cabinet for an operation to cut off Germany's main source of iron ore, which was being supplied by neutral Sweden. He wanted neutral Norway's waters mined so that the vital raw material could not be ferried during the winter months to Germany via the northern port of Narvik. Repeatedly, his schemes were rejected or postponed.

The French government was adamant that action should be taken to assist the Finns. In February 1940, the Anglo-French Supreme War Council met in Paris and fused together different plans so that an expeditionary force would be dispatched to seize the Swedish ore-fields and to prepare a base to assist Finland's resistance to the Russians. The latter proposal risked sparking all-out war with the Soviet Union. Fortuitously, it was shelved before being put into operation because, on 13 March, the Finns accepted a timely truce with Moscow. But Churchill's plan to mine Norwegian territorial waters and land troops at Narvik was finally given the go-ahead.

Both Churchill and Chamberlain were sure that restricting the Reich's ability to receive its supply of iron ore would seriously impact upon its war-making capacity. Actually they were misled in this respect because the stockpiles already in German hands exceeded estimates. However, at the time, criticism was strongest from those squeamish at what amounted to a proposed violation of Scandinavian neutrality. Was this not the sort of action totalitarian states sank to? What would President Roosevelt think? Churchill was not impressed by these arguments, especially when the neutral states involved were supplying the enemy. 'Each one hopes that if he feeds the crocodile enough, the crocodile will eat him last. All of them hope that the storm will pass before their turn comes to be devoured' he had warned of the neutral states in January, 'and if at any time Britain and France, wearying of the struggle, were to make a shameful peace, nothing would remain for the smaller states of Europe, with their shipping and their possessions, but to be divided between the

ON THIS DAY
30 MARCH 1940

• A splinter group of Chinese Nationalist Kuomintang politicians controversially form a government in Nanjing (Nanking) acceptable to the Japanese occupation forces. This is the city that, in the 'Rape of Nanking' of 1937–8, witnessed hundreds of thousands of Chinese deaths in an orgy of Japanese military brutality. The Axis powers recognize the new government, but the Allies and the United States do not.

• Hitler indicates support for sending arms to the Soviet Union, a lip service to the amity of the Nazi-Soviet Pact.

opposite, though similar, barbarisms of Nazidom and Bolshevism.' It was a theme he returned to when making another world broadcast at the end of March.

People often ask me, will the war be long or short? It might have been a very short war – perhaps indeed there might have been no war – if all the neutral states who share our convictions upon fundamental matters, and who openly or secretly sympathize with us, had stood together at one signal and in one line. We did not count on this, we did not expect it, and therefore we are not disappointed or dismayed. We trust in God, and in our own arm uplifted in a cause which we devoutly feel carries with it the larger hopes and harmonies of mankind. But the fact that many of the smaller states of Europe are terrorized by Nazi violence and brutality into supplying Germany with the materials of modern war – this fact may condemn the whole world to a prolonged ordeal with grievous unmeasured consequences in many lands. Therefore I cannot assure you that the war will be short and still less that it will be easy.

'It would not be right . . . that their weakness should feed the aggressor's strength and fill to overflowing the cup of human woe'

It is, I think, our duty to try so far as our strength lies not only to win the war, but to curtail as far as possible its devouring course. Some few weeks ago I spoke about the action of the neutral states who have the misfortune to be Germany's neighbours. We have the greatest sympathy for these forlorn countries, and we understand their dangers and their point of view; but it would not be right, or in the general interest, that their weakness should feed the aggressor's strength and fill to overflowing the cup of human woe. There can be no justice if in a mortal struggle the aggressor tramples down every sentiment of humanity, and if those who resist him remain entangled in the tatters of violated legal conventions. Hardly a day passes without fresh outrages of a barbarous character being inflicted upon the shipping and sailors of all European countries. Their ships are sunk by mine or by torpedo, or by bombs from the air, and their crews are murdered or left to perish, unless we are able to rescue them. Swedes, Norwegians, Danes and even Italians, and many more I could mention, have been the victims of Hitler's murderous rage. In his frenzy, this wicked man and the criminal regime which he has conceived and erected, increasingly turn their malice upon the weak, upon the lonely, and above all upon the unarmed vessels of countries with which Germany is still supposed to be in friendly relations.

'Interpretations of neutrality which give all the advantages to the aggressor and inflict all the disadvantages upon the defenders of freedom'

Such a form of warfare has never been practised since the effectual suppression of piracy on the high seas. And this is the monstrous power which even the very neutrals who have suffered, and are suffering most, are forced to supply with the means of future aggression.

This is the power before whom, even while they writhe in anger, they are forced to bow, and whose victory would mean their own enslavement. Why, only yesterday, while the sailors from a British submarine were carrying ashore on stretchers eight emaciated Dutchmen whom they had rescued from six days' exposure in an open boat, Dutch aviators in Holland, in the name of strict and impartial neutrality, were shooting down a British aircraft which had lost its way. I do not reproach the Dutch, our valiant allies of bygone centuries; my heart goes out to them in their peril and distress, dwelling as they do in the cage with the tiger. But when we are asked to take as a matter of course interpretations of neutrality which give all the advantages to the aggressor and inflict all the disadvantages upon the defenders of freedom, I recall a saying of the late Lord Balfour: 'This is a singularly ill-contrived world, but not so ill-contrived as that.'

'All these outrages upon the sea, which are so clearly visible'

All these outrages upon the sea, which are so clearly visible, pale before the villainous deeds which are wrought upon the helpless Czechs and Austrians, and they sink almost into insignificance before the hideous agony of Poland. What a frightful fate has overtaken Poland! Here was a community of nearly 35,000,000 of people, with all the organization of a modern government, and all the traditions of an ancient state, which in a few weeks was dashed out of civilized existence to become an incoherent multitude of tortured and starving men, women and children, ground beneath the heel of two rival forms of withering and blasting tyranny. The other day in a well-known British harbour I inspected the crew of a Polish destroyer. I have rarely seen a finer body of men. I was stirred by their discipline and bearing. Yet how tragic was their plight! Their ship was afloat, but their country had foundered! But as I looked around upon all the great ships of war which lay at their anchors, and at all the preparations which were being made on every side to carry this war forward at all costs as long as may be necessary, I comforted myself with the thought that when these Polish sailors have finished their work with the British Navy, we will take particular care that they once more have a home to go to. Although the fate of Poland stares them in the face, there are thoughtless dilettanti or purblind worldlings who sometimes ask us: 'What is it that Britain and France are fighting for?' To this I answer: 'If we left off fighting you would soon find out.'

We shall follow this war wherever it leads us; but we have no wish to broaden the area of conflict. At the outbreak, seven months ago, we did not know that Italy would not be our enemy. We were not sure that Japan would not be our enemy. Many people, on the other hand, had hoped that Russia would re-enter the comity of nations and help to shield working folk all over the world from Nazi aggression. But none of these things, bad or good, has happened. We have no quarrel with the Italian or Japanese peoples. We have tried, and we shall try, our best to live on good terms with them.

'We are determined to bring such a hideous state of alarm and menace to an end'

All's quiet upon the Western Front; and today, this Saturday, so far, nothing has happened on the sea or in the air. But more than a million German soldiers, including all their active divisions and armoured divisions, are drawn up ready to attack, at a few hours' notice, all along the frontiers of Luxembourg, of Belgium and of Holland. At any moment these neutral countries may be subjected to an avalanche of steel and fire; and the decision rests in the hands of a haunted, morbid being, who, to their eternal shame, the German peoples in their bewilderment have worshipped as a god. That is the situation of Europe tonight. And can anyone wonder that we are determined to bring such a hideous state of alarm and menace to an end, and to bring it to an end as soon as may be, and to bring it to an end once and for all? Few there are tonight who, looking back on these last seven months, would doubt that the British and French peoples were right to draw the sword of justice and of retribution. Fewer still there are who would wish to sheathe it till its sombre, righteous work is done.

'Hitler's sudden overrunning of the vast region of Norway'

House of Commons, London, 8 May 1940

On the Norwegian campaign

Such was the confidence in London that the proposed operation to cut off German supplies of iron-ore from Narvik would succeed that on 2 April, Neville Chamberlain assured the public that Hitler had 'missed the bus'.

The prime minister's prediction was ill-timed. Before the British expedition arrived off the Norwegian coast, the Germans got there first. On 9 April – just as the Royal Navy was beginning to lay mines within Norway's territorial waters – the Wehrmacht launched full-scale invasions of Norway and Denmark. Rather than countermand the order, the British campaign proceeded regardless. On the waves, the operation went relatively well. The German Navy came under heavy attack, losing seven destroyers. But the campaign in Norway itself was a disaster. British troops came ashore on either side of Trondheim. But despite outnumbering the German defenders, the landing parties were lightly armed and poorly supplied for the snowbound conditions in which they would have to operate. What was more, the Germans – having got to the Norwegian airfields first – had air superiority. Fearing disaster, the Trondheim objective was cancelled and the landing party evacuated by sea. Meanwhile, Major-General Mackesy, in charge of the Narvik operation, decided he dare not risk a direct assault on the town, preferring to put ashore parties at various other points and wait several weeks in the Arctic conditions. The Norway campaign, which should have been cancelled when the German invasion forestalled it, was descending into farce.

The attack on Narvik had still not gone ahead when, on 7 May, the House of Commons began debating the matter. Chamberlain had decided to make the Labour Party's criticism the subject of a vote of confidence. In doing so he raised the stakes, for there was now a fractious mood in the nation that even normally loyal MPs were starting to reflect. Blame was apportioned not to Churchill, who had largely conceived the Narvik part of the campaign, but to the government generally and the prime minister in particular. Several prominent Tory MPs joined the abuse hurled at Chamberlain from the Opposition benches.

Winding up the debate for the government the following day, Churchill found himself defending the record of colleagues who had previously been his opponents during the years of appeasement. But he did not shirk from the task, despite the aged former wartime prime minister, David Lloyd George, gesturing to him with the advice 'not to allow himself to be converted into an air-raid shelter to keep the splinters from hitting his colleagues'.

Churchill apportioned most of his speech to discussing and dismissing the alternative options for how the Norway campaign might have been better handled. In particular, he defended the decision to abandon the attack

ON THIS DAY
8 MAY 1940

- Belgium and the Netherlands brace themselves for imminent German invasion, which duly begins, by blitzkrieg, on 10 May. Both countries face insuperable odds, and the Netherlands is overwhelmed in a few days.

- In China, Japanese forces seize territory in Hupeh province.

- In British newspapers, obituaries appear of George Lansbury, the Labour Party's avowedly pacifist leader from 1931 to 1935, who has died the previous day.

on Trondheim, which had 'saved us in the upshot from a most disastrous entanglement. It often happens in war that an operation which is successful on a small scale becomes vicious if it is multiplied by three, four or five times.'

Churchill's advocacy was insufficient to save the desperateness of the government's position. The debate was won, but the majority – which should have exceeded 200 – was cut to 81. Some MPs started abusively shouting 'Go! Go! Go! Go!' at the prime minister as he made his way out of the chamber. Stung, Chamberlain recognized his government could not continue in these partisan conditions. A new coalition was needed that would include and implicate the Labour and Liberal parties in the responsibility of the war. The Labour Party made clear it would not serve under Chamberlain. It would only work with a new prime minister. But who would it be? There were only two clear choices: the calm and experienced foreign secretary, Lord Halifax, or the rash but far more determined Winston Churchill.

'Our numerical deficiency in the air . . . will condemn us for some time to come to a great deal of difficulty and suffering and danger'

I would like to say a few things about the subject of the Norwegian campaign and also about the general war. In this war we are frequently asked, 'Why do you not take the initiative, why do you repeatedly wait and wonder where the enemy is going to strike you next?' Obviously, he has many choices open. We always seem to be waiting, and when we are struck, then we take some action. 'Why', it is asked, 'is the next blow not going to be struck by Britain?' The reason for this serious disadvantage of our not having the initiative is one which cannot speedily be removed, and it is our failure in the last five years to maintain or regain air parity in numbers with Germany. That is an old story, and it is a long story – a very long story, let me remind the House – because for the first two years, when I, with some friends, was pressing this upon the House, it was not only the government who objected, but both the Opposition parties. In the last two years or so, they came around, and gave great and valuable aid, but the fact remains that we failed to achieve the air parity which was considered to be vital to our security. The fact of our numerical deficiency in the air, in spite of our superiority in quality, both in men and material – which is I believe established – has condemned us and will condemn us for some time to come, to a great deal of difficulty and suffering and danger, which we must endure with firmness, until more favourable conditions can be established, as assuredly they will be established ...

'The Nazi empire of Hungryland'

Churchill explained how the landings around Trondheim had fared and why they were called off, before concluding, rather optimistically:

My right honourable friend the Member for Caernarvon [David Lloyd George] said we must not mention calculations of profit and loss, but I do not agree. Calculations of profit and loss are our life. We win by these calculations of the ships we sink. It seems to me that, although Hitler's sudden overrunning of the vast region of Norway has had astonishing and unwelcome effects, nevertheless, the advantages rest substantially with us. I will give some of the facts which are worth mentioning. Hitler has certainly lost ten lives for one – not that he cares for that, I agree. He has condemned a large part of the Scandinavian peninsula and Denmark to enter the Nazi empire of Hungryland. He has committed an act of self-blockade. We see no reason why our control over the commerce of the seas should not become even more effective now that the Norwegian corridor exists no longer, and now that unhappy Denmark, when her reserves have been devoured, will no longer be the purveyor of bacon and butter and the channel of trade and communications with the outer world.

'We have taken into our service a very large amount of Danish shipping'

… Although Hitler has treacherously received a large part of Norway it is perhaps forgotten that, like our own people, the Norwegians live largely by the sea. The French and the British Mercantile Marine can now rely upon the invaluable support and cooperation of the Norwegian merchant fleet, the fourth largest in the world, and on the services of seamen whose skill and daring are well known. Also we have taken into our service a very large amount of Danish shipping which will be of the greatest assistance. These are notable facts when we remember that the British and French losses through enemy action since the war are barely 800,000 tons, and the captures and the building have already made good three-quarters of that loss.

ALL BEHIND YOU, WINSTON

'Blood, toil, tears and sweat'

House of Commons, London, 13 May 1940

On becoming prime minister and the need for unity

On 10 May 1940, British politics was in flux with the prime minister, Neville Chamberlain, seemingly about to fall. That very day, Germany invaded the neutral countries of Luxembourg, Belgium and the Netherlands. The long awaited war in the west had begun.

The British and French armies accepted Belgium's urgent call for assistance and began their pre-planned advance into the country to meet the invading Germans. The phoney war was over. No more would time and energy be spent on fringe campaigns and diversionary tactics. Here was the great moment, with the massed German divisions smashing on through Belgium, just as they had done in August 1914, triggering the last catastrophe for civilization. Then as now, the ensuing battle seemed destined to decide both the war and the fate of the world.

Chamberlain's first thought was that this fresh crisis necessitated his staying on as prime minister, at least until the Battle of France was won. He was soon persuaded that, on the contrary, the crisis meant he had to go immediately. Despite this, many – and probably most – Conservative MPs worried about Churchill's temperament and were concerned that he was not a good Tory Party man. They wanted the 'Establishment' figure of Lord Halifax to lead the new cross-party National government.

Despite being implicated in Chamberlain's pre-war appeasement policy, the tall, devoutly Anglican, deeply honourable foreign secretary would probably have been acceptable to the Labour and Liberal leadership too. But it was hardly ideal that Britain should be led by a peer of the realm who would be answering questions in the hereditary House of Lords rather than in the democratic House of Commons at a moment when the humblest in the land were being asked to make the ultimate sacrifice. It was not in keeping with the spirit of the moment. Ironically it was Winston Spencer Churchill, born in Blenheim Palace, the cousin of a duke, who was credited with a far surer command of the wider nation's confidence.

Halifax recognized the difficulties a peerage presented (no legal mechanism for renouncing the title existed at that time). Nor could he have looked forward gladly to a situation in which Churchill performed much of the government's powers of persuasion in the Commons and a great deal of the arguing in the War Cabinet. Thus, when Chamberlain summoned Halifax and Churchill to discuss which of them should succeed him, Churchill allowed his rival for

ON THIS DAY
13 MAY 1940

- Belgian forces destroy the bridges across the River Meuse in an unsuccessful attempt to stem the German onslaught.

- German Panzer divisions which, under their strategic master General Heinz Guderian, have traversed the 'impenetrable' Ardennes region, now cross the River Meuse at Sedan and begin their destruction of the insufficiently numerous French forces there.

- In Britain, the precautionary internment of German and Austrian 'aliens' gets underway. In fact, many of them are refugees from Nazi Europe, and throughout the war the feared 'fifth column' proves minimal in numbers and impact.

power to do the talking. With becoming modesty, Halifax duly talked himself out of the premiership. Chamberlain felt obliged to advise King George VI to send for Churchill as the new prime minister. In the early evening of 10 May, the 65-year-old war veteran duly arrived at Buckingham Palace to receive the commission to form a new cross-party government.

That night, Churchill went to bed – as he later put it – feeling 'a profound sense of relief. At last I had authority to give directions over the whole scene. I felt as if I were walking with destiny, and that all my past life had been but a preparation for this hour and for this trial.'

On Friday evening last I received His Majesty's commission to form a new administration. It was the evident wish and will of Parliament and the nation that this should be conceived on the broadest possible basis and that it should include all parties, both those who supported the late government and also the parties of the Opposition. I have completed the most important part of this task. A War Cabinet has been formed of five Members, representing, with the Opposition Liberals, the unity of the nation. The three party leaders have agreed to serve, either in the War Cabinet or in high executive office. The three fighting services have been filled. It was necessary that this should be done in one single day, on account of the extreme urgency and rigour of events. A number of other key positions were filled yesterday, and I am submitting a further list to His Majesty tonight. I hope to complete the appointment of the principal ministers during tomorrow. The appointment of the other ministers usually takes a little longer, but I trust that, when Parliament meets again, this part of my task will be completed, and that the administration will be complete in all respects.

I considered it in the public interest to suggest that the House should be summoned to meet today. Mr Speaker agreed, and took the necessary steps, in accordance with the powers conferred upon him by the Resolution of the House. At the end of the proceedings today, the adjournment of the House will be proposed until Tuesday, May 21, with, of course, provision for earlier meeting if need be. The business to be considered during that week will be notified to Members at the earliest opportunity. I now invite the House, by the resolution which stands in my name, to record its approval of the steps taken and to declare its confidence in the new government.

'I have nothing to offer but blood, toil, tears and sweat.'

To form an administration of this scale and complexity is a serious undertaking in itself, but it must be remembered that we are in the preliminary stage of one of the greatest battles in history, that we are in action at many points in Norway and in Holland, that we have to be prepared in the Mediterranean, that the air battle is continuous and that many preparations have to be made here at home. In this crisis I hope I may be pardoned if I do not address the House at any length today. I hope that any of my friends and colleagues, or former colleagues, who are affected by the political reconstruction, will make all allowance for any lack of ceremony with which it has been necessary to act. I would say to the House, as I said to those who have joined this government: 'I have nothing to offer but blood, toil, tears and sweat.'

'What is our aim? I can answer with one word: victory – victory at all costs, victory in spite of all terror, victory, however long and hard the road may be; for without victory, there is no survival'

We have before us an ordeal of the most grievous kind. We have before us many, many long months of struggle and of suffering. You ask what is our policy? I will say: It is to wage war, by sea, land and air, with all our might and with all the strength that God can give us: to wage war against a monstrous tyranny, never surpassed in the dark, lamentable catalogue of human crime. That is our policy. You ask, what is our aim? I can answer in one word: victory – victory at all costs, victory in spite of all terror, victory, however long and hard the road may be; for without victory, there is no survival. Let that be realized; no survival for the British Empire; no survival for all that the British Empire has stood for, no survival for the urge and impulse of the ages, that mankind will move forward towards its goal. But I take up my task with buoyancy and hope. I feel sure that our cause will not be suffered to fail among men. At this time I feel entitled to claim the aid of all, and I say, 'Come, then, let us go forward together with our united strength.'

'Arm yourselves, and be ye men of valour'

World broadcast, 19 May 1940

On the battle for France

Upon becoming prime minister, Churchill immediately set about forming the new cross-party coalition government. For his deputy, he appointed Clement Attlee, the leader of the Labour Party. But while he may no longer have been prime minister, Neville Chamberlain remained the leader of the Conservative Party, which was still overwhelmingly the majority group in the House of Commons. As such, he had the potential to bring down the new government at any moment. Well aware that they needed to continue as colleagues, Churchill kept Chamberlain in the War Cabinet alongside Lord Halifax, the Tory foreign secretary assumed to have been Chamberlain's preferred choice of successor. If they showed Churchill the same loyalty that he had shown them in the first eight months of war, he might survive.

It was not just morale in Whitehall and Westminster that Churchill had to bolster. In far greater need of reassurance was the French government. On 16 May, the new British prime minister flew to Paris to try and support his opposite number, Paul Reynaud and the French High Command.

> ## ON THIS DAY
> ### 19 MAY 1940
>
> • In France, Amiens and Arras are now in the front line, and the following day Amiens falls to German forces.
>
> • A French Cabinet reshuffle has brought the iconic First World War figure of Marshall Philippe Pétain, now 84 years old, into government as vice-premier; it is hoped that he will rally the French people.
>
> • In Britain, at the secret centre at Bletchley Park, code-breakers working on the captured Enigma machines are now successfully deciphering Luftwaffe communications.

The latter was in a state of shock and bewilderment. The German blitzkrieg was punching through the lines of defence, out-manoeuvring and out-thinking the British and French generals at every turn. The main thrust of the Panzer divisions had come not against the heavily defended Maginot Line but through the Ardennes (which the Allied planners had assumed was virtually impassable) and on to the banks of the Meuse. Despite having fewer men and tanks than the defenders, it was the attackers who were winning.

To the north, the Netherlands was overwhelmed first – in a mere four days. With German paratroopers capturing key positions and Rotterdam in flames, the Dutch Army surrendered on 14 May. The Belgians too were in a desperate and by now almost hopeless situation. The mighty Eben Emael fortress was seized. Brussels fell on 17 May.

By the time Churchill delivered his first broadcast as prime minister, German soldiers were trampling across French soil for the third time in living memory.

I speak to you for the first time as prime minister in a solemn hour for the life of our country, of our Empire, of our allies, and, above all, of the cause of freedom. A tremendous battle is raging in France and Flanders. The Germans, by a remarkable combination of air bombing and heavily armoured tanks, have broken through the French defences north of the Maginot Line, and strong columns of their armoured vehicles are ravaging the open country, which for the first day or two was without defenders. They have penetrated deeply and spread alarm and confusion in their track. Behind them there are now appearing infantry in lorries, and behind them, again, the large masses are moving forward. The regroupment of the French armies to make head against, and also to strike at, this intruding wedge has been proceeding for several days, largely assisted by the magnificent efforts of the Royal Air Force.

'We must not allow ourselves to be intimidated'

We must not allow ourselves to be intimidated by the presence of these armoured vehicles in unexpected places behind our lines. If they are behind our front, the French are also at many points fighting actively behind theirs. Both sides are therefore in an extremely dangerous position. And if the French Army, and our own Army, are well handled, as I believe they will be; if the French retain that genius for recovery and counter-attack for which they have so long been famous; and if the British Army shows the dogged endurance and solid fighting power of which there have been so many examples in the past – then a sudden transformation of the scene might spring into being.

'It would be foolish . . . to disguise the gravity of the hour'

It would be foolish, however, to disguise the gravity of the hour. It would be still more foolish to lose heart and courage or to suppose that well-trained, well-equipped armies numbering three or four millions of men can be overcome in the space of a few weeks, or even months, by a scoop, or raid of mechanized vehicles, however formidable. We may look with confidence to the stabilization of the front in France, and to the general engagement of the masses, which will enable the qualities of the French and British soldiers to be matched squarely against those of their adversaries. For myself, I have invincible confidence in the French Army and its leaders. Only a very small part of that splendid army has yet been heavily engaged; and only a very small part of France has yet been invaded. There is good evidence to show that practically the whole of the specialized and mechanized forces of the enemy have been already thrown into the battle; and we know that very heavy losses have been inflicted upon them. No officer or man, no brigade or division, which grapples at close quarters with the enemy, wherever encountered, can fail to make a worthy contribution to the general result. The armies must cast away the idea of resisting behind concrete lines or natural obstacles, and must realize that mastery can only be regained by furious and unrelenting assault. And this spirit must not only animate the High Command, but must inspire every fighting man.

In the air – often at serious odds – often at odds hitherto thought overwhelming – we have been clawing down three or four to one of our enemies; and the relative balance of the British and German Air Forces is now considerably more favourable to us than at the beginning of the battle. In cutting down the German bombers, we are fighting our own battle as well as that of France. My confidence in our ability to fight it out to the finish with the German Air Force has been strengthened by the fierce encounters which have taken place and are taking place. At the same time, our heavy bombers are striking nightly at the tap-root of German mechanized power, and have already inflicted serious damage upon the oil refineries on which the Nazi effort to dominate the world directly depends.

'Is not this the appointed time for all to make the utmost exertions in their power?'

We must expect that as soon as stability is reached on the Western Front, the bulk of that hideous apparatus of aggression which gashed Holland into ruin and slavery in a few days, will be turned upon us. I am sure I speak for all when I say we are ready to face it; to endure it; and to retaliate against it – to any extent that the unwritten laws of war permit. There will be many men, and many women, in this island who when the ordeal comes upon them, as come it will, will feel comfort, and even a pride – that they are sharing the perils of our lads at the front – soldiers, sailors and airmen, God bless them – and are drawing away from them a part at least of the onslaught they have to bear. Is not this the appointed time for all to make the utmost exertions in their power? If the battle is to be won, we must provide our men with ever-increasing quantities of the weapons and ammunition they need. We must have, and have quickly, more aeroplanes, more tanks, more shells, more guns. There is imperious need for these vital munitions. They increase our strength against the powerfully armed enemy. They replace the wastage of the obstinate struggle; and the knowledge that wastage will speedily be replaced enables us to draw more readily upon our reserves and throw them in now that everything counts so much.

'We shall not hesitate to take every step . . . to call forth from our people the last ounce and the last inch of effort of which they are capable'

Our task is not only to win the battle, but to win the war. After this battle in France abates its force, there will come the battle for our island – for all that Britain is, and all that Britain means. That will be the struggle. In that supreme emergency we shall not hesitate to take every step, even the most drastic, to call forth from our people the last ounce and the last inch of effort of which they are capable. The interests of property, the hours of labour, are nothing compared with the struggle for life and honour, for right and freedom, to which we have vowed ourselves.

I have received from the Chiefs of the French Republic, and in particular from its indomitable prime minister, Monsieur Reynaud, the most sacred pledges that whatever happens they will fight to the end, be it bitter or be it glorious. Nay, if we fight to the end, it can only be glorious.

'Conquer we shall'

Having received His Majesty's commission, I have formed an administration of men and women of every party and of almost every point of view. We have differed and quarrelled in the past; but now one bond unites us all – to wage war until victory is won, and never to surrender ourselves to servitude and shame, whatever the cost and the agony may be. This is one of the most awe-striking periods in the long history of France and Britain. It is also beyond doubt the most sublime. Side by side, unaided except by their kith and kin in the great Dominions and by the wide empires which rest beneath their shield – side by side, the British and French peoples have advanced to rescue not only Europe but mankind from the foulest and most soul-destroying tyranny which has ever darkened and stained the pages of history. Behind them – behind us – behind the armies and fleets of Britain and France – gather a group of shattered states and bludgeoned races: the Czechs, the Poles, the Norwegians, the Danes, the Dutch, the Belgians – upon all of whom the long night of barbarism will descend, unbroken even by a star of hope, unless we conquer, as conquer we must; as conquer we shall.

'Arm yourselves, and be ye men of valour'

Today is Trinity Sunday. Centuries ago words were written to be a call and a spur to the faithful servants of truth and justice: 'Arm yourselves, and be ye men of valour, and be in readiness for the conflict; for it is better for us to perish in battle than to look upon the outrage of our nation and our altar. As the Will of God is in Heaven, even so let it be.'

'Fight them on the beaches'

House of Commons, London, 4 June 1940

On Dunkirk and the spirit of resistance

For the Allies, the die was cast when German tanks came within sight of the English Channel near Abbeville on 20 May. In doing so, they severed the British Expeditionary Force (BEF) and French troops in Flanders from the rest of the French Army. From Abbeville, the panzers swooped north to attack the Channel ports, cutting off the retreat of the BEF. Surrounded, the BEF could be pummelled into surrender. If this happened there would be insufficient troops remaining to defend Britain from the expected invasion.

Boulogne and Calais were both under attack by 23 May. These assaults brought the Germans to within ten miles of the one remaining Channel port from which the British Army could yet escape – Dunkirk. Had the panzers pressed on, they could have taken Dunkirk easily but at the vital moment Hitler ordered them to halt and await resupply. Perhaps fearful that they were already overstretched, the Führer believed they faced treacherously boggy conditions. Reichsmarschall Hermann Goering was meanwhile urging him to let the Luftwaffe deliver the *coup de grâce*.

A half-hearted attempt at a breakout near Arras having failed, the BEF continued to fall back towards this one free harbour. The British flank was opened-up further when the Belgian king ordered his troops to surrender. Churchill, meanwhile, instructed the British troops defending Calais to fight to the death so that the German advance on Dunkirk could be held up long enough for a rescue mission to be attempted.

The first troops were lifted from Dunkirk's harbour and beaches on the night of 27 May, but only 11,400 got away. There were still more than 200,000 British and 160,000 French troops desperately trying to escape the encircling jaws of the enemy.

On this arithmetic, the situation appeared hopeless. In the War Cabinet, Halifax suggested Britain enter into negotiations via Mussolini to explore terms for a negotiated peace. Churchill was appalled, asserting that there was no possibility of 'decent terms' being gained and that 'Nations which went down fighting rose again, but those who surrendered tamely were finished.' Taking his case to the full Cabinet, Churchill assured the assembled ministers that 'If this long island story of ours is to end at last, let it end only when each one of us lies choking in his own blood upon the ground.' Stirred, several colleagues began cheering him and banged the table in support. Shored up, he returned to the War Cabinet. There, at this critical juncture, his onetime adversary, Neville Chamberlain, swung round to offer him full support. Britain would not sue for peace. She would, if need be, go down fighting.

It was then that the epic of Dunkirk – some called it the miracle – intervened. The Germans were being held off while the Royal Navy – supplemented by reservists and

ON THIS DAY
4 JUNE 1940

• In the small hours, HMS *Shikari* is the last ship to evacuate men from the beaches of Dunkirk.

• As the Dunkirk 'miracle' concludes, Allied troops begin their evacuation from Norway after the unsuccessful Scandinavian intervention.

• Ernest Bevin, who is the powerful Cabinet member responsible for labour and national service, prepares to announce wartime regulations that ban strikes and ensure that the state controls the levers of power in vital industries such as munitions and engineering.

volunteers who risked their lives to steer their small ships, sailing boats, fishing vessels, even pleasure-steamers – came to the rescue of the stranded men.

Overhead, the Luftwaffe circled in for the kill, bombing and strafing the evacuees and their ships. Over 200 of the 860 vessels involved were sunk. But by the time the last boats left on 4 June and the Dunkirk beachhead was finally overrun, 224,318 British and 111,172 French troops had been rescued. Almost all their weapons and armour had been left behind in the scramble to get away, but considering that the initial estimate had been that only 20,000–45,000 might be evacuated, the retreat took on the mantle of a deliverance. By the skin of its teeth, it seemed, Britain might yet be saved.

When a week ago today I asked the House to fix this afternoon as the occasion for a statement, I feared it would be my hard lot to announce the greatest military disaster in our long history. I thought – and some good judges agreed with me – that perhaps 20,000 or 30,000 men might be re-embarked. But it certainly seemed that the whole of the French First Army and the whole of the British Expeditionary Force north of the Amiens–Abbeville gap, would be broken up in the open field or else would have to capitulate for lack of food and ammunition. These were the hard and heavy tidings for which I called upon the House and the nation to prepare themselves a week ago. The whole root and core and brain of the British Army, on which and around which we were to build, and are to build, the great British armies in the later years of the war, seemed about to perish upon the field or to be led into an ignominious and starving captivity.

'King Leopold . . . surrendered his army and exposed our whole flank and means of retreat'

That was the prospect a week ago. But another blow which might well have proved final was yet to fall upon us. The king of the Belgians had called upon us to come to his aid. Had not this ruler and his government severed themselves from the Allies, who rescued their country from extinction in the late war, and had they not sought refuge in what has proved to be a fatal neutrality, the French and British armies might well at the outset have saved not only Belgium but perhaps even Poland. Yet at the last moment when Belgium was already invaded, King Leopold called upon us to come to his aid, and even at the last moment we came. He and his brave, efficient army, nearly half a million strong, guarded our left flank and thus kept open our only line of retreat to the sea. Suddenly, without prior consultation, with the least possible notice, without the advice of his ministers and upon his own personal act, he sent a plenipotentiary to the German Command, surrendered his army and exposed our whole flank and means of retreat.

I asked the House a week ago to suspend its judgment because the facts were not clear, but I do not feel that any reason now exists why we should not form our own opinions upon this pitiful episode. The surrender of the Belgian Army compelled the British at the shortest notice to cover a flank to the sea more than thirty miles in length. Otherwise all would have been cut off, and all would have shared the fate to which King Leopold had condemned the finest army his country had ever formed. So in doing this and in exposing this flank, as anyone who followed the operations on the map will see, contact was lost between the British and two out of the three corps forming the First French Army, who were still farther from the coast than we were, and it seemed impossible that any large number of Allied troops could reach the coast.

'Pressing in upon the narrow exit . . . the enemy began to fire with cannon upon the beaches'

The enemy attacked on all sides with great strength and fierceness, and their main power, the power of their far more numerous air force, was thrown into the battle or else concentrated upon Dunkirk and the beaches. Pressing in upon the narrow exit, both from the east and from the west, the enemy began to fire with cannon upon the beaches by which alone the shipping could approach or depart. They sowed magnetic mines in the channels and seas; they sent repeated waves of hostile aircraft, sometimes more than a hundred strong in one formation, to cast their bombs upon the single pier that remained, and upon the sand dunes upon which the troops had their eyes for shelter. Their U-boats, one of which was sunk, and their motor launches took their toll of the vast traffic which now began. For four or five days an intense struggle reigned. All their armoured divisions – or what was left of them – together with great masses of infantry and artillery, hurled themselves in vain upon the ever-narrowing, ever-contracting appendix within which the British and French armies fought.

'Making trip after trip across the dangerous waters, bringing with them always men whom they had rescued'

Meanwhile, the Royal Navy, with the willing help of countless merchant seamen, strained every nerve to embark the British and Allied troops; 220 light warships and 650 other vessels were engaged. They had to operate upon the difficult coast, often in adverse weather, under an almost ceaseless hail of bombs and an increasing concentration of artillery fire. Nor were the seas, as I have said, themselves free from mines and torpedoes. It was in conditions such as these that our men carried on, with little or no rest, for days and nights on end, making trip after trip across the dangerous waters, bringing with them always men whom they had rescued. The numbers they have brought back are the measure of their devotion and their courage. The hospital ships, which brought off many thousands of British and French wounded, being so plainly marked were a special target for Nazi bombs; but the men and women on board them never faltered in their duty.

'Wars are not won by evacuations'

Meanwhile, the Royal Air Force, which had already been intervening in the battle, so far as its range would allow, from home bases, now used part of its main metropolitan fighter strength, and struck at the German bombers, and at the fighters which in large numbers protected them. This struggle was protracted and fierce. Suddenly the scene has cleared, the crash and thunder has for the moment – but only for the moment – died away. A miracle of deliverance, achieved by valour, by perseverance, by perfect discipline, by faultless service, by resource, by skill, by unconquerable fidelity, is manifest to us all. The enemy was hurled back by the retreating British and French troops. He was so roughly handled that he did not hurry their departure seriously. The Royal Air Force engaged the main strength of the German Air Force, and inflicted upon them losses of at least four to one; and the Navy, using nearly 1000 ships of all kinds, carried over 335,000 men, French and British, out of the jaws of death and shame, to their native land and to the tasks which lie immediately ahead. We must be very careful not to assign to this deliverance the attributes of a victory. Wars are not won by evacuations. But there was a victory inside this deliverance, which should be noted. It was gained by the Air Force. Many of our soldiers coming back have not seen the Air Force at work; they saw only the bombers which escaped its protective attack. They underrate its achievements. I have heard much talk of this; that is why I go out of my way to say this. I will tell you about it.

This was a great trial of strength between the British and German Air Forces. Can you conceive a greater objective for the Germans in the air than to make evacuation from these beaches impossible, and to sink all these ships which were displayed, almost to the extent of thousands? Could there have been an objective of greater military importance and significance for the whole purpose of the war than this? They tried hard, and they were beaten back; they were frustrated in their task. We got the Army away; and they have paid fourfold for any losses which they have inflicted. Very large formations of German aeroplanes – and we know that they are a very brave race – have turned on several occasions from the attack of one-quarter of their number of the Royal Air Force, and have dispersed in different directions. Twelve aeroplanes have been hunted by two. One aeroplane was driven into the water and cast away, by the mere charge of a British aeroplane, which had no more ammunition. All of our types – the Hurricane, the Spitfire and the new Defiant – and all our pilots have been vindicated as superior to what they have at present to face.

'I will pay my tribute to these young airmen . . . holding in their hands these instruments of colossal and shattering power'

When we consider how much greater would be our advantage in defending the air above this island against an overseas attack, I must say that I find in these facts a sure basis upon which practical and reassuring thoughts may rest. I will pay my tribute to these young airmen. The great French Army was very largely, for the time being, cast back and disturbed by the onrush of a few thousands of armoured vehicles. May it not also be that the cause of civilization itself will be defended by the skill and devotion of a few thousand airmen? There never had been, I suppose, in all the world, in all the history of war, such an opportunity for youth. The Knights of the Round Table, the Crusaders, all fall back into the past: not only distant but prosaic; these young men, going forth every morn to guard their native land and all that we stand for, holding in their hands these instruments of colossal and shattering power, of whom it may be said that

> 'Every morn brought forth a noble chance
> And every chance brought forth a noble knight'

deserve our gratitude, as do all of the brave men who, in so many ways and on so many occasions, are ready, and continue ready, to give life and all for their native land.

I return to the Army. In the long series of very fierce battles, now on this front, now on that, fighting on three fronts at once, battles fought by two or three divisions against an equal or somewhat larger number of the enemy, and fought fiercely on some of the old grounds that so many of us knew so well, in these battles our losses in men have exceeded 30,000 killed, wounded and missing. I take occasion to express the sympathy of the House to all who have suffered bereavement or who are still anxious. The President of the Board of Trade [Sir Andrew Duncan] is not here today. His son has been killed, and many in the House have felt the pangs of affliction in the sharpest form. But I will say this about the missing. We have had a large number of wounded come home safely to this country, but I would say about the missing that there may be very many reported missing who will come back home, some day, in one way or another. In the confusion of this fight it is inevitable that many have been left in positions where honour required no further resistance from them.

'Work is proceeding everywhere, night and day, Sundays and weekdays . . . already the flow of munitions has leapt forward'

Against this loss of over 30,000 men, we can set a far heavier loss certainly inflicted upon the enemy. But our losses in material are enormous. We have perhaps lost one-third of the men we lost in the opening days of the battle of March 21, 1918, but we have lost nearly as many guns – nearly 1000 – and all our transport, all the armoured vehicles that were with the Army in the north. This loss will impose a further delay on the expansion of our military strength. That expansion had not been proceeding as fast as we had hoped. The best of all we had to give had gone to the British Expeditionary Force, and although they had not the numbers of tanks and some articles of equipment which were desirable, they were a very well and finely equipped army. They had the first-fruits of all that our industry had to give, and that is gone. And now here is this further delay. How long it will be, how long it will last, depends upon the exertions which we make in this island. An effort the like of which has never been seen in our records is now being made. Work is proceeding everywhere, night and day, Sundays and weekdays. Capital and labour have cast aside their interests, rights and customs and put them into the common stock. Already the flow of munitions has leapt forward. There is no reason why we should not in a few months overtake the sudden and serious loss that has come upon us, without retarding the development of our general programme.

Nevertheless, our thankfulness at the escape of our Army and so many men, whose loved ones have passed through an agonizing week, must not blind us to the fact that what has happened in France and Belgium is a colossal military disaster. The French Army has been weakened, the Belgian Army has been lost, a large part of those fortified lines upon which so much faith had been reposed is gone, many valuable mining districts and factories have passed into the enemy's possession, the whole of the Channel ports are in his hands, with all the tragic consequences that follow from that, and we must expect another blow to be struck almost immediately at us or at France. We are told that Herr Hitler has a plan for invading the British Isles. This has often been thought of before. When Napoleon lay at Boulogne for a year with his flat-bottomed boats and his Grand Army, he was told by someone, 'There are bitter weeds in England.' There are certainly a great many more of them since the British Expeditionary Force returned . . .

'We shall fight on the beaches, we shall fight on the landing grounds, we shall fight in the fields and in the streets, we shall fight in the hills; we shall never surrender'

I have, myself, full confidence that if all do their duty, if nothing is neglected, and if the best arrangements are made, as they are being made, we shall prove ourselves once again able to defend our island home, to ride out the storm of war, and to outlive the menace of tyranny, if necessary for years, if necessary alone. At any rate, that is what we are going to try to do. That is the resolve of His Majesty's government – every man of them. That is the will of Parliament and the nation. The British Empire and the French Republic, linked together in their cause and in their need, will defend to the death their native soil, aiding each other like good comrades to the utmost of their strength. Even though large tracts of Europe and many old and famous states have fallen or may fall into the grip of the Gestapo and all the odious apparatus of Nazi rule, we shall not flag or fail. We shall go on to the end, we shall fight in France, we shall fight on the seas and oceans, we shall fight with growing confidence and growing strength in the air, we shall defend our island, whatever the cost may be, we shall fight on the beaches, we shall fight on the landing grounds, we shall fight in the fields and in the streets, we shall fight in the hills; we shall never surrender, and even if, which I do not for a moment believe, this island or a large part of it were subjugated and starving, then our Empire beyond the seas, armed and guarded by the British Fleet, would carry on the struggle, until, in God's good time, the New World, with all its power and might, steps forth to the rescue and the liberation of the Old.

'Their finest hour'

House of Commons, London,
later broadcast on 18 June 1940

On preparations for a
'Battle of Britain'

The escape from Dunkirk did not look like much of a deliverance for the French left to face the unrelenting fury of the Wehrmacht as it struck on south towards the Marne. There, the German advance had famously been halted in the desperate days of 1914, but this time was very different. On 7 June, the new French commander-in-chief, General Weygand, concluded the situation was irretrievable and began pressing his government to seek an armistice.

Two days later, the French government fled Paris. Flying over to discuss the crisis on 11 June, Churchill found France's political heads holed up near Briare, in the Loire. The British prime minister's offer of troop reinforcements (but no more precious aircraft – which were now needed for Britain's defence) did little to lift the spirits of a divided cabinet. Not so easily deflated, he made the journey again after they had moved on to Tours. But it was clear the defeatists were in the ascendancy. It was not as if there were any grounds for optimism. Churchill was with them when the news arrived that Paris had fallen, without a fight.

By then there was also a new fascist foe. On 10 June, with the timing of a dedicated opportunist, Mussolini had joined his Axis partner in the fight. Britain and France were now at war with Italy too. Nothing Churchill could do, not even the rather desperate offer of an Anglo-French union, could shake what had become the majority view at Tours that further resistance was useless. On 16 June, Reynaud bowed to the inevitable and resigned. Marshal Pétain – a hero of France's heroic defence of Verdun in the last war – formed a new government and immediately sued for peace.

ON THIS DAY
18 JUNE 1940

• Attempting to rally France in its hour of crisis, the tank officer General de Gaulle broadcasts from London, urging continued resistance.

• With Italy joining the Axis, the war becomes truly global, as Britain's East African colonies and mandates take on the Italian forces in Abyssinia (Ethiopia), the independent African country Italy overran in 1935–6.

• In Germany, Mussolini and Hitler discuss terms for any peace with France, and Il Duce's ambitions for territorial acquisition in southern France are quashed by Hitler.

Hitler's terms were agreed on 22 June, the signatures extracted in the same railway carriage – preserved at Compiègne – in which Germany's defeated envoys had signed the armistice in 1918. It was, as Hitler fully intended, a moment of supreme revenge. His army had won in 43 days what in all the bloodbath of the First World War the Kaiser's legions had failed to achieve in 4 years.

Hitler had grounds for satisfaction. On 24 June, he boasted that 'the war in the West is ended'. The statement was at odds with his fast evolving plans for the remaining foe across the English Channel. What terms would he offer there? Urging the public to brace itself, Churchill insisted only that the Battle of Britain was about to begin.

'Whatever happened in France would make no difference to the resolve of Britain'

The disastrous military events which have happened during the past fortnight have not come to me with any sense of surprise. Indeed, I indicated a fortnight ago as clearly as I could to the House that the worst possibilities were open; and I made it perfectly clear then that whatever happened in France would make no difference to the resolve of Britain and the British Empire to fight on, 'if necessary for years, if necessary alone'. During the last few days we have successfully brought off the great majority of the troops we had on the lines of communication in France; and seven-eighths of the troops we have sent to France since the beginning of the war – that is to say, about 350,000 out of 400,000 men – are safely back in this country. Others are still fighting with the French, and fighting with considerable success in their local encounters against the enemy. We have also brought back a great mass of stores, rifles and munitions of all kinds which had been accumulated in France during the last nine months.

'We intend to call up, drill and train further large numbers'

We have, therefore, in this island today a very large and powerful military force. This force comprises all our best trained and our finest troops, including scores of thousands of those who have already measured their quality against the Germans and found themselves at no disadvantage. We have under arms at the present time in this island over a million and a quarter men. Behind these we have the Local Defence Volunteers, numbering half a million, only a portion of whom, however, are yet armed with rifles or other firearms. We have incorporated into our defence forces every man for whom we have a weapon. We expect very large additions to our weapons in the near future, and in preparation for this we intend forthwith to call up, drill and train further large numbers. Those who are not called up, or else are employed upon the vast business of munitions production in all its branches – and their ramifications are innumerable – will serve their country best by remaining at their ordinary work until they receive their summons. We have also over here Dominions armies. The Canadians had actually landed in France, but have now been safely withdrawn, much disappointed, but in perfect order, with all their artillery and equipment. And these very high-class forces from the Dominions will now take part in the defence of the mother country.

Lest the account which I have given of these large forces should raise the question: Why did they not take part in the great battle in France? I must make it clear that, apart from the divisions training and organizing at home, only twelve divisions were equipped to fight upon a scale which justified their being sent abroad. And this was fully up to the number which the French had been led to expect would be available in France at the ninth month of the war. The rest of our forces at home have a fighting value for home defence which will, of course, steadily increase every week that passes. Thus, the invasion of Great Britain would at this time require the transportation across the sea of hostile armies on a very large scale, and after they had been so transported they would have to be continually maintained with all the masses of munitions and supplies which are required for continuous battle – as continuous battle it will surely be.

Churchill made clear that the Royal Navy remained the first line of defence, ready to intercept any sizeable invasion armada 'long before it reached the coast' while minefields and coastal defences would account for those who got closer to the shore.

'Can we break Hitler's air weapon'

This brings me, naturally, to the great question of invasion from the air, and of the impending struggle between the British and German Air Forces. It seems quite clear that no invasion on a scale beyond the capacity of our land forces to crush speedily is likely to take place from the air until our Air Force has been definitely overpowered. In the meantime, there may be raids by parachute troops and attempted descents of airborne soldiers. We should be able to give those gentry a warm reception, both in the air and on the ground, if they reach it in any condition to continue the dispute. But the great question is: Can we break Hitler's air weapon? Now, of course, it is a very great pity that we have not got an Air Force at least equal to that of the most powerful enemy within striking distance of these shores. But we have a very powerful Air Force which has proved itself far superior in quality, both in men and in many types of machine, to what we have met so far in the numerous and fierce air battles which have been fought with the Germans. In France, where we were at a considerable disadvantage and lost many machines on the ground when they were standing around the aerodromes, we were accustomed to inflict in the air losses of as much as two to two-and-a-half to one. In the fighting over Dunkirk, which was a sort of no-man's-land, we undoubtedly beat the German Air Force, and gained the mastery of the local air, inflicting here a loss of three or four to one day after day. Anyone who looks at the photographs which were published a week or so ago of the re-embarkation, showing the masses of troops assembled on the beach and forming an ideal target for hours at a time, must realize that this re-embarkation would not have been possible unless the enemy had resigned all hope of recovering air superiority at that time and at that place.

In the defence of this island the advantages to the defenders will be much greater than they were in the fighting around Dunkirk. We hope to improve on the rate of three or four to one which was realized at Dunkirk; and in addition all our injured machines and their crews which get down safely – and, surprisingly, a very great many injured machines and men do get down safely in modern air fighting – all of these will fall, in an attack upon these islands, on friendly soil and live to fight another day; whereas all the injured enemy machines and their complements will be total losses as far as the war is concerned.

'Our fighter pilots – those splendid men, this brilliant youth – who will have the glory of saving their native land, their island home, and all they love'

During the great battle in France, we gave very powerful and continuous aid to the French Army, both by fighters and bombers; but in spite of every kind of pressure we never would allow the entire metropolitan fighter strength of the Air Force to be consumed. This decision was painful, but it was also right, because the fortunes of the battle in France could not have been decisively affected even if we had thrown in our entire fighter force. That battle was lost by the unfortunate strategical opening, by the extraordinary and unforeseen power of the armoured columns and by the great preponderance of the German Army in numbers. Our fighter Air Force might easily have been exhausted as a mere accident in that great struggle, and then we should have found ourselves at the present time in a very serious plight. But as it is, I am happy to inform the House that our fighter strength is stronger at the present time relatively to the Germans, who have suffered terrible losses, than it has ever been; and consequently we believe ourselves possessed of the capacity to continue the war in the air under better conditions than we have ever experienced before. I look forward confidently to the exploits of our fighter pilots – these splendid men, this brilliant youth – who will have the glory of saving their native land, their island home, and all they love, from the most deadly of all attacks.

'Every man and every woman will have the chance to show the finest qualities of their race'

There remains, of course, the danger of bombing attacks, which will certainly be made very soon upon us by the bomber forces of the enemy. It is true that the German bomber force is superior in numbers to ours; but we have a very large bomber force also, which we shall use to strike at military targets in Germany without intermission. I do not at all underrate the severity of the ordeal which lies before us; but I believe our countrymen will show themselves capable of standing up to it, like the brave men of Barcelona, and will be able to stand up to it, and carry on in spite of it, at least as well as any other people in the world. Much will depend upon this; every man and every woman will have the chance to show the finest qualities of their race, and render the highest service to their cause. For all of us, at this time, whatever our sphere, our station, our occupation or our duties, it will be a help to remember the famous lines:

> 'He nothing common did or mean,
> Upon that memorable scene.'

'Messages couched in the most moving terms in which they endorse our decision to fight on'

I have thought it right upon this occasion to give the House and the country some indication of the solid, practical grounds upon which we base our inflexible resolve to continue the war. There are a good many people who say, 'Never mind. Win or lose, sink or swim, better die than submit to tyranny – and such a tyranny.' And I do not dissociate myself from them. But I can assure them that our professional advisers of the three Services unitedly advise that we should carry on the war, and that there are good and reasonable hopes of final victory. We have fully informed and consulted all the self-governing Dominions, these great communities far beyond the oceans who have been built up on our laws and on our civilization, and who are absolutely free to choose their course, but are absolutely devoted to the ancient motherland, and who feel themselves inspired by the same emotions which lead me to stake our all upon duty and honour. We have fully consulted them, and I have received from their prime ministers, Mr Mackenzie King of Canada, Mr Menzies of Australia, Mr Fraser of New Zealand and General Smuts of South Africa – that wonderful man, with his immense profound mind, and his eye watching from a distance the whole panorama of European affairs – I have received from all these eminent men, who all have governments behind them elected on wide franchises, who are all there because they represent the will of their people, messages couched in the most moving terms in which they endorse our decision to fight on, and declare themselves ready to share our fortunes and to persevere to the end. That is what we are going to do.

We may now ask ourselves: In what way has our position worsened since the beginning of the war? It has worsened by the fact that the Germans have conquered a large part of the coastline of Western Europe, and many small countries have been overrun by them. This aggravates the possibilities of air attack and adds to our naval preoccupations. It in no way diminishes, but on the contrary definitely increases, the power of our long-distance blockade. Similarly, the entrance of Italy into the war increases the power of our long-distance blockade. We have stopped the worst leak by that. We do not know whether military resistance will come to an end in France or not, but should it do so, then of course the Germans will be able to concentrate their forces, both military and industrial, upon us. But for the reasons I have given to the House these will not be found so easy to apply. If invasion has become more imminent, as no doubt it has, we, being relieved from the task of maintaining a large army in France, have far larger and more efficient forces to meet it.

If Hitler can bring under his despotic control the industries of the countries he has conquered, this will add greatly to his already vast armament output. On the other hand, this will not happen immediately, and we are now assured of immense, continuous and increasing support in supplies and munitions of all kinds from the United States; and especially of aeroplanes and pilots from the Dominions and across the oceans, coming from regions which are beyond the reach of enemy bombers.

'The winter will impose a strain upon the Nazi regime, with almost all Europe writhing and starving under its cruel heel'

I do not see how any of these factors can operate to our detriment on balance before the winter comes; and the winter will impose a strain upon the Nazi regime, with almost all Europe writhing and starving under its cruel heel, which, for all their ruthlessness, will run them very hard. We must not forget that from the moment when we declared war on September 3 it was always possible for Germany to turn all her Air Force upon this country, together with any other devices of invasion she might conceive, and that France could have done little or nothing to prevent her doing so. We have, therefore, lived under this danger, in principle and in a slightly modified form, during all these months. In the meanwhile, however, we have enormously improved our methods of defence, and we have learned, what we had no right to assume at the beginning, namely, that the individual aircraft and the individual British pilot have a sure and definite superiority. Therefore, in casting up this dread balance-sheet and contemplating our dangers with a disillusioned eye, I see great reason for intense vigilance and exertion, but none whatever for panic or despair.

During the first four years of the last war the Allies experienced nothing but disaster and disappointment. That was our constant fear: one blow after another, terrible losses, frightful dangers. Everything miscarried. And yet at the end of those four years the morale of the Allies was higher than that of the Germans, who had moved from one aggressive triumph to another, and who stood everywhere triumphant invaders of the lands into which they had broken. During that war we repeatedly asked ourselves the question: How are we going to win? and no one was able ever to answer it with much precision, until at the end, quite suddenly, quite unexpectedly, our terrible foe collapsed before us, and we were so glutted with victory that in our folly we threw it away.

We do not yet know what will happen in France or whether the French resistance will be prolonged, both in France and in the French Empire overseas. The French government will be throwing away great opportunities and casting adrift their future if they do not continue the war in accordance with their treaty obligations, from which we have not felt able to release them. The House will have read the historic declaration in which, at the desire of many Frenchmen – and of our own hearts – we have proclaimed our willingness at the darkest hour in French history to conclude a union of common citizenship in this struggle. However matters may go in France or with the French government, or other French governments, we in this island and in the British Empire will never lose our sense of comradeship with the French people. If we are now called upon to endure what they have been suffering, we shall emulate their courage, and if final victory rewards our toils they shall share the gains, aye, and freedom shall be restored to all. We abate nothing of our just demands; not one jot or tittle do we recede. Czechs, Poles, Norwegians, Dutch, Belgians have joined their causes to our own. All these shall be restored.

'If the British Empire and its Commonwealth last for a thousand years, men will still say, "This was their finest hour"'

What General Weygand called the Battle of France is over. I expect that the Battle of Britain is about to begin. Upon this battle depends the survival of Christian civilization. Upon it depends our own British life, and the long continuity of our institutions and our Empire. The whole fury and might of the enemy must very soon be turned on us. Hitler knows that he will have to break us in this island or lose the war. If we can stand up to him, all Europe may be free and the life of the world may move forward into broad, sunlit uplands. But if we fail, then the whole world, including the United States, including all that we have known and cared for, will sink into the abyss of a new dark age made more sinister, and perhaps more protracted, by the lights of perverted science. Let us therefore brace ourselves to our duties, and so bear ourselves that, if the British Empire and its Commonwealth last for a thousand years, men will still say, 'This was their finest hour.'

'What we were to do about the French Fleet'

House of Commons, London, 4 July 1940

On destroying part of the French fleet

There was considerable Anglo-French mutual recrimination over responsibility for the disaster that had befallen France. Always a Francophile in his heart, Churchill refused to dwell upon such matters. He was quick to insist that France would rise again and equally swift in his endorsement of Charles de Gaulle, who had established himself in London as the leader in exile of the 'Free French'. The lanky and imperiously mannered general had moral authority but commanded only a rump of soldiers and sailors who had escaped with him across the English Channel. He would be achieving nothing without his host's assistance.

De Gaulle's compatriots left behind in northern France were now under direct German occupation. The south, meanwhile, was to be administered by Marshal Pétain's government which had set itself up in the spa town of Vichy. Existing on the sufferance of the Germans, the price of the Vichy regime's survival was inevitably its ability to do Germany's bidding. One of Pétain's first acts was to order the arrest of his predecessor, Paul Reynaud, and those other senior politicians deemed to be enemies of cohabitation with the Nazis.

French citizens still at liberty – in the unoccupied colonies or on the high seas – were forced to decide to which authority their allegiance lay. Those administering the colonies in northwest Africa opted to back Vichy as the legitimate government. Interpreting France's armistice terms as potentially putting her navy at Germany's disposal, Churchill was especially anxious that the French warships should either come over to the British or 'Free French' side or put themselves out of German reach.

On 3 July, the Royal Navy sailed towards Mers el-Kebir, the French naval base at Oran in Algeria. Nine hours of negotiation followed, during which the French Admiral Gensoul was given the options of sailing to British ports in order to join the Free French in the war against Germany, handing his ships over to British personnel, berthing the ships in the French West Indies where they could be demilitarized, or putting the ships himself beyond use by scuttling them. But none of these options tempted Gensoul as much as doing what he saw as his duty of loyalty to the terms Pétain's new government had agreed with the Germans. It thus fell to the Royal Navy to enact the unsavoury task of opening fire on those who had been allies only days previously. Over 1300 French sailors were killed in the bombardment which succeeded in putting the better part of the French Navy beyond the Axis's grasp.

There was outrage in France. Pétain's government responded by breaking off diplomatic relations. But in Westminster the reaction was not what might have been expected. The terrible episode demonstrated that in Winston Churchill Britain had at last found a leader who would not shrink from determined and resolute action. When he

ON THIS DAY
4 JULY 1940

• The more numerous Italian forces make inroads into Sudan, in East Africa.

• Two policemen are killed in New York, when a timebomb explodes in the British section of the 1939–40 World's Fair exhibition.

• A military court under the emerging French Vichy regime imposes a custodial sentence and fine on General de Gaulle in his absence.

finished his solemn account of what had happened, there was an eruption of cheering from all sides of the House of Commons. It was the first time even Neville Chamberlain's supporters among Conservative MPs deemed his successor worthy of a standing ovation. For Churchill, personally, it was a pivotal moment.

It is with sincere sorrow that I must now announce to the House the measures which we have felt bound to take in order to prevent the French Fleet from falling into German hands. When two nations are fighting together under long and solemn alliance against a common foe, one of them may be stricken down and overwhelmed, and may be forced to ask its ally to release it from its obligations. But the least that could be expected was that the French government, in abandoning the conflict and leaving its whole weight to fall upon Great Britain and the British Empire, would have been careful not to inflict needless injury upon their faithful comrade, in whose final victory the sole chance of French freedom lay, and lies.

As the House will remember, we offered to give full release to the French from their treaty obligations, although these were designed for precisely the case which arose, on one condition, namely, that the French Fleet should be sailed for British harbours before the separate armistice negotiations with the enemy were completed. This was not done, but on the contrary, in spite of every kind of private and personal promise and assurance given by Admiral Darlan to the First Lord and to his naval colleague the First Sea Lord of the British Admiralty, an armistice was signed which was bound to place the French Fleet as effectively in the power of Germany and its Italian following as that portion of the French Fleet [that] was placed in our power when many of them, being unable to reach African ports, came into the harbours of Portsmouth and Plymouth about ten days ago. Thus I must place on record that what might have been a mortal injury was done to us by the Bordeaux government with full knowledge of the consequences and of our dangers, and after rejecting all our appeals at the moment when they were abandoning the alliance, and breaking the engagements which fortified it.

'This callous and perhaps even malevolent treatment . . . from the Bordeaux government . . . will not be condoned by history'

There was another example of this callous and perhaps even malevolent treatment which we received, not indeed from the French nation, who have never been and apparently never are to be consulted upon these transactions, but from the Bordeaux government. This is the instance. There were over 400 German air pilots who were prisoners in France, many of them, perhaps most of them, shot down by the Royal Air Force. I obtained from Monsieur Reynaud a personal promise that these pilots should be sent for safe keeping to England, and orders were given by him to that effect; but when Monsieur Reynaud fell, these pilots were delivered over to Germany in order, no doubt, to win favour for the Bordeaux government with their German masters, and to win it without regard to the injury done to us. The German Air Force already feels acutely the shortage of high-grade pilots, and it seemed to me particularly odious, if I may use the word, that these 400 skilled men should be handed over with the sure knowledge that they would be used to bomb this country, and thus force our airmen to shoot them down for the second time over. Such wrongful deeds I am sure will not be condoned by history, and I firmly believe that a generation of Frenchmen will arise who will clear their national honour from all countenance of them.

'Early yesterday morning ... we took the greater part of the French Fleet under our control'

I said last week that we must now look with particular attention to our own salvation. I have never in my experience seen discussed in a Cabinet so grim and sombre a question as what we were to do about the French Fleet. It shows how strong were the reasons for the course which we thought it our duty to take, that every member of the Cabinet had the same conviction about what should be done and there was not the slightest hesitation or divergence among them, and that the three service ministers, as well as men like the minister of information and the secretary of state for the colonies, particularly noted for their long friendship with France, when they were consulted were equally convinced that no other decision than that which we took was possible. We took that decision, and it was a decision to which, with aching hearts but with clear vision, we unitedly came. Accordingly early yesterday morning, July 3, after all preparations had been made, we took the greater part of the French Fleet under our control, or else called upon them, with adequate force, to comply with our requirements. Two battleships, two light cruisers, some submarines, including a very large one, the *Surcouf*, eight destroyers and approximately 200 smaller but extremely useful minesweeping and anti-submarine craft which lay, for the most part at Portsmouth and Plymouth, though there were some at Sheerness, were boarded by superior forces, after brief notice had been given wherever possible to their captains.

This operation was successfully carried out without resistance or bloodshed except in one instance. A scuffle arose through a misunderstanding in the submarine *Surcouf*, in which one British leading seaman was killed and two British officers and one rating wounded and one French officer killed and one wounded. For the rest, the French sailors, in the main, cheerfully accepted the end of a period of uncertainty. A considerable number, 800 to 900, have expressed an ardent desire to continue the war, and some have asked for British nationality. This we are ready to grant without prejudice to the other Frenchmen, numbered by thousands, who prefer to fight on with us as Frenchmen. All the rest of those crews will be immediately repatriated to French ports, if the French government are able to make arrangements for their reception by permission of their German rulers. We are also repatriating all French troops who were in this country, excepting those who, of their own free will, have volunteered to follow General de Gaulle in the French Forces of Liberation of whom he is chief. Several French submarines have also joined us independently, and we have accepted their services.

'I fear the loss of life among the French and in the harbour must have been very heavy'

Churchill then narrated the sequence of events that caused the Royal Navy to attack the French Fleet at Mers el-Kebir.

... I need hardly say that the French ships fought, albeit in this unnatural cause, with the characteristic courage of the French Navy, and every allowance must be made for Admiral Gensoul and his officers who felt themselves obliged to obey the orders they received from their government and could not look behind that government to see the German dictation. I fear the loss of life among the French and in the harbour must have been very heavy, as we were compelled to use a severe measure of force and several immense explosions were heard. None of the British ships taking part in the action was in any way affected in gun-power or mobility by the heavy fire directed upon them. I have not yet received any reports of our casualties, but Admiral Somerville's Fleet is, in all military respects, intact and ready for further action. The Italian Navy, for whose reception we had also made arrangements and which is, of course, considerably stronger numerically than the Fleet we used at Oran, kept prudently out of the way. However, we trust that their turn will come during the operations which we shall pursue to secure the effectual command of the Mediterranean.

> ## 'I leave the judgment of our action, with confidence, to Parliament. I leave it to the nation, and I leave it to the United States. I leave it to the world and history.'

A large proportion of the French Fleet has, therefore, passed into our hands or has been put out of action or otherwise withheld from Germany by yesterday's events. The House will not expect me to say anything about other French ships which are at large except that it is our inflexible resolve to do everything that is possible in order to prevent them falling into the German grip. I leave the judgment of our action, with confidence, to Parliament. I leave it to the nation, and I leave it to the United States. I leave it to the world and history …

Churchill quoted a message of resolve and the need to maintain morale, which was being sent to those in positions of authority, before coming to his conclusion.

… In conclusion, I feel that we are entitled to the confidence of the House and that we shall not fail in our duty, however painful. The action we have already taken should be, in itself, sufficient to dispose once and for all of the lies and rumours which have been so industriously spread by German propaganda and through Fifth Column activities that we have the slightest intention of entering into negotiations in any form and through any channel with the German and Italian governments. We shall, on the contrary, prosecute the war with the utmost vigour by all the means that are open to us until the righteous purposes for which we entered upon it have been fulfilled.

'The war of the unknown warriors'

World broadcast, 14 July 1940

On the need to pull together for victory

The speed with which France had collapsed under the German blitzkrieg naturally begged the question whether Britain would prove any more resilient when her time came. Churchill had to demonstrate not just to his own countrymen and women but to the wider world – and the United States in particular – that circumstances would dictate a different conclusion. When delivering this international broadcast he therefore chose to emphasize the extent to which the withdrawal from France actually improved the United Kingdom's chances, transforming the island into a giant armed camp, far more defendable than those countries that had succumbed to date. It was crucial, too, that a sense of activity and broad participation should keep defeatist attitudes at bay. If Britons thought their fate rested solely with a few politicians and generals, some of whom they held responsible for getting the country into its current peril, fear and discontent could result. Churchill's speech, entitled 'The war of the unknown warriors', emphasized that victory was dependent upon everyone – no matter how obscure or lowly – playing their part.

ON THIS DAY
14 JULY 1940

- Contingents of Free French forces in London celebrate their native country's Bastille Day, with General de Gaulle laying a wreath at the Cenotaph in Whitehall.

- A British commando raid on the Channel Islands, now occupied by German forces, becomes a catalogue of accidents: clearly, there is a lot to learn about sabotage, and later in July the War Cabinet decides to set up the Special Operations Executive (SOE)

- The Baltic states (Latvia, Lithuania, Estonia), occupied by the Red Army under the terms of the Nazi-Soviet Non-Aggression Pact, 'vote' to become Soviet republics.

During the last fortnight the British Navy, in addition to blockading what is left of the German Fleet and chasing the Italian Fleet, has had imposed upon it the sad duty of putting effectually out of action for the duration of the war the capital ships of the French Navy. These, under the armistice terms, signed in the railway coach at Compiègne, would have been placed within the power of Nazi Germany. The transference of these ships to Hitler would have endangered the security of both Great Britain and the United States. We therefore had no choice but to act as we did, and to act forthwith. Our painful task is now complete. Although the unfinished battleship the *Jean Bart* still rests in a Moroccan harbour and there are a number of French warships at Toulon and in various French ports all over the world, these are not in a condition or of a character to derange our preponderance of naval power. As long, therefore, as they make no attempt to return to ports controlled by Germany or Italy, we shall not molest them in any way. That melancholy phase in our relations with France has, so far as we are concerned, come to an end.

'Faith is given to us, to help and comfort us when we stand in awe before the unfurling scroll of human destiny'

Let us think rather of the future. Today is the fourteenth of July, the national festival of France. A year ago in Paris I watched the stately parade down the Champs Elysées of the

French Army and the French Empire. Who can foresee what the course of other years will bring? Faith is given to us, to help and comfort us when we stand in awe before the unfurling scroll of human destiny. And I proclaim my faith that some of us will live to see a fourteenth of July when a liberated France will once again rejoice in her greatness and in her glory, and once again stand forward as the champion of the freedom and the rights of man. When the day dawns, as dawn it will, the soul of France will turn with comprehension and with kindness to those Frenchmen and Frenchwomen, wherever they may be, who in the darkest hour did not despair of the Republic.

'You need not bear malice because of your friend's cries of delirium and gestures of agony'

In the meantime, we shall not waste our breath nor cumber our thought with reproaches. When you have a friend and comrade at whose side you have faced tremendous struggles, and your friend is smitten down by a stunning blow, it may be necessary to make sure that the weapon that has fallen from his hands shall not be added to the resources of your common enemy. But you need not bear malice because of your friend's cries of delirium and gestures of agony. You must not add to his pain; you must work for his recovery. The association of interest between Britain and France remains. The cause remains. Duty inescapable remains. So long as our pathway to victory is not impeded, we are ready to discharge such offices of good will towards the French government as may be possible, and to foster the trade and help the administration of those parts of the great French Empire which are now cut off from captive France, but which maintain their freedom. Subject to the iron demands of the war which we are waging against Hitler and all his works, we shall try so to conduct ourselves that every true French heart will beat and glow at the way we carry on the struggle; and that not only France, but all the oppressed countries in Europe may feel that each British victory is a step towards the liberation of the Continent from the foulest thralldom into which it has ever been cast.

All goes to show that the war will be long and hard. No one can tell where it will spread. One thing is certain: the peoples of Europe will not be ruled for long by the Nazi Gestapo, nor will the world yield itself to Hitler's gospel of hatred, appetite and domination.

'We await undismayed the impending assault'

And now it has come to us to stand alone in the breach, and face the worst that the tyrant's might and enmity can do. Bearing ourselves humbly before God, but conscious that we serve an unfolding purpose, we are ready to defend our native land against the invasion by which it is threatened. We are fighting by ourselves alone; but we are not fighting for ourselves alone. Here in this strong City of Refuge which enshrines the title-deeds of human progress and is of deep consequence to Christian civilization; here, girt about by the seas and oceans where the Navy reigns; shielded from above by the prowess and devotion of our airmen – we await undismayed the impending assault. Perhaps it will come tonight. Perhaps it will come next week. Perhaps it will never come. We must show ourselves equally capable of meeting a sudden violent shock, or what is perhaps a harder test, a prolonged vigil. But be the ordeal sharp or long, or both, we shall seek no terms, we shall tolerate no parley; we may show mercy – we shall ask for none.

I can easily understand how sympathetic onlookers across the Atlantic, or anxious friends in the yet unravished countries of Europe, who cannot measure our resources or our resolve, may have feared for our survival when they saw so many states and kingdoms torn to pieces in a few weeks or even days by the monstrous force of the Nazi war machine. But Hitler has not yet been withstood by a great nation with a will-power the equal of his own. Many of these countries have been poisoned by intrigue before they were struck down by violence. They have been rotted from within before they were smitten from without. How else can you explain what has happened to France? – to the French Army, to the French people, to the leaders of the French people?

'We would rather see London laid in ruins and ashes than that it should be tamely and abjectly enslaved'

But here, in our island, we are in good health, and in good heart. We have seen how Hitler prepared in scientific detail the plans for destroying the neighbour countries of Germany. He had his plans for Poland and his plans for Norway. He had his plans for Denmark. He had his plans all worked out for the doom of the peaceful, trustful Dutch; and, of course, for the Belgians. We have seen how the French were undermined and overthrown. We may therefore be sure that there is a plan – perhaps built up over years – for destroying Great Britain, which after all has the honour to be his main and foremost enemy. All I can say is that any plan for invading Britain which Hitler made two months ago must have had to be entirely re-cast in order to meet our new position. Two months ago – nay, one month ago – our first and main effort was to keep our best army in France. All our regular troops, all our output of munitions, and a very large part of our Air Force, had to be sent to France and maintained in action there. But now we have it all at home. Never before in the last war – or in this – have we had in this island an Army comparable in quality, equipment or numbers to that which stands here on guard tonight. We have a million and a half men in the British Army under arms tonight, and every week of June and July has seen their organization, their defences and their striking power advance by leaps and bounds. No praise is too high for the officers and men – aye, and civilians – who have made this immense transformation in so short a time. Behind these soldiers of the Regular Army, as a means of destruction for parachutists, airborne invaders, and any traitors that may be found in our midst (but I do not believe there are many – woe betide them, they will get short shrift), behind the Regular Army we have more than a million of the Local Defence Volunteers, or, as they are much better called, the 'Home Guard'. These officers and men, a large proportion of whom have been through the last war, have the strongest desire to attack and come to close quarters with the enemy wherever he may appear. Should the invader come to Britain, there will be no placid lying down of the people in submission before him as we have seen, alas, in other countries. We shall defend every village, every town, and every city. The vast mass of London itself, fought street by street, could easily devour an entire hostile army; and we would rather see London laid in ruins and ashes than that it should be tamely and abjectly enslaved. I am bound to state these facts, because it is necessary to inform our people of our intentions, and thus to reassure them.

This has been a great week for the Royal Air Force, and for the Fighter Command. They have shot down more than five to one of the German aircraft which have tried to molest our convoys in the Channel, or have ventured to cross the British coastline. These are of course, only the preliminary encounters to the great air battles which lie ahead. But I know of no reason why we should be discontented with the results so far achieved; although, of course, we hope to improve upon them as the fighting becomes more widespread and comes more inland. Around all lies the power of the Royal Navy. With over a thousand armed ships under the white ensign, patrolling the seas, the Navy, which is capable of transferring its force very readily to the protection of any part of the British Empire which may be threatened, is capable also of keeping open communication with the New World, from whom, as the struggle deepens, increasing aid will come. Is it not remarkable that after ten months of unlimited U-boat and air attack upon our commerce, our food reserves are higher than they have ever been, and we have a substantially larger tonnage under our own flag, apart from great numbers of foreign ships in our control, than we had at the beginning of the war?

'While we toil through the dark valley we can see the sunlight on the uplands beyond'

Why do I dwell on all this? Not, surely, to induce any slackening of effort or vigilance. On the contrary. These must be redoubled, and we must prepare not only for the summer, but for the winter; not only for 1941, but for 1942; when the war will, I trust, take a different form from the defensive, in which it has hitherto been bound. I dwell on these elements in our strength – on these resources which we have mobilized and control – I dwell on them because it is right to show that the good cause can command the means of survival; and that while we toil through the dark valley we can see the sunlight on the uplands beyond.

I stand at the head of a government representing all parties in the state – all creeds, all classes, every recognizable section of opinion. We are ranged beneath the Crown of our ancient monarchy. We are supported by a free Parliament and a free press; but there is one bond which unites us all and sustains us in the public regard – namely (as is increasingly becoming known), that we are prepared to proceed to all extremities, to endure them and to enforce them; that is our bond of union in His Majesty's government tonight. Thus only, in times like these, can nations preserve their freedom; and thus only can they uphold the cause entrusted to their care.

'This is a war of the unknown warriors'

But all depends now upon the whole life-strength of the British race in every part of the world and of all our associated peoples and of all our well-wishers in every land, doing their utmost night and day, giving all, daring all, enduring all – to the utmost – to the end. This is no war of chieftains or of princes, of dynasties or national ambition; it is a war of peoples and of causes. There are vast numbers not only in this island but in every land, who will render faithful service in this war, but whose names will never be known, whose deeds will never be recorded. This is a war of the unknown warriors; but let all strive without failing in faith or in duty, and the dark curse of Hitler will be lifted from our age.

'Never in the field of
human conflict'

House of Commons, London, 20 August 1940

On the war's first year and the
Battle of Britain

On 13 August Hitler unleashed upon Britain *Adler Tag* (Eagle Day), the greatest air assault the world had yet seen. The aim was to annihilate the Royal Air Force. Destroying Britain's air protection might prove enough to force its politicians to negotiate peace. But if stubbornness persisted, the Luftwaffe's attainment of air superiority would give Germany the edge if Hitler gave the go-ahead for *Operation Seelöwe* (Operation Sea Lion) – the invasion of Britain. Despite the Führer's nervousness about so great an undertaking, on 16 July he had ordered those tasked with planning the invasion to be ready to put it into action in mid-August.

The Luftwaffe high command predicted victory within a fortnight. It was hardly an arrogant assumption given that they outnumbered the RAF by three to one. In the dogfights that had taken place largely over the English Channel during June and July, the RAF had lost pilots at a rate of attrition that would extinguish Britain's trained personnel before it exhausted Germany's supply of airmen.

But playing over their home turf, the British had several key advantages. In particular, they benefited from the early warning provided by radar, the speed and manoeuvrability of the Spitfire and Hurricane fighter planes, the ability to return shot-down but unscathed pilots to their bases ready to face the next wave of attack and the selfless bravery of pilots – many of them scarcely in their twenties – determined to defend their homeland. The pilots were supplemented by equally resolute airmen from the British Commonwealth and those skilled French, Czech and Polish pilots who had managed to make it across the Channel.

The Luftwaffe's first targets were the radar transmitters, but the German planes failed to put them out of long-term action. They were also determined to destroy the airfields from which the RAF could operate. On 15 August, the Luftwaffe launched a great assault on the RAF's bases. Every available fighter was sent up into the air to engage the onslaught. A desperate struggle ensued on one of the most important days of the conflict. By dusk, 75 enemy aircraft had been shot down for the RAF's loss of 34. Yet, more importantly, while several of Fighter Command's bases sustained heavy damage, none was put out of action for long. Another massive attack was seen off three days later, the tally going in Britain's favour by 71 to 27.

This was not the end. Wave after wave, day after day, the Luftwaffe kept coming. But despite their vast superiority in numbers, they were still denied the opportunity to deliver the knock-out punch. The summer skies over southern England and the Channel were criss-crossed with trailer smoke from the dogfights.

ON THIS DAY
20 AUGUST 1940

• Over 100 RAF bombers attack targets in France and the Low Countries, while Italian planes bomb the strategically essential British outpost of Gibraltar. Mussolini also begins blockading British Mediterranean ports, as part of the Anglo-Italian struggle for naval control in the region.

• An assassin armed with an ice-pick fatally wounds the exiled Russian revolutionary Leon Trotsky at his home in Mexico City. He has been a vehement critic of Stalin.

• Large and coordinated attacks by Chinese communists in northern China severely damage the communications of the occupying Japanese forces.

In a war of mechanization and mass slaughter, here was a duelling contest in which pilot took on pilot.

Churchill went up to Fighter Command's operations rooms to observe the course of battle unfold on the giant maps, plotting tables and early warning technology installed there. Deeply stirred, it was as he was coming away from one of these early visits, that the words came to him, 'Never in the field of human conflict was so much owed by so many to so few.' Redolent of Shakespeare's King Henry V assuring his troops — 'We few, we happy few' — before the Battle of Agincourt, it hit a chord with the nation when on 20 August he repeated the phrase in what became one of his most famous speeches.

'Throughout all Europe for one man killed or wounded in the first year perhaps five were killed or wounded in 1914–15'

Almost a year has passed since the war began, and it is natural for us, I think, to pause on our journey at this milestone and survey the dark, wide field. It is also useful to compare the first year of this second war against German aggression with its forerunner a quarter of a century ago. Although this war is in fact only a continuation of the last, very great differences in its character are apparent. In the last war millions of men fought by hurling enormous masses of steel at one another. 'Men and shells' was the cry, and prodigious slaughter was the consequence. In this war nothing of this kind has yet appeared. It is a conflict of strategy, of organization, of technical apparatus, of science, mechanics and morale. The British casualties in the first twelve months of the Great War amounted to 365,000. In this war, I am thankful to say, British killed, wounded, prisoners and missing, including civilians, do not exceed 92,000, and of these a large proportion are alive as prisoners of war. Looking more widely around, one may say that throughout all Europe for one man killed or wounded in the first year perhaps five were killed or wounded in 1914–15.

The slaughter is only a small fraction, but the consequences to the belligerents have been even more deadly. We have seen great countries with powerful armies dashed out of coherent existence in a few weeks. We have seen the French Republic and the renowned French Army beaten into complete and total submission with less than the casualties which they suffered in any one of half a dozen of the battles of 1914–18. The entire body – it might almost seem at times the soul – of France has succumbed to physical effects incomparably less terrible than those which were sustained with fortitude and undaunted will-power 25 years ago. Although up to the present the loss of life has been mercifully diminished, the decisions reached in the course of the struggle are even more profound upon the fate of nations than anything that has ever happened since barbaric times. Moves are made upon the scientific and strategic boards, advantages are gained by mechanical means, as a result of which scores of millions of men become incapable of further resistance, or judge themselves incapable of further resistance, and a fearful game of chess proceeds from check to mate by which the unhappy players seem to be inexorably bound.

'The trenches are dug in the towns and street. Every village is fortified. Every road is barred. The front line runs through the factories'

There is another more obvious difference from 1914. The whole of the warring nations are engaged, not only soldiers, but the entire population, men, women and children. The fronts are everywhere. The trenches are dug in the towns and streets. Every village is fortified. Every road is barred. The front line runs through the factories. The workmen are soldiers with different weapons but the same courage. These are great and distinctive changes from what many of us saw in the struggle of a quarter of a century ago. There seems to be every reason to believe that this new kind of war is well suited to the genius and the resources of the British nation and the British Empire and that, once we get properly equipped and properly started, a war of this kind will be more favourable to us than the sombre mass slaughters of the Somme and Passchendaele. If it is a case of the whole nation fighting and suffering together, that ought to suit us, because we are the most united of all the nations, because we entered the war upon the national will and with our eyes open, and because we have been nurtured in freedom and individual responsibility and are the products, not of totalitarian uniformity but of tolerance and variety. If all these qualities are turned, as they are being turned, to the arts of war, we may be able to show the enemy quite a lot of things that they have not thought of yet. Since the Germans drove the Jews out and lowered their technical standards, our science is definitely ahead of theirs. Our geographical position, the command of the sea, and the friendship of the United States enable us to draw resources from the whole world and to manufacture weapons of war of every kind, but especially of the superfine kinds, on a scale hitherto practised only by Nazi Germany.

'The honour to be the sole champion of the liberties of all Europe'

Hitler is now sprawled over Europe. Our offensive springs are being slowly compressed, and we must resolutely and methodically prepare ourselves for the campaigns of 1941 and 1942. Two or three years are not a long time, even in our short, precarious lives. They are nothing in the history of the nation, and when we are doing the finest thing in the world, and have the honour to be the sole champion of the liberties of all Europe, we must not grudge these years or weary as we toil and struggle through them. It does not follow that our energies in future years will be exclusively confined to defending ourselves and our possessions. Many opportunities may lie open to amphibious power, and we must be ready to take advantage of them. One of the ways to bring this war to a speedy end is to convince the enemy, not by words, but by deeds, that we have both the will and the means, not only to go on indefinitely but to strike heavy and unexpected blows. The road to victory may not be so long as we expect. But we have no right to count upon this. Be it long or short, rough or smooth, we mean to reach our journey's end …

'Few would have believed we could survive'

Rather more than a quarter of a year has passed since the new government came into power in this country. What a cataract of disaster has poured out upon us since then. The trustful Dutch overwhelmed; their beloved and respected sovereign driven into exile; the peaceful city of Rotterdam the scene of a massacre as hideous and brutal as anything in the Thirty Years War. Belgium invaded and beaten down; our own fine Expeditionary Force, which King Leopold called to his rescue, cut off and almost captured, escaping as it seemed only by a miracle and with the loss of all its equipment; our ally, France, out; Italy in against us; all France in the power of the enemy, all its arsenals and vast masses of military material converted or convertible to the enemy's use; a puppet government set up at Vichy which may at any moment be forced to become our foe; the whole western seaboard of Europe from the North Cape to the Spanish frontier in German hands; all the ports, all the airfields on this immense front, employed against us as potential springboards of invasion. Moreover, the German air-power, numerically so far outstripping ours, has been brought so close to our island that what we used to dread greatly has come to pass and the hostile bombers not only reach our shores in a few minutes and from many directions, but can be escorted by their fighting aircraft. Why, sir, if we had been confronted at the beginning of May with such a prospect, it would have seemed incredible that at the end of a period of horror and disaster, or at this point in a period of horror and, we should stand erect, sure of ourselves, masters of our fate and with the conviction of final victory burning unquenchable in our hearts. Few would have believed we could survive; none would have believed that we should today not only feel stronger but should actually be stronger than we have ever been before.

'Death and ruin have become small things compared with the shame of defeat or failure in duty'

Let us see what has happened on the other side of the scales. The British nation and the British Empire finding themselves alone, stood undismayed against disaster. No one flinched or wavered; nay, some who formerly thought of peace, now think only of war. Our people are united and resolved, as they have never been before. Death and ruin have become small things compared with the shame of defeat or failure in duty. We cannot tell what lies ahead. It may be that even greater ordeals lie before us. We shall face whatever is coming to us. We are sure of ourselves and of our cause and that is the supreme fact which has emerged in these months of trial.

'We have not only fortified our hearts but our island'

Meanwhile, we have not only fortified our hearts but our island. We have rearmed and rebuilt our armies in a degree which would have been deemed impossible a few months ago. We have ferried across the Atlantic, in the month of July, thanks to our friends over there, an immense mass of munitions of all kinds, cannon, rifles, machine-guns, cartridges and shell, all safely landed without the loss of a gun or a round. The output of our own factories, working as they have never worked before, has poured forth to the troops. The whole British Army is at home. More than 2,000,000 determined men have rifles and bayonets in their hands tonight and three-quarters of them are in regular military formations. We have never had armies like this in our island in time of war. The whole island bristles against invaders, from the sea or from the air. As I explained to the House in the middle of June, the stronger our Army at home, the larger must the invading expedition be, and the larger the invading expedition, the less difficult will be the task of the Navy in detecting its assembly and in intercepting and destroying it on passage; and the greater also would be the difficulty of feeding and supplying the invaders if ever they landed, in the teeth of continuous naval and air attack on their communications. All this is classical and venerable doctrine. As in Nelson's day, the maxim holds, 'Our first line of defence is the enemy's ports.' Now air reconnaissance and photography have brought to an old principle a new and potent aid.

Our Navy is far stronger than it was at the beginning of the war. The great flow of new construction set on foot at the outbreak is now beginning to come in. We hope our friends across the ocean will send us a timely reinforcement to bridge the gap between the peace flotillas of 1939 and the war flotillas of 1941. There is no difficulty in sending such aid. The seas and oceans are open. The U-boats are contained. The magnetic mine is, up to the present time, effectively mastered. The merchant tonnage under the British flag, after a year of unlimited U-boat war, after eight months of intensive mining attack, is larger than when we began. We have in addition, under our control, at least 4,000,000 tons of shipping from the captive countries which has taken refuge here or in the harbours of the Empire. Our stocks of food of all kinds are far more abundant than in the days of peace and a large and growing programme of food production is on foot.

'The people have a right to know that there are solid grounds for the confidence which we feel'

Why do I say all this? Not assuredly to boast; not assuredly to give the slightest countenance to complacency. The dangers we face are still enormous, but so are our advantages and resources. I recount them because the people have a right to know that there are solid grounds for the confidence which we feel, and that we have good reason to believe ourselves capable, as I said in a very dark hour two months ago, of continuing the war 'if necessary alone, if necessary for years'. I say it also because the fact that the British Empire stands invincible, and that Nazidom is still being resisted, will kindle again the spark of hope in the breasts of hundreds of millions of downtrodden or despairing men and women throughout Europe, and far beyond its bounds, and that from these sparks there will presently come cleansing and devouring flame.

'Herr Hitler could not admit defeat in his air attack on Great Britain'

The great air battle which has been in progress over this island for the last few weeks has recently attained a high intensity. It is too soon to attempt to assign limits either to its scale or to its duration. We must certainly expect that greater efforts will be made by the enemy than any he has so far put forth. Hostile airfields are still being developed in France and the Low Countries, and the movement of squadrons and material for attacking us is still proceeding. It is quite plain that Herr Hitler could not admit defeat in his air attack on Great Britain without sustaining most serious injury. If, after all his boastings and blood-curdling threats and lurid accounts trumpeted around the world of the damage he has inflicted, of the vast numbers of our Air Force he has shot down, so he says, with so little loss to himself; if after tales of the panic-stricken British crushed in their holes cursing the plutocratic Parliament which has led them to such a plight; if after all this his whole air onslaught were forced after a while tamely to peter out, the Führer's reputation for veracity of statement might be seriously impugned. We may be sure, therefore, that he will continue as long as he has the strength to do so, and as long as any preoccupations he may have in respect of the Russian Air Force allow him to do so.

On the other hand, the conditions and course of the fighting have so far been favourable to us. I told the House two months ago that whereas in France our fighter aircraft were wont to inflict a loss of two or three to one upon the Germans, and in the fighting at Dunkirk, which was a kind of no-man's-land, a loss of about three or four to one, we expected that in an attack on this island we should achieve a larger ratio. This has certainly come true. It must also be remembered that all the enemy machines and pilots which are shot down over our island, or over the seas which surround it, are either destroyed or captured; whereas a considerable proportion of our machines, and also of our pilots, are saved, and soon again in many cases come into action.

A vast and admirable system of salvage, directed by the Ministry of Aircraft Production, ensures the speediest return to the fighting line of damaged machines, and the most provident and speedy use of all the spare parts and material. At the same time the splendid, nay, astounding increase in the output and repair of British aircraft and engines which Lord Beaverbrook has achieved by a genius of organization and drive, which looks like magic, has given us overflowing reserves of every type of aircraft, and an ever-mounting stream of production both in quantity and quality. The enemy is, of course, far more numerous than we are. But our new production already, as I am advised, largely exceeds his, and the American production is only just beginning to flow in. It is a fact, as I see from my daily returns, that our bomber and fighter strength now, after all this fighting, are larger than they have ever been. We believe that we shall be able to continue the air struggle indefinitely and as long as the enemy pleases, and the longer it continues the more rapid will be our approach, first towards that parity, and then into that superiority in the air, upon which in a large measure the decision of the war depends.

'Never in the field of human conflict was so much owed by so many to so few'

The gratitude of every home in our island, in our Empire, and indeed throughout the world, except in the abodes of the guilty, goes out to the British airmen who, undaunted by odds, unwearied in their constant challenge and mortal danger, are turning the tide of the world war by their prowess and by their devotion. Never in the field of human conflict was so much owed by so many to so few. All hearts go out to the fighter pilots, whose brilliant actions we see with our own eyes day after day; but we must never forget that all the time, night after night, month after month, our bomber squadrons travel far into Germany, find their targets in the darkness by the highest navigational skill, aim their attacks, often under the heaviest fire, often with serious loss, with deliberate careful discrimination, and inflict shattering blows upon the whole of the technical and war-making structure of the Nazi power. On no part of the Royal Air Force does the weight of the war fall more heavily than on the daylight bombers who will play an invaluable part in the case of invasion and whose unflinching zeal it has been necessary in the meanwhile on numerous occasions to restrain.

We are able to verify the results of bombing military targets in Germany, not only by reports which reach us through many sources, but also, of course, by photography. I have no hesitation in saying that this process of bombing the military industries and communications of Germany and the air bases and storage depots from which we are attacked, which process will continue upon an ever-increasing scale until the end of the war, and may in another year attain dimensions hitherto undreamed of, affords one at least of the most certain, if not the shortest of all the roads to victory. Even if the Nazi legions stood triumphant on the Black Sea, or indeed upon the Caspian, even if Hitler were at the gates of India, it would profit him nothing if at the same time the entire economic and scientific apparatus of German war-power lay shattered and pulverized at home . . .

Churchill then turned to the strategic implications of France's exit from the war. In contrast to the 'men of Vichy', General de Gaulle stood ready to keep Anglo-French comradeship together. 'These Free Frenchmen have been condemned to death by Vichy, but the day will come, as surely as the sun will rise tomorrow, when their names will be held in honour, and their names will be graven in stone in the streets and villages of a France restored in a liberated Europe to its full freedom and its ancient name.' Finally, Churchill explained the deal he had done with President Roosevelt to lease to the United States a number of British bases ...

'Like the Mississippi, it just keeps rolling along. Let it roll. Let it roll on full flood, inexorable, irresistible, benignant, to broader lands and better days'

Presently we learned that anxiety was also felt in the United States about the air and naval defence of their Atlantic seaboard, and President Roosevelt has recently made it clear that he would like to discuss with us, and with the Dominion of Canada and with Newfoundland, the development of American naval and air facilities in Newfoundland and in the West Indies. There is, of course, no question of any transference of sovereignty – that has never been suggested – or of any action being taken, without the consent or against the wishes of the various colonies concerned, but for our part, His Majesty's government are entirely willing to accord defence facilities to the United States on a 99 years' leasehold basis, and we feel sure that our interests no less than theirs, and the interests of the colonies themselves and of Canada and Newfoundland will be served thereby. These are important steps. Undoubtedly this process means that these two great organizations of the English-speaking democracies, the British Empire and the United States, will have to be somewhat mixed up together in some of their affairs for mutual and general advantage. For my own part, looking out upon the future, I do not view the process with any misgivings. I could not stop it if I wished; no one can stop it. Like the Mississippi, it just keeps rolling along. Let it roll. Let it roll on full flood, inexorable, irresistible, benignant, to broader lands and better days.

'Let God defend the right'

Broadcast, 11 September 1940

On possible invasion and the Blitz

By the end of August, the RAF was running dangerously low of trained pilots to plug its losses while many airfields were so badly hit as to be virtually inoperable. Yet, the Luftwaffe too was feeling the strain, its pilots incredulous that, despite having supposedly wiped out the estimated strength of Britain's air force, the sky was still inexplicably full of Spitfires and Hurricanes. Frustrated, the Luftwaffe changed tactics, switching from concentrating on shooting at aircraft and hitting airbases to saturation bombing of Britain's cities and civilian population.

London was unintentionally lightly bombed on 24 August. This was just a foreshadow of what was to follow. Intelligence intercepts on 6 September convinced the government that the invasion was coming in the next 24 hours. In fact, what was being signalled was the commencement in earnest on 7 September of the 'Blitz' and the beginning of 57 nights in which the capital city came under continuous attack.

High losses in the first daytime raids convinced the Luftwaffe of the necessity of flying under cloak of darkness. Consequently, the job of shooting down the bombers increasingly fell to those on the ground, with searchlights desperately sweeping the night sky in the hope of giving the anti-aircraft guns a target to lock on to.

ON THIS DAY
11 SEPTEMBER 1940

- London's Lord Mayor inaugurates the Air Raid Relief Fund.

- Italian troops continue building up in occupied Albania, for what will become an attempted invasion of Greece.

- Officials assess the modest damage to Buckingham Palace, hit by a bomb the previous day. The palace will be hit again two days later, smashing windows just yards from the king and queen, but they resist Churchill's exhortations for them to leave London.

To escape annihilation on the ground, Londoners spent their nights in grim and often deeply unsanitary shelters. Many took sanctuary in Underground stations and tunnels, the ground shaking above them as once familiar homes, offices and department stores came crashing down under the relentless pounding from the skies. The next morning, the citizens emerged from their burrows to go off to work, picking their way through the ruins of their city. To many observers, their apparent insouciance was remarkable.

Nor were Londoners left to endure alone. Hull, Liverpool, Cardiff, Southampton and Bristol were among the other major targets. Visiting sites of devastation, Churchill was especially struck by the people's sense of resolve. When he arrived to inspect a London air-raid shelter that had been destroyed the previous night with great loss of life, he was mobbed by bereaved survivors assuring him: 'We thought you'd come. We can take it. Give it 'em back.' When, eventually, Churchill was moved on, a woman was heard turning to her neighbours and pointing out 'You see, he really cares, he's crying.'

When I said in the House of Commons the other day that I thought it improbable that the enemy's air attack in September could be more than three times as great as it was in August, I was not, of course, referring to barbarous attacks upon the civil population, but to the great air battle which is being fought out between our fighters and the German Air Force.

You will understand that whenever the weather is favourable waves of German bombers, protected by fighters often 500 or 400 at a time, surge over this island, especially the promontory of Kent, in the hope of attacking military and other objectives by daylight. However, they are met by our fighter squadrons and nearly always broken up; and their losses average three to one in machines and six to one in pilots.

'This effort of the Germans to secure daylight mastery of the air over England is . . . the crux of the whole war'

This effort of the Germans to secure daylight mastery of the air over England is, of course, the crux of the whole war. So far it has failed conspicuously. It has cost them very dear, and we have felt stronger and actually are relatively a good deal stronger, than when the hard fighting began in July. There is no doubt that Herr Hitler is using up his fighter force at a very high rate, and that if he goes on for many more weeks he will wear down and ruin this vital part of his Air Force. That will give us a very great advantage.

On the other hand, for him to try to invade this country without having secured mastery in the air would be a very hazardous undertaking. Nevertheless, all his preparations for invasion on a great scale are steadily going forward. Several hundreds of self-propelled barges are moving down the coasts of Europe, from the German and Dutch harbours to the ports of northern France; from Dunkirk to Brest; and beyond Brest to the French harbours in the Bay of Biscay.

Besides this, convoys of merchant ships in tens of dozens are being moved through the Straits of Dover into the Channel, dodging along from port to port under the protection of the new batteries which the Germans have built on the French shore. There are now considerable gatherings of shipping in the German, Dutch, Belgian and French harbours – all the way from Hamburg to Brest. Finally, there are some preparations made of ships to carry an invading force from the Norwegian harbours.

'A heavy, full-scale invasion of this island is being prepared'

Behind these clusters of ships or barges, there stand very large numbers of German troops, awaiting the order to go on board and set out on their very dangerous and uncertain voyage across the seas. We cannot tell when they will try to come; we cannot be sure that in fact they will try at all; but no one should blind himself to the fact that a heavy, full-scale invasion of this island is being prepared with all the usual German thoroughness and method, and that it may be launched now – upon England, upon Scotland, or upon Ireland, or upon all three.

If this invasion is going to be tried at all, it does not seem that it can be long delayed. The weather may break at any time. Besides this, it is difficult for the enemy to keep these gatherings of ships waiting about indefinitely, while they are bombed every night by our bombers, and very often shelled by our warships which are waiting for them outside.

'It ranks with the days when the Spanish Armada was approaching'

Therefore, we must regard the next week or so as a very important period in our history. It ranks with the days when the Spanish Armada was approaching the Channel, and Drake was finishing his game of bowls; or when Nelson stood between us and Napoleon's Grand Army at Boulogne. We have read all about this in the history books; but what is happening now is on a far greater scale and of far more consequence to the life and future of the world and its civilization than these brave old days of the past.

Every man and woman will therefore prepare himself to do his duty, whatever it may be, with special pride and care. Our fleets and flotillas are very powerful and numerous; our Air Force is at the highest strength it has ever reached, and it is conscious of its proved superiority, not indeed in numbers, but in men and machines. Our shores are well fortified and strongly manned, and behind them, ready to attack the invaders, we have a far larger and better-equipped mobile Army than we have ever had before.

'Let God defend the right'

Besides this, we have more than a million and a half men of the Home Guard, who are just as much soldiers of the Regular Army as the Grenadier Guards, and who are determined to fight for every inch of the ground in every village and in every street.

It is with devout but sure confidence that I say: Let God defend the right.

'These cruel, wanton, indiscriminate bombings of London'

These cruel, wanton, indiscriminate bombings of London are, of course, a part of Hitler's invasion plans. He hopes, by killing large numbers of civilians, and women and children, that he will terrorize and cow the people of this mighty imperial city, and make them a burden and an anxiety to the government and thus distract our attention unduly from the ferocious onslaught he is preparing. Little does he know the spirit of the British nation, or the tough fibre of the Londoners, whose forebears played a leading part in the establishment of Parliamentary institutions and who have been bred to value freedom far above their lives. This wicked man, the repository and embodiment of many forms of soul-destroying hatred, this monstrous product of former wrongs and shame, has now resolved to try to break our famous island race by a process of indiscriminate slaughter and destruction. What he has done is to kindle a fire in British hearts, here and all over the world, which will glow long after all traces of the conflagration he has caused in London have been removed. He has lighted a fire which will burn with a steady and consuming flame until the last vestiges of Nazi tyranny have been burnt out of Europe, and until the Old World – and the New – can join hands to rebuild the temples of man's freedom and man's honour, upon foundations which will not soon or easily be overthrown.

This is a time for everyone to stand together, and hold firm, as they are doing. I express my admiration for the exemplary manner in which all the Air Raid Precautions services of London are being discharged, especially the Fire Brigade, whose work has been so heavy and also dangerous. All the world that is still free marvels at the composure and fortitude with which the citizens of London are facing and surmounting the great ordeal to which they are subjected, the end of which or the severity of which cannot yet be foreseen.

'We shall draw from the heart of suffering itself the means of inspiration and survival'

It is a message of good cheer to our fighting forces on the seas, in the air, and in our waiting armies in all their posts and stations, that we send them from this capital city. They know that they have behind them a people who will not flinch or weary of the struggle – hard and protracted though it will be; but that we shall rather draw from the heart of suffering itself the means of inspiration and survival, and of a victory won not only for our own time, but for the long and better days that are to come.

'Frenchmen – rearm your spirits'

Broadcast in French and English, 21 October 1940

On realities in France and the courage of the French people

Although it continued into October, the Battle of Britain was effectively won after a titanic aerial encounter on 15 September, when two great waves of German assault were driven off. The British people did not realize it at the time, but that day's tally – 60 Luftwaffe planes shot down for the loss of 26 RAF aircraft – convinced Hitler that continuing the struggle for air superiority was fruitless. Two days later he postponed plans for the invasion of Britain, first until further notice and, soon after, until the spring of 1941. The destruction of Britain's cities from the air would continue, with devastating losses for the civilian population. Coventry was decimated in November and London continued to be subjected to the Blitz until May 1941. But the essential victory was won, the country had saved itself from defeat and occupation.

It was the first time Hitler's ambitions had been checked. It gave hope to Britain's well-wishers across the seas. Meanwhile, Churchill was especially keen to see the 'Free French' under Charles de Gaulle demonstrate that they too could strike a blow for freedom. London approved plans for winning over the colonies of French West Africa from the German-collaborating Vichy regime. A Royal Navy squadron was assigned to carry de Gaulle and his Free French forces to Dakar. But rather than welcoming them as liberators, on 23 September the French garrison there demonstrated its loyalty to Vichy by opening fire. With the British ships taking hits, the decision was taken to about turn and withdraw. Put bluntly, the Dakar expedition was a fiasco: saving Britain from invasion was one matter, but reclaiming other parts of the world for the greater cause still appeared beyond the armed forces' powers.

'Dieu protège la France'

Frenchmen! For more than thirty years in peace and war I have marched with you, and I am marching still along the same road. Tonight I speak to you at your firesides wherever you may be, or whatever your fortunes are. I repeat the prayer around the louis d'or, 'Dieu protège la France'. Here at home in England, under the fire of the Boche, we do not forget the ties and links that unite us to France, and we are persevering steadfastly and in good heart in the cause of European freedom and fair dealing for the common people of all countries, for which, with you, we drew the sword. When good people get into trouble because they are attacked and heavily smitten by the vile and wicked, they must be very careful not to get at loggerheads with one another. The common enemy is always trying to bring this about, and, of course, in bad luck a lot of things happen which play into the enemy's hands. We must just make the best of things as they come along.

'It is not defeat that France will now be made to suffer at German hands, but the doom of complete obliteration'

Here in London, which Herr Hitler says he will reduce to ashes, and which his aeroplanes are now bombarding, our people are bearing up unflinchingly. Our Air Force has more than held its own. We are waiting for the long-promised invasion. So are the fishes. But, of course, this for us is only the beginning. Now in 1940, in spite of occasional losses, we have, as ever, command of the seas. In 1941 we shall have the command of the air. Remember what that means. Herr Hitler with his tanks and other mechanical weapons, and also by Fifth Column intrigue with traitors, has managed to subjugate for the time being most of the finest races in Europe, and his little Italian accomplice is trotting along hopefully and hungrily, but rather wearily and very timidly, at his side. They both wish to carve up France and her Empire as if it were a fowl: to one a leg, to another a wing or perhaps part of the breast. Not only the French Empire will be devoured by these two ugly customers, but Alsace-Lorraine will go once again under the German yoke, and Nice, Savoy and Corsica – Napoleon's Corsica – will be torn from the fair realm of France. But Herr Hitler is not thinking only of stealing other people's territories, or flinging gobbets of them to his little confederate. I tell you truly what you must believe when I say this evil man, this monstrous abortion of hatred and defeat, is resolved on nothing less than the complete wiping out of the French nation, and the disintegration of its whole life and future. By all kinds of sly and savage means, he is plotting and working to quench forever the fountain of characteristic French culture and of French inspiration to the world. All Europe, if he has his way, will be reduced to one uniform Bocheland, to be exploited, pillaged, and bullied by his Nazi gangsters. You will excuse my speaking frankly because this is not a time to mince words. It is not defeat that France will now be made to suffer at German hands, but the doom of complete obliteration. Army, Navy, Air Force, religion, law, language, culture, institutions, literature, history, tradition, all are to be effaced by the brute strength of a triumphant army and the scientific low-cunning of a ruthless police force.

'Frenchmen – rearm your spirits before it is too late'

Frenchmen   rearm your spirits before it is too late. Remember how Napoleon said before one of his battles: 'These same Prussians who are so boastful today were three to one at Jena, and six to one at Montmirail.' Never will I believe that the soul of France is dead. Never will I believe that her place amongst the greatest nations of the world has been lost forever! All these schemes and crimes of Herr Hitler's are bringing upon him and upon all who belong to his system a retribution which many of us will live to see. The story is not yet finished, but it will not be so long. We are on his track, and so are our friends across the Atlantic Ocean, and your friends across the Atlantic Ocean. If he cannot destroy us, we will surely destroy him and all his gang, and all their works. Therefore, have hope and faith, for all will come right.

'If you cannot help us, at least you will not hinder us'

Now what is it we British ask of you in this present hard and bitter time? What we ask at this moment in our struggle to win the victory which we will share with you, is that if you cannot help us, at least you will not hinder us. Presently you will be able to weight the arm that strikes for you, and you ought to do so. But even now we believe that Frenchmen, wherever they may be, feel their hearts warm and a proud blood tingle in their veins when we have some success in the air or on the sea, or presently – for that will come – upon the land.

Remember we shall never stop, never weary, and never give in, and that our whole people and Empire have vowed themselves to the task of cleansing Europe from the Nazi pestilence and saving the world from the new Dark Ages. Do not imagine, as the German-controlled wireless tells you, that we English seek to take your ships and colonies. We seek to beat the life and soul out of Hitler and Hitlerism. That alone, that all the time, that to the end. We do not covet anything from any nation except their respect. Those Frenchmen who are in the French Empire, and those who are in so-called unoccupied France, may see their way from time to time to useful action. I will not go into details. Hostile ears are listening. As for those, to whom English hearts go out in full, because they see them under the sharp discipline, oppression and spying of the Hun – as to those Frenchmen in the occupied regions, to them I say, when they think of the future let them remember the words which Gambetta, that great Frenchman, uttered after 1870 [when France was losing the Franco-Prussian War] about the future of France and what was to come: 'Think of it always: speak of it never.'

'Brightly will it shine on the brave and true, kindly upon all who suffer for the cause, glorious upon the tombs of heroes'

Good night then: sleep to gather strength for the morning. For the morning will come. Brightly will it shine on the brave and true, kindly upon all who suffer for the cause, glorious upon the tombs of heroes. Thus will shine the dawn. Vive la France! Long live also the forward march of the common people in all the lands towards their just and true inheritance, and towards the broader and fuller age.

'The silence of Neville Chamberlain's tomb'

House of Commons, London, 12 November 1940

On the death of the former prime minister

The threat of invasion forced many of Britain's old political foes to work together. But the relationship Churchill built with his predecessor and pre-war opponent, Neville Chamberlain, matured well beyond the requirements of necessity. By throwing the weight of the Conservative Party that he still led behind his successor as prime minister, Chamberlain put the national interest beyond petty personal disappointment. His far-sighted and patriotic magnanimity contrasted favourably with the poisonous and calamitous loathing that fatally divided France's political leaders in their time of trial.

Despite their previous differences and wholly different personalities, Churchill and Chamberlain ended up admiring each other's qualities. But Chamberlain's physical powers were waning fast and, in increasing pain, he found himself forced to remove himself from 11 Downing Street to a house in Hampshire, leant to him by an aunt.

ON THIS DAY
12 NOVEMBER 1940

- The Italian navy counts the costs of the overnight raids by the Royal Navy's Fleet Air Arm. In a short time, three Italian battleships have been destroyed and four other ships badly damaged, in the harbour of Taranto, in Italy's heel.

- In Berlin, Hitler releases a new war directive, aimed at drawing General Franco's Spanish government into the war: it is destined to fail.

- The Russian foreign minister Molotov visits Berlin. He rebuffs Hitler's attempts to persuade the Soviet Union to fight the British, and instead presses his host about Nazi intentions in Eastern Europe. The Non-Aggression Pact is under severe strain.

Churchill continued to show him consideration, sending him official papers and having the latest news from the Battle of Britain telephoned through to him. However by 3 October, a sharp deterioration in Chamberlain's health forced him to resign both from the War Cabinet and as leader of the Conservative Party. It was a testament of how perceptions of Churchill had changed that he proceeded to assume the dual reins of the premiership and the Conservative Party leadership unopposed and without any significant protest, even from Tories who had previously distrusted him.

Finally, on 9 November, Chamberlain died, claimed by bowel cancer and worn down by the struggles of peace and war. He was 71. It fell to Churchill to deliver a eulogy of remarkable power and perspicacity.

Since we last met, the House has suffered a very grievous loss in the death of one of its most distinguished Members, and of a statesman and public servant who, during the best part of three memorable years, was First Minister of the Crown.

'With this shield, however the fates may play, we march always in the ranks of honour'

The fierce and bitter controversies which hung around him in recent times were hushed by the news of his illness and are silenced by his death. In paying a tribute of respect and of regard to an eminent man who has been taken from us, no one is obliged to alter the opinions which he has formed or expressed upon issues which have become a part of history; but at the Lychgate we may all pass our own conduct and our own judgments under a searching review. It is not given to human beings, happily for them, for otherwise life would be intolerable, to foresee or to predict to any large extent the unfolding course of events. In one phase men seem to have been right, in another they seem to have been wrong. Then again, a few years later, when the perspective of time has lengthened, all stands in a different setting. There is a new proportion. There is another scale of values. History with its flickering lamp stumbles along the trail of the past, trying to reconstruct its scenes, to revive its echoes, and kindle with pale gleams the passion of former days. What is the worth of all this? The only guide to a man is his conscience; the only shield to his memory is the rectitude and sincerity of his actions. It is very imprudent to walk through life without this shield, because we are so often mocked by the failure of our hopes and the upsetting of our calculations; but with this shield, however the fates may play, we march always in the ranks of honour.

'The verdict of history'

It fell to Neville Chamberlain in one of the supreme crises of the world to be contradicted by events, to be disappointed in his hopes, and to be deceived and cheated by a wicked man. But what were these hopes in which he was disappointed? What were these wishes in which he was frustrated? What was that faith that was abused? They were surely among the most noble and benevolent instincts of the human heart – the love of peace, the toil for peace, the strife for peace, the pursuit of peace, even at great peril, and certainly to the utter disdain of popularity or clamour. Whatever else history may or may not say about these terrible, tremendous years, we can be sure that Neville Chamberlain acted with perfect sincerity according to his lights and strove to the utmost of his capacity and authority, which were powerful, to save the world from the awful, devastating struggle in which we are now engaged. This alone will stand him in good stead as far as what is called the verdict of history is concerned.

'What do these ravings and outpourings count before the silence of Neville Chamberlain's tomb'

But it is also a help to our country and to our whole Empire, and to our decent faithful way of living that, however long the struggle may last, or however dark may be the clouds which overhang our path, no future generation of English-speaking folks – for that is the tribunal to which we appeal – will doubt that, even at a great cost to ourselves in technical preparation, we were guiltless of the bloodshed, terror and misery which have engulfed so many lands and peoples, and yet seek new victims still. Herr Hitler protests with frantic words and gestures that he has only desired peace. What do these ravings and outpourings count before the silence of Neville Chamberlain's tomb?

'Give us the tools
and we will finish
the job'

World broadcast, 9 February 1941

On the urgent need for US war supplies

On 31 July 1940, just as the Luftwaffe was gearing up to crush Britain's air defence, Churchill sent an urgent appeal to President Roosevelt, begging to be given 'fifty or sixty of your oldest destroyers' and concluding, 'Mr President, with great respect I must tell you that in the long history of the world this is a thing to do now.'

So desperate seemed Britain's plight that any such gift looked destined only to end up in Hitler's hands, given the likelihood that Britain would, like every other European nation before it, fold under the weight of the Nazi onslaught. It was the RAF's defiance in the Battle of Britain which began to change this perception. Thus it was that in September Roosevelt agreed the 'bases for destroyers' deal with Churchill, in which the United States gave 50 of its older destroyers to the Royal Navy in return for 99-year leases on British bases in the Pacific.

With so much shipping being sunk by the U-boats, the agreement was timely as well as hugely symbolic. For all its hopes of staying out the war, America was becoming increasingly entangled in Britain's struggle for survival. The latter had switched wholly to a war economy in which the needs of military production took precedence. For the population, rationing was spreading beyond the already strict food allowances and by the summer included clothing too.

Distorting the economy towards military rather than commercial enterprises had a drawback: diminishing trade denied Britain the dollars to pay for American armaments. The United States demanded payment in the form of Britain's remaining gold reserves and the liquidation of what assets she still held in America. It was a hard bargain but in December, Roosevelt came up with a new initiative, announcing a giant mortgage scheme whereby the cost of purchases would be borne by the United States, with repayment or replacement in kind to follow once Britain was able to do so. This Lend-Lease Bill passed the House of Representatives in February and the Senate in March 1941.

Diplomatic ties were being strengthened further with Lord Halifax's arrival in Washington, D.C. as Britain's new ambassador. Roosevelt's personal representative, Harry Hopkins, came over to London and immediately formed a positive impression of Churchill. These signs of Anglo-American rapprochement certainly worried Hitler. Frustrated by the aid being given to the Atlantic convoys supplying Britain, on 30 January 1941 he announced that US ships risked being torpedoed.

ON THIS DAY
9 FEBRUARY 1941

• The Royal Navy bombards the port of Genoa, in northern Italy.

• General Franco's government in Spain prepares to sign an agreement with Germany to resist any Allied attack. However, frustratingly for Hitler, Franco has consistently refused to enter the war on the Axis side.

• Pétain decides to make Admiral Darlan the new vice premier of the Vichy regime, announcing his decision the next day. Darlan will eventually return to the Allied side in late 1942, following the liberation of French North Africa. He is then regarded by some, including the United States, as a potential replacement leader of the Free French, but he is assassinated in December 1942.

Meanwhile, British forces had found a theatre of war beyond their homeland in which they could score devastating victories. Italy's entry into the war had dealt Britain a strategic blow, imperilling her hold upon the Mediterranean. But in November 1940, Fleet Air Arm pilots, flying Fairy Swordfishes, torpedoed the Italian fleet at Taranto, at one stroke halving Mussolini's battleship strength. This tipped the balance in the Mediterranean in Britain's favour (and, unintentionally, gave the Japanese war planners a valuable case study in how airpower could destroy sea power).

The following month, General Wavell, commander-in-chief in the Middle East, ordered an attack on a major Italian incursion into Egypt. The Italians – despite their vast numerical superiority – were so completely outfought that the British and Empire troops, making the most of their Matilda tanks, turned an assault into an all-out offensive, pushing the beleaguered opponents back towards Tobruk, which surrendered in January.

At the same time, Mussolini's forces failed to make the most of their overwhelming numbers in Italian East Africa (Somaliland, Eritrea and Ethiopia) to threaten the small British forces guarding Kenya and Sudan. Instead, by February 1941, it was the British who took the initiative and all Italian East Africa would soon be conquered. Even the Italian invasion of Greece had gone badly, forcing the resignation of Marshal Badoglio, the Supreme Commander of the Italian Army.

Churchill began his world broadcast by reflecting on the failure of the Blitz to destroy British resolve before moving on to Mussolini's travails both in the Balkans where the Italian invaders had been mauled by the Greeks and in Libya where they had been bested by the British: 'The whole Italian Army in the east of Libya, which was reputed to exceed 150,000 men, has been captured or destroyed' Churchill announced. 'The entire province of Cyrenaica – nearly as big as England and Wales – has been conquered' and this was 'only part of the story of the decline and fall of the Italian Empire, that will not take a future Gibbon so long to write as the original work'.

'The United States intend to supply us with all that is necessary for victory'

But after all, the fate of this war is going to be settled by what happens on the oceans, in the air and – above all – in this island. It seems now to be certain that the government and people of the United States intend to supply us with all that is necessary for victory. In the last war the United States sent 2,000,000 men across the Atlantic. But this is not a war of vast armies, firing immense masses of shells at one another. We do not need the gallant armies which are forming throughout the American Union. We do not need them this year, nor next year; nor any year that I can foresee. But we do need most urgently an immense and continuous supply of war materials and technical apparatus of all kinds. We need them here and we need to bring them here. We shall need a great mass of shipping in 1942, far more than we can build ourselves, if we are to maintain and augment our war effort in the West and in the East.

'His clutching fingers reach out on both sides of us into the ocean'

These facts are, of course, all well known to the enemy, and we must therefore expect that Herr Hitler will do his utmost to prey upon our shipping and to reduce the volume of American supplies entering these islands. Having conquered France and Norway, his clutching fingers reach out on both sides of us into the ocean. I have never underrated this danger, and you know I have never concealed it from you. Therefore, I hope you will believe me when I say that I have complete confidence in the Royal Navy, aided by the Air Force of the Coastal Command, and that in one way or another I am sure they will be able to meet every changing phase of this truly mortal struggle, and that sustained by the courage of our merchant seamen, and the dockers and workmen of all our ports, we shall outwit, outmanoeuvre, outfight and outlast the worst that the enemy's malice and ingenuity can contrive.

I have left the greatest issue to the end. You will have seen that Sir John Dill, our principal military adviser, the Chief of the Imperial General Staff, has warned us all that Hitler may be forced by the strategic, economic and political stresses in Europe, to try to invade these islands in the near future. That is a warning which no one should disregard. Naturally, we are working night and day to have everything ready. Of course, we are far stronger than we ever were before, incomparably stronger than we were in July, August and September. Our Navy is more powerful, our flotillas are more numerous; we are far stronger, actually and relatively, in the air above these islands, than we were when our Fighter Command beat off and beat down the Nazi attack last autumn. Our Army is more numerous, more mobile and far better equipped and trained than in September, and still more than in July.

'I put my faith in the simple unaffected resolve to conquer or die'

I have the greatest confidence in our commander-in-chief, General Brooke, and in the generals of proved ability who, under him, guard the different quarters of our land. But most of all I put my faith in the simple unaffected resolve to conquer or die which will animate and inspire nearly 4,000,000 Britons with serviceable weapons in their hands. It is not an easy military operation to invade an island like Great Britain, without the command of the sea and without the command of the air, and then to face what will be waiting for the invader here. But I must drop one word of caution; for next to cowardice and treachery, over-confidence, leading to neglect or slothfulness, is the worst of martial crimes. Therefore, I drop one word of caution. A Nazi invasion of Great Britain last autumn would have been a more or less improvised affair. Hitler took it for granted that when France gave in we should give in; but we did not give in. And he had to think again. An invasion now will be supported by a much more carefully prepared tackle and equipment of landing-craft and other apparatus, all of which will have been planned and manufactured in the winter months. We must all be prepared to meet gas attacks, parachute attacks and glider attacks, with constancy, forethought and practised skill.

I must again emphasize what General Dill has said, and what I pointed out myself last year. In order to win the war Hitler must destroy Great Britain. He may carry havoc into the Balkan states; he may tear great provinces out of Russia; he may march to the Caspian; he may march to the gates of India. All this will avail him nothing. It may spread his curse more widely throughout Europe and Asia, but it will not avert his doom. With every month that passes the many proud and once happy countries he is now holding down by brute force and vile intrigue are learning to hate the Prussian yoke and the Nazi name as nothing has ever been hated so fiercely and so widely among men before. And all the time, masters of the sea and air, the British Empire – nay, in a certain sense, the whole English-speaking world – will be on his track, bearing with them the swords of justice.

'Put your confidence in us'

The other day, President Roosevelt gave his opponent [Wendell Willkie] in the late presidential election a letter of introduction to me, and in it he wrote out a verse, in his own handwriting, from Longfellow which, he said, 'applies to you people as it does to us'. Here is the verse:

> Sail on, O Ship of State!
> Sail on, O Union, strong and great!
> Humanity with all its fears,
> With all the hopes of future years,
> Is hanging breathless on thy fate!

What is the answer that I shall give, in your name, to this great man, the thrice-chosen head of a nation of 130,000,000? Here is the answer which I will give to President Roosevelt: Put your confidence in us. Give us your faith and your blessing, and, under Providence, all will be well.

'Give us the tools, and we will finish the job'

We shall not fail or falter; we shall not weaken or tire. Neither the sudden shock of battle, nor the long-drawn trials of vigilance and exertion will wear us down. Give us the tools, and we will finish the job.

'Westward, look, the land is bright'

World broadcast, 27 April 1941

On Balkan events and the
Battle of the Atlantic

Having humiliated the Italian Army in successive victories, the British, Australian and New Zealand forces were within sight of taking Tripoli and removing the Italian presence entirely from North Africa. But just when they had the opportunity to finish the job, Churchill – with full War Cabinet and military backing – ordered a major diversion of troops to the Balkans. He had been impressed by the Greek resistance to Mussolini's attempted invasion and hoped a sizeable troop deployment there would foster a Balkan alliance against the Axis Powers.

The consequence was the worst of both worlds. Enough soldiers were detached from the North African operation to prevent the *coup de grâce* being delivered there but they were nonetheless insufficient in strength to meet the massive German invasion of Yugoslavia and Greece, which was launched in April. By the end of the month the Royal Yugoslav Army had been defeated, the Germans had entered Athens and the British had been forced into another mass seaborne evacuation, this time to Crete, in which, like Dunkirk, they had to leave their hardware (and 12,000 prisoners) behind. Nor was there any let-up when they arrived on Crete. In May, German paratroopers launched a daring invasion of the island. Fierce fighting ensued and for a while the battle's outcome hung in the balance. The Germans were outnumbered, especially in the early stages, but their tenacity – and dive bombers – prevailed and in June the remaining 16,500 British and Allied troops were evacuated yet again. The only positive aspect was that the losses which his crack paratroopers suffered in the fight put Hitler off launching subsequent airborne assaults.

ON THIS DAY
27 APRIL 1941

- On the Greek mainland, German forces, having transformed the failing Italian invasion of the country, establish control of Athens.

- In the Mediterranean, the Royal Navy aircraft carrier Ark Royal deliver some much-needed Hurricane fighter aircraft to the beleaguered but strategically vital island of Malta, which is being regularly pounded by the Luftwaffe.

- Churchill prepares to order that, in the Far Eastern theatre, Singapore and Malaya cannot be reinforced.

Strategically, the diversion of British and Commonwealth troops from North Africa could not have been worse timed, for in February the German tank commander, Erwin Rommel, arrived in Tripoli with orders to stave off Italy's defeat. Although he started with relatively few tanks, he enjoyed air superiority and the vital element of surprise. During April, he did to the British what they had recently done to the Italians, swiftly driving them out of northern Libya (but for a garrison grimly holding out in Tobruk) and back over the Egyptian border.

The news on the Home Front was not much better. Hitler had responded to RAF raids on Germany first with rhetoric – promising Britain 100 bombs for every one she dropped until Churchill was removed – and then, with deeds. Over 30,000 British civilians had already been killed in the bombing raids. On 10 May the Luftwaffe launched a huge attack on London. Amid the carnage and destruction, in which over 1400 more civilians met their doom, the home of British democracy, the House of Commons, was destroyed. Driven to see the wreckage, Churchill assured his chauffeur, 'I shall never live to sit in the Commons Chamber again.'

I was asked last week whether I was aware of some uneasiness which it was said existed in the country on account of the gravity, as it was described, of the war situation. So I thought it would be a good thing to go and see for myself what this 'uneasiness' amounted to, and I went to some of our great cities and seaports which had been most heavily bombed, and to some of the places where the poorest people had got it worst. I have come back not only reassured, but refreshed. To leave the offices in Whitehall with their ceaseless hum of activity and stress, and to go out to the front, by which I mean the streets and wharves of London or Liverpool, Manchester, Cardiff, Swansea or Bristol, is like going out of a hothouse on to the bridge of a fighting ship. It is a tonic which I should recommend any who are suffering from fretfulness to take in strong doses when they have need of it.

'It is quite true that I have seen many painful scenes of havoc'

It is quite true that I have seen many painful scenes of havoc, and of fine buildings and acres of cottage homes blasted into rubble-heaps of ruin. But it is just in those very places where the malice of the savage enemy has done its worst, and where the ordeal of the men, women and children has been most severe, that I found their morale most high and splendid. Indeed, I felt encompassed by an exaltation of spirit in the people which seemed to lift mankind and its troubles above the level of material facts into that joyous serenity we think belongs to a better world than this.

Of their kindness to me I cannot speak, because I have never sought it or dreamed of it, and can never deserve it. I can only assure you that I and my colleagues, or comrades rather – for that is what the are – will toil with every scrap of life and strength, according to the lights that are granted to us, not to fail these people or be wholly unworthy of their faithful and generous regard. The British nation is stirred and moved as it has never been at any time in its long, eventful, famous history, and it is no hackneyed trope of speech to say that they mean to conquer or to die.

'This is indeed the grand heroic period of our history, and the light of glory shines on all'

What a triumph the life of these battered cities is, over the worst that fire and bomb can do. What a vindication of the civilized and decent way of living we have been trying to work for and work towards in our island. What a proof of the virtues of free institutions. What a test of the quality of our local authorities, and of institutions and customs and societies so steadily built. This ordeal by fire has even a certain sense exhilarated the manhood and womanhood of Britain. The sublime but also terrible and sombre experiences and emotions of the battlefield which for centuries had been reserved for the soldiers and sailors, are now shared, for good or ill, by the entire population. All are proud to be under the fire of the enemy. Old men, little children, the crippled veterans of former wars, aged women, the ordinary hard-pressed citizen or subject of the king, as he likes to call himself, the sturdy workmen who swing the hammers or load the ships; skilful craftsmen; the members of every kind of ARP [Air Raid Precaution] service, are proud to feel that they stand in the line together with our fighting men, when one of the greatest of causes is being fought out, as fought out it will be, to the end. This is indeed the grand heroic period of our history, and the light of glory shines on all.

You may imagine how deeply I feel my own responsibility to all these people; my responsibility to bear my part in bringing them safely out of this long, stern, scowling valley through which we are marching, and not to demand from them their sacrifices and exertions in vain.

'Honour should be our guide'

I have thought in this difficult period, when so much fighting and so many critical and complicated manoeuvres are going on, that it is above all things important that our policy and conduct should be upon the highest level, and that honour should be our guide. Very few people realize how small were the forces with which General Wavell, that fine commander whom we cheered in good days and will back through bad – how small were the forces which took the bulk of the Italian masses in Libya prisoners. In none of his successive victories could General Wavell maintain in the desert or bring into action more than two divisions, or about 30,000 men. When we reached Benghazi, and what was left of Mussolini's legions scurried back along the dusty road to Tripoli, a call was made upon us which we could not resist. Let me tell you about that call.

'In their mortal peril the Greeks turned to us for succour'

You will remember how in November the Italian dictator fell upon the unoffending Greeks, and without reason and without warning invaded their country, and how the Greek nation, reviving their classic fame, hurled his armies back at the double-quick. Meanwhile Hitler, who had been creeping and worming his way steadily forward, doping and poisoning and pinioning, one after the other, Hungary, Romania and Bulgaria, suddenly made it clear that he would come to the rescue of his fellow-criminal. The lack of unity among the Balkan states had enabled him to build up a mighty army in their midst. While nearly all the Greek troops were busy beating the Italians, the tremendous German military machine suddenly towered up on their other frontier. In their mortal peril the Greeks turned to us for succour. Strained as were our own resources, we could not say them nay. By solemn guarantee given before the war, Great Britain had promised them her help. They declared they would fight for their native soil even if neither of their neighbours made common cause with them, and even if we left them to their fate. But we could not do that. There are rules against that kind of thing; and to break those rules would be fatal to the honour of the British Empire, without which we could neither hope nor deserve to win this hard war. Military defeat or miscalculation can be redeemed. The fortunes of war are fickle and changing. But an act of shame would deprive us of the respect which we now enjoy throughout the world, and this would sap the vitals of our strength.

'That gleaming flash of resolve which lifts the hearts of men and nations, and springs from the spiritual foundations of human life itself'

During the last year we have gained by our bearing and conduct a potent hold upon the sentiments of the people of the United States. Never, never in our history, have we been held in such admiration and regard across the Atlantic Ocean. In that great republic, now in much travail and stress of soul, it is customary to use all the many valid, solid arguments about American interests and American safety, which depend upon the destruction of Hitler and his foul gang and even fouler doctrines. But in the long run – believe me, for I know – the action of the United States will be dictated, not by methodical calculations of profit and loss, but by moral sentiment, and by that gleaming flash of resolve which lifts the hearts of men and nations, and springs from the spiritual foundations of human life itself.

Churchill then defended the decision to divert forces from North Africa to the Balkan theatre of operations. The resolve it gave to those Yugoslavs determined to prevent their government siding with the Axis powers might have been decisive, he claimed, had the Germans not overrun the country before they could properly mobilize their forces. He conceded that 'our forces in Libya have sustained a vexatious and damaging defeat' but that no matter what Hitler achieved 'he must either conquer this island by invasion, or he must cut the ocean life-line which joins us to the United States.' Survival thus depended upon winning the Battle of the Atlantic.

... when you think how easy it is to sink ships at sea and how hard it is to build them and protect them, and when you remember that we have never less than 2000 ships afloat and 300 or 400 in the danger zone; when you think of the great armies we are maintaining and reinforcing in the East, and of the worldwide traffic we have to carry on – when you remember all this, can you wonder that it is the Battle of the Atlantic which holds the first place in the thoughts of those upon whom rests the responsibility for procuring the victory?

'The Battle of the Atlantic will be long and hard'

It was therefore with indescribable relief that I learned of the tremendous decisions lately taken by the president and people of the United States. The American Fleet and flying boats have been ordered to patrol the wide waters of the western hemisphere, and to warn the peaceful shipping of all nations outside the combat zone of the presence of lurking U-boats or aiding cruisers belonging to the two aggressor nations. We British shall therefore be able to concentrate our protecting forces far more upon the routes nearer home, and to take a far heavier toll of the U-boats there. I have felt for some time that something like this was bound to happen. The president and Congress of the United States, having newly fortified themselves by contact with their electors, have solemnly pledged their aid to Britain in this war because they deem our cause just, and because they know their own interests and safety would be endangered if we were destroyed. They are taxing themselves heavily. They have passed great legislation. They have turned a large part of their gigantic industry to making the munitions which we need. They have even given us or lent us valuable weapons of their own. I could not believe that they would allow the high purposes to which they have set themselves to be frustrated and the products of their skill and labour sunk to the bottom of the sea. U-boat warfare as conducted by Germany is entirely contrary to international agreements freely subscribed to by Germany only a few years ago. There is no effective blockade, but only a merciless murder and marauding over wide, indiscriminate areas utterly beyond the control of the German sea-power. When I said ten weeks ago: 'Give us the tools and we will finish the job', I meant, give them to us: put them within our reach – and that is what it now seems the Americans are going to do. And that is why I feel a very strong conviction that though the Battle of the Atlantic will be long and hard, and its issue is by no means yet determined, it has entered upon a more grim but at the same time a far more favourable phase. When you come to think of it, the United States are very closely bound up with us now, and have engaged themselves deeply in giving us moral, material and, within the limits I have mentioned, naval support.

'The cause of freedom shall not be trampled down'

It is worthwhile therefore to take a look on both sides of the ocean at the forces which are facing each other in this awful struggle, from which there can be no drawing back. No prudent and far-seeing man can doubt that the eventual and total defeat of Hitler and Mussolini is certain, in view of the respective declared resolves of the British and American democracies. There are less than 70,000,000 malignant Huns – some of whom are curable and others killable – many of whom are already engaged in holding down Austrians, Czechs, Poles, French, and the many other ancient races they now bully and pillage. The peoples of the British Empire and of the United States number nearly 200,000,000 in their homelands and in the British Dominions alone. They possess the unchallengeable command of the oceans, and will soon obtain decisive superiority in the air. They have more wealth, more technical resources, and they make more steel, than the whole of the rest of the world put together. They are determined that the cause of freedom shall not be trampled down, nor the tide of world progress turned backwards, by the criminal dictators.

While therefore we naturally view with sorrow and anxiety much that is happening in Europe and in Africa, and may happen in Asia, we must not lose our sense of proportion and thus become discouraged or alarmed. When we face with a steady eye the difficulties which lie before us, we may derive new confidence from remembering those we have already overcome. Nothing that is happening now is comparable in gravity with the dangers through which we passed last year. Nothing that can happen in the East is comparable with what is happening in the West.

'But westward, look, the land is bright'

Last time I spoke to you I quoted the lines of Longfellow which President Roosevelt had written out for me in his own hand. I have some other lines [from Arthur Hugh Clough's 'Say Not the Struggle Naught Availeth'] which are less well known but which seem apt and appropriate to our fortunes tonight, and I believe they will be so judged wherever the English language is spoken or the flag of freedom flies:

> For while the tired waves, vainly breaking,
>   Seem here no painful inch to gain,
> Far back, through creeks and inlets making.
>   Comes silent, flooding in, the main.
>
> And not by eastern windows only,
>   When daylight comes, comes in the light;
> In front the sun climbs slow, how slowly!
>   But westward, look, the land is bright.

'The fourth climacteric'

World broadcast, 22 June 1941

On the German invasion of the
Soviet Union

During June 1941, British Intelligence deciphered German radio signals indicating a huge build up of Wehrmacht divisions close to the Soviet border. Stalin's Russia was still at peace with Hitler's Reich under the terms of their mutual Non-Aggression Pact. Churchill decided he needed to warn Stalin. But the communist dictator appeared to take little notice. On the evening of 21 June, Churchill told his dinner guests, 'a German attack on Russia is certain and Russia will assuredly be defeated'.

The next morning Churchill awoke to the news that Germany had invaded the Soviet Union across a 1500-mile front stretching from Finland to the Black Sea. During the day, as he worked on the speech he would broadcast to the world that evening, the prime minister received an almost unending succession of gloomy consuls on how many weeks the Red Army could last. The assessments had the opposite effect on his mood, and he started voicing his new-found optimism that the Soviet Union would not prove such a push-over. Recognizing that his enemy's enemy was his friend, Churchill, the virulent anti-Bolshevik, swiftly led his War Cabinet into sending the reeling Russians much needed supplies, including 200 fighter aircraft. As he had assured his assistant private secretary, Jock Colville, 'If Hitler invaded Hell I would at least make a favourable reference to the Devil.'

ON THIS DAY
22 JUNE 1941

- Germany's Operation Barbarossa against its former Non-Agression Pact ally, the Soviet Union, kicks off at 03:15, involving 151 divisions and massive armoured and air support. Hitler, expectant of rapid success, broadcasts to his people. The invasion is soon supported by Germany's allies, including troops from Finland, Romania and Hungary. Stalin's armed forces, though sizeable, are unprepared, hampered by obsolete armour and planes, and have been demoralised and damaged by political purges of officers.

- Free French, Australian and British troops begin to establish their authority in Damascus, having fought for over two weeks to win Syria from the surprisingly robust Vichy forces defending it.

'Those were the three climacterics. The fourth is now upon us'

I have taken occasion to speak to you tonight because we have reached one of the climacterics of the war. The first of these intense turning-points was a year ago when France fell prostrate under the German hammer, and when we had to face the storm alone. The second was when the Royal Air Force beat the Hun raiders out of the daylight air, and thus warded off the Nazi invasion of our island while we were still ill-armed and ill-prepared. The third turning-point was when the president and Congress of the United States passed the Lease-and-Lend enactment, devoting nearly 2000 millions Sterling of the wealth of the New World to help us to defend our liberties and their own. Those were the three climacterics. The fourth is now upon us.

'At 4 o'clock this morning Hitler attacked and invaded Russia'

At 4 o'clock this morning Hitler attacked and invaded Russia. All his usual formalities of perfidy were observed with scrupulous technique. A non-aggression treaty had been solemnly signed and was in force between the two countries. No complaint had been made by Germany of its non-fulfilment. Under its cloak of false confidence, the German armies drew up in immense strength along a line which stretches from the White Sea to the Black Sea; and their air fleets and armoured divisions slowly and methodically took their stations. Then, suddenly, without declaration of war, without even an ultimatum, German bombs rained down from the air upon the Russian cities, the German troops violated the frontiers; and an hour later the German Ambassador, who till the night before was lavishing his assurances of friendship, almost of alliance, upon the Russians, called upon the Russian Foreign Minister to tell him that a state of war existed between Germany and Russia.

Thus was repeated on a far larger scale the same kind of outrage against every form of signed compact and international faith which we have witnessed in Norway, Denmark, Holland and Belgium, and which Hitler's accomplice and jackal Mussolini so faithfully imitated in the case of Greece.

All this was no surprise to me. In fact I gave clear and precise warnings to Stalin of what was coming. I gave him warning as I have given warning to others before. I can only hope that this warning did not fall unheeded. All we know at present is that the Russian people are defending their native soil and that their leaders have called upon them to resist to the utmost.

'Hitler is a monster of wickedness, insatiable in his lust for blood and plunder'

Hitler is a monster of wickedness, insatiable in his lust for blood and plunder. Not content with having all Europe under his heel, or else terrorized into various forms of abject submission, he must now carry his work of butchery and desolation among the vast multitudes of Russia and of Asia. The terrible military machine, which we and the rest of the civilized world so foolishly, so supinely, so insensately allowed the Nazi gangsters to build up year by year from almost nothing, cannot stand idle lest it rust or fall to pieces. It must be in continual motion, grinding up human lives and trampling down the homes and the rights of hundreds of millions of men. Moreover it must be fed, not only with flesh but with oil.

'The diabolic emblem of the swastika'

So now this bloodthirsty guttersnipe must launch his mechanized armies upon new fields of slaughter, pillage and devastation. Poor as are the Russian peasants, workmen and soldiers, he must steal from them their daily bread; he must devour their harvests; he must rob them of the oil which drives their ploughs; and thus produce a famine without example in human history. And even the carnage and ruin which his victory, should he gain it – he has not gained it yet – will bring upon the Russian people, will itself be only a stepping-stone to the attempt to plunge the 400,000,000 or 500,000,000 who live in China, and the 350,000,000 who live in India, into that bottomless pit of human degradation over which the diabolic emblem of the swastika flaunts itself. It is not too much to say here this summer evening that the lives and happiness of 1,000,000,000 additional people are now menaced with brutal Nazi violence. That is enough to make us hold our breath. But presently I shall show you something else that lies behind, and something that touches very nearly the life of Britain and of the United States.

'I see also the dull, drilled, docile, brutish masses of the Hun soldiery plodding on like a swarm of crawling locusts'

The Nazi regime is indistinguishable from the worst features of Communism. It is devoid of all theme and principle except appetite and racial domination. It excels all forms of human wickedness in the efficiency of its cruelty and ferocious aggression. No one has been a more consistent opponent of Communism than I have for the last 25 years. I will unsay no word that I have spoken about it. But all this fades away before the spectacle which is now unfolding. The past with its crimes, its follies and its tragedies, flashes away. I see the Russian soldiers standing on the threshold of their native land, guarding the fields which their fathers have tilled from time immemorial. I see them guarding their homes where mothers and wives pray – ah yes, for there are times when all pray – for the safety of their loved ones, the return of the bread-winner, of their champion, of their protector. I see the 10,000 villages of Russia, where the means of existence was wrung so hardly from the soil, but where there are still primordial human joys, where maidens laugh and children play. I see advancing upon all this in hideous onslaught the Nazi war machine, with its clanking, heel-clicking, dandified Prussian officers, its crafty expert agents fresh from the cowing and tying-down of a dozen countries. I see also the dull, drilled, docile, brutish masses of the Hun soldiery plodding on like a swarm of crawling locusts. I see the German bombers and fighters in the sky, still smarting from many a British whipping, delighted to find what they believe is an easier and a safer prey.

Behind all this glare, behind all this storm, I see that small group of villainous men who plan, organize and launch this cataract of horrors upon mankind. And then my mind goes back across the years to the days when the Russian armies were our allies against the same deadly foe; when they fought with so much valour and constancy, and helped to gain a victory all share in [from] which, alas, they were – through no fault of ours – utterly cut off. I have lived through all this, and you will pardon me if I express my feelings and the stir of old memories.

'We are resolved to destroy Hitler and every vestige of the Nazi regime'

But now I have to declare the decision of His Majesty's government – and I feel sure it is a decision in which the great Dominions will, in due course, concur – for we must speak out now at once, without a day's delay. I have to make the declaration, but can you doubt what our policy will be? We have but one aim and one single, irrevocable purpose. We are resolved to destroy Hitler and every vestige of the Nazi regime. From this nothing will turn us – nothing. We will never parley, we will never negotiate with Hitler or any of his gang. We shall fight him by land, we shall fight him by sea, we shall fight him in the air, until with God's help we have rid the earth of his shadow and liberated its peoples from his yoke. Any man or state who fights on against Nazidom will have our aid. Any man or state who marches with

Hitler is our foe. This applies not only to organized states but to all representatives of that vile race of quislings who make themselves the tools and agents of the Nazi regime against their fellow-countrymen and the lands of their birth. They – these quislings – like the Nazi leaders themselves, if not disposed of by their fellow-countrymen, which would save trouble, will be delivered by us on the morrow of victory to the justice of the Allied tribunals. That is our policy and that is our declaration. It follows, therefore, that we shall give whatever help we can to Russia and the Russian people. We shall appeal to all our friends and allies in every part of the world to take the same course and pursue it, as we shall, faithfully and steadfastly to the end.

'We shall bomb Germany by day as well as by night . . . making the German people taste and gulp each month a sharper dose of the miseries they have showered upon mankind'

We have offered the government of Soviet Russia any technical or economic assistance which is in our power, and which is likely to be of service to them. We shall bomb Germany by day as well as by night in ever-increasing measure, casting upon them month by month a heavier discharge of bombs, and making the German people taste and gulp each month a sharper dose of the miseries they have showered upon mankind. It is noteworthy that only yesterday the Royal Air Force, fighting inland over French territory, cut down with very small loss to themselves 28 of the Hun fighting machines in the air above the French soil they have invaded, defiled and profess to hold. But this is only a beginning. From now forward the main expansion of our Air Force proceeds with gathering speed. In another six months the weight of the help we are receiving from the United States in war materials of all kinds, and especially in heavy bombers, will begin to tell.

This is no class war, but a war in which the whole British Empire and Commonwealth of Nations is engaged without distinction of race, creed or party. It is not for me to speak of the action of the United States, but this I will say: if Hitler imagines that his attack on Soviet Russia will cause the slightest division of aims or slackening of effort in the great democracies who are resolved upon his doom, he is woefully mistaken. On the contrary, we shall be fortified and encouraged in our efforts to rescue mankind from his tyranny. We shall be strengthened and not weakened in determination and in resources.

This is no time to moralize on the follies of countries and governments which have allowed themselves to be struck down one by one, when by united action they could have saved themselves and saved the world from this catastrophe. But when I spoke a few minutes ago of Hitler's blood-lust and the hateful appetites which have impelled or lured him on his Russian adventure, I said there was one deeper motive behind his outrage. He wishes to destroy the Russian power because he hopes that if he succeeds in this, he will be able to bring back the main strength of his army and air force from the East and hurl it upon this island, which he knows he must conquer or suffer the penalty of his crimes. His invasion of Russia is no more than a prelude to an attempted invasion of the British Isles. He hopes, no doubt, that all this may be accomplished before the winter comes, and that he can overwhelm Great Britain before the Fleet and air-power of the United States may intervene. He hopes that he may once again repeat, upon a greater scale than ever before, that process of destroying his enemies one by one, by which he has so long thrived and prospered, and that then the scene will be clear for the final act, without which all his conquests would be in vain – namely, the subjugation of the Western Hemisphere to his will and to his system.

'The Russian danger is therefore our danger . . . Let us redouble our exertions, and strike with united strength while life and power remain.'

The Russian danger is therefore our danger, and the danger of the United States, just as the cause of any Russian fighting for his hearth and home is the cause of free men and free peoples in every quarter of the globe. Let us learn the lessons already taught by such cruel experience. Let us redouble our exertions, and strike with united strength while life and power remain.

'The tunnel may be dark and long'

World broadcast, London, 24 August 1941

On meeting Roosevelt and signing
the Atlantic Charter

The news coming in from the Eastern Front in the summer of 1941 was almost uniformly bad: the Germans were pressing further and further into Soviet territory. While pledging what aid he could spare to Stalin, Churchill also had to stay focused on the imperative – drawing the United States deeper into the Allied cause – as this remained the most likely means of ultimate deliverance.

President Roosevelt and Churchill had been in regular contact for the previous two years, but the president was keen for them both to meet. So, on 3 August 1941 Churchill boarded the battleship HMS *Prince of Wales* to sail across the Atlantic to meet him – the first time that Churchill had slipped out of Britain since France's collapse a year previously.

Six days later, the *Prince of Wales* reached its rendezvous point in Placentia Bay, off Argentia, Newfoundland. There, Churchill boarded the USS *Augusta* to be received by the president. The two men had met only once before, fleetingly, in 1919. The following day, Roosevelt joined the singing on the deck of the *Prince of Wales* where a church service was held with rousing hymns handpicked by the prime minister.

Roosevelt's pledge to make the United States the 'arsenal of democracy' had been given a boost in March when Congress finally passed the Lend-Lease Act. This circumvented existing neutrality laws so that war *matériel* could be shipped to Britain without the latter – already cash-strapped – having to pay upfront. But the Battle of the Atlantic was raging. In April alone, 700,000 tons of shipping was sunk. While Roosevelt and Churchill built their personal relationship to the accompanying harmony of 'For those in peril on the sea', the British and American chiefs of staff worried about how the U-boat gauntlet could be run without embroiling the US Navy in the fighting.

The meeting of these two great leaders of what remained of the free world also produced a document for public consumption: an eight-point declaration that came to be called the 'Atlantic Charter', which stated the postwar aims of Britain and the United States. They committed themselves to 'seek no aggrandisement, territorial or other' nor to press for 'territorial changes that do not accord with the freely expressed wishes of the peoples concerned'. They promised to 'respect the right of all peoples to choose the form of government under which they will live; and they wish to see sovereign rights and self-government restored to those who have been forcibly deprived of them'. There were also appeals for a future of economic cooperation and rising living standards and equitable trade for all nations, together with freedom of the seas and eventual worldwide reduction in armaments.

ON THIS DAY
24 AUGUST 1941

- In Germany, the secret policy of murdering the mentally ill, in effect since 1939, is ended on Hitler's orders. Over 70,000 have died.

- In Vichy France, new laws enact the death penalty for those fighting the regime, i.e. the Resistance or Maquis.

- In the Ukraine, German forces encounter stubborn Soviet resistance.

- British and Soviet forces prepare to invade neutral Iran the following morning, because of worries about Iranian–German ties and to secure oil supplies.

The Atlantic Charter was a ringing endorsement of freedom and self-determination, which at face value positioned Britain and America clearly on the moral high ground. At the same time there were some British imperialists who questioned whether their prime minister's agreement to let people choose their own destiny was entirely compatible with the strict maintenance of colonial rule.

For Churchill, this was an argument for another day. The key issue was whether his discussions with Roosevelt would bring America's entry into the war any closer. The prime minister drew encouragement from the rapport he had built with the president. Shortly afterwards, the US Navy began escorting British convoys as far as the mid-Atlantic, and U-boats surfacing within range of these escort ships risked being fired upon by the American vessels. If a motive to enter the war was being sought, the likelihood of a major Atlantic incident with the Germans was clearly growing. Furthermore, Washington's declining relations with Tokyo in the Pacific promised to be a second danger zone in which the United States might find itself pushed into a war – for which eventuality Churchill was quick to promise British involvement.

When Roosevelt returned from Placentia Bay, he swiftly reassured his fellow Americans that they were no nearer to getting sucked into the conflict. This was hardly surprising given that opinion polls suggested three-quarters of his nation opposed entering the war. Watching ominously as the Soviet Union appeared to be heading towards collapse under the Wehrmacht's onslaught, Churchill could not suppress a fear that by the time the United States did get dragged in the situation would be almost irretrievable.

I thought you would like me to tell you something about the voyage which I made across the ocean to meet our great friend, the president of the United States. Exactly where we met is a secret, but I don't think I shall be indiscreet if I go so far as to say that it was 'somewhere in the Atlantic'.

In a spacious, landlocked bay which reminded me of the west coast of Scotland, powerful American warships protected by strong flotillas and far-ranging aircraft awaited our arrival, and, as it were, stretched out a hand to help us in. Our party arrived in the newest, or almost the newest, British battleship, the *Prince of Wales*, with a modern escort of British and Canadian destroyers; and there for three days I spent my time in company, and I think I may say in comradeship, with Mr Roosevelt; while all the time the chiefs of the staff and the naval and military commanders both of the British Empire and of the United States sat together in continual council.

'I am the servant of King and Parliament'

President Roosevelt is the thrice-chosen head of the most powerful state and community in the world. I am the servant of King and Parliament at present charged with the principal direction of our affairs in these fateful times, and it is my duty also to make sure, as I have made sure, that anything I say or do in the exercise of my office is approved and sustained by the whole British Commonwealth of Nations. Therefore this meeting was bound to be important, because of the enormous forces at present only partially mobilized but steadily mobilizing which are at the disposal of these two major groupings of the human family: the British Empire and the United States, who, fortunately for the progress of mankind, happen to speak the same language, and very largely think the same thoughts, or anyhow think a lot of the same thoughts.

The meeting was therefore symbolic. That is its prime importance. It symbolizes, in a form and manner which everyone can understand in every land and in every clime, the deep underlying unities which stir and at decisive moments rule the English-speaking peoples throughout the world. Would it be presumptuous for me to say that it symbolizes something even more majestic – namely, the marshalling of the good forces of the world against the evil forces which are now so formidable and triumphant and which have cast their cruel spell over the whole of Europe and a large part of Asia?

'Lead them forward . . . to the broad high road of freedom and justice'

This was a meeting which marks forever in the pages of history the taking-up by the English-speaking nations, amid all this peril, tumult and confusion, of the guidance of the fortunes of the broad toiling masses in all the continents; and our loyal effort without any clog of selfish interest to lead them forward out of the miseries into which they have been plunged back to the broad high road of freedom and justice. This is the highest honour and the most glorious opportunity which could ever have come to any branch of the human race.

Churchill spoke about Hitler's aggression against the Soviet Union: 'Here is a devil who, in a mere spasm of his pride and lust for domination, can condemn two or three millions, perhaps it may be many more, of human beings, to speedy and violent death.' He then turned to the Pacific and the brooding menace from the Japanese forces:

... Now they stretch a grasping hand into the southern seas of China, they snatch Indo-China from the wretched Vichy French; they menace by their movement Siam; menace Singapore, the British link with Australasia; and menace the Philippine Islands under the protection of the United States. It is certain that this has got to stop. Every effort will be made to secure a peaceful settlement. The United States are labouring with infinite patience to arrive at a fair and amicable settlement which will give Japan the utmost reassurance for her legitimate interests. We earnestly hope these negotiations will succeed. But this I must say: that if these hopes should fail we shall of course range ourselves unhesitatingly at the side of the United States.

'Make a way for others to march . . . which will certainly be painful.'

And thus we come back to the quiet bay somewhere in the Atlantic where misty sunshine plays on great ships which carry the White Ensign, or the Stars and Stripes. We had the idea, when we met there – the president and I – that without attempting to draw up final and formal peace aims, or war aims, it was necessary to give all peoples, especially the oppressed and conquered peoples, a simple, rough-and-ready wartime statement of the goal towards which the British Commonwealth and the United States mean to make their way, and thus make a way for others to march with them upon a road which will certainly be painful, and may be long.

There are, however, two distinct and marked differences in this joint declaration from the attitude adopted by the Allies during the latter part of the last war; and no one should overlook them. The United States and Great Britain do not now assume that there will never be any more war again. On the contrary, we intend to take ample precautions to prevent its renewal in any period we can foresee by effectively disarming the guilty nations while remaining suitably protected ourselves.

'What is this New Order? . . . It is the rule of the Herrenvolk'

The second difference is this: that instead of trying to ruin German trade by all kinds of additional trade barriers and hindrances as was the mood of 1917, we have definitely adopted the view that it is not in the interests of the world and of our two countries that any large nation should be unprosperous or shut out from the means of making a decent living for itself and its people by its industry and enterprise. These are far-reaching changes of principle upon which all countries should ponder. Above all, it was necessary to give hope and the assurance of final victory to those many scores of millions of men and women who are battling for life and freedom, or who are already bent down under the Nazi yoke. Hitler and his confederates have for some time past been adjuring, bullying and beseeching the populations whom they have wronged and injured, to bow to their fate, to resign themselves to their servitude, and for the sake of some mitigations and indulgences, to 'collaborate' – that is the word – in what is called the New Order in Europe.

What is this New Order which they seek to fasten first upon Europe and if possible – for their ambitions are boundless – upon all the continents of the globe? It is the rule of the Herrenvolk – the master-race – who are to put an end to democracy, to parliaments, to the fundamental freedoms and decencies of ordinary men and women, to the historic rights of nations; and give them in exchange the iron rule of Prussia, the universal goose-step, and a strict, efficient discipline enforced upon the working-class by the political police, with the German concentration camps and firing parties, now so busy in a dozen lands, always handy in the background. There is the New Order.

'The tunnel may be dark and long, but at the end there is light'

Napoleon in his glory and his genius spread his empire far and wide. There was a time when only the snows of Russia and the white cliffs of Dover with their guardian fleets stood between him and the dominion of the world. Napoleon's armies had a theme: they carried with them the surges of the French Revolution. 'Liberty, Equality and Fraternity' – that was the cry. There was a sweeping away of outworn medieval systems and aristocratic privilege. There was the land for the people, a new code of law. Nevertheless, Napoleon's empire vanished like a dream. But Hitler, Hitler has no theme, naught but mania, appetite and exploitation. He has, however, weapons and machinery for grinding down and for holding down conquered countries which are the product, the sadly perverted product, of modern science.

The ordeals, therefore, of the conquered peoples will be hard. We must give them hope; we must give them the conviction that their sufferings and their resistances will not be in vain. The tunnel may be dark and long, but at the end there is light. That is the symbolism and that is the message of the Atlantic meeting. Do not despair, brave Norwegians: your land shall be cleansed not only from the invader but from the filthy quislings who are his tools. Be sure of yourselves, Czechs: your independence shall be restored. Poles, the heroism of your people standing up to cruel oppressors, the courage of your soldiers, sailors and airmen, shall not be forgotten: your country shall live again and resume its rightful part in the new organization of Europe. Lift up your heads, gallant Frenchmen: not all the infamies of Darlan and of Laval shall stand between you and the restoration of your birthright. Tough, stout-hearted Dutch, Belgians, Luxembourgers, tormented, mishandled, shamefully castaway peoples of Yugoslavia, glorious Greece, now subjected to the crowning insult of the rule of the Italian jackanapes; yield not an inch! Keep your souls clean from all contact with the Nazis; make them feel even in their fleeting hour of brutish triumph that they are the moral outcasts of mankind! Help is coming; mighty forces are arming in your behalf. Have faith. Have hope. Deliverance is sure.

There is the signal which we have flashed across the water; and if it reaches the hearts of those to whom it is sent, they will endure with fortitude and tenacity their present misfortunes in the sure faith that they, too, are still serving the common cause and that their efforts will not be in vain.

You will perhaps have noticed that the president of the United States and the British representative, in what is aptly called the 'Atlantic Charter', have jointly pledged their countries to the final destruction of the Nazi tyranny. That is a solemn and grave undertaking. It must be made good; it will be made good. And, of course, many practical arrangements to fulfil that purpose have been and are being organized and set in motion.

'How near is the United States to war?'

The question has been asked: how near is the United States to war? There is certainly one man who knows the answer to that question. If Hitler has not yet declared war upon the United States, it is surely not out of his love for American institutions; it is certainly not because he could not find a pretext. He has murdered half a dozen countries for far less. Fear of immediately redoubling the tremendous energies now being employed against him is no doubt a restraining influence. But the real reason is, I am sure, to be found in the method to which he has so faithfully adhered and by which he has gained so much.

What is that method? It is a very simple method. One by one: that is his plan; that is his guiding rule; that is the trick by which he has enslaved so large a portion of the world. Three and a half years ago I appealed to my fellow countrymen to take the lead in weaving together a strong defensive union within the principles of the League of Nations, a union of all the countries who felt themselves in ever-growing danger. But none would listen; all stood idle while Germany rearmed. Czechoslovakia was subjugated; a French government deserted their faithful ally and broke a plighted word in that ally's hour of need. Russia was cajoled and deceived into a kind of neutrality or partnership, while the French Army was being annihilated. The Low Countries and the Scandinavian countries, acting with France and Great Britain in good time, even after the war had begun, might have altered its course, and would have had, at any rate, a fighting chance. The Balkan states had only to stand together to save themselves from the ruin by which they are now engulfed. But one by one they were undermined and overwhelmed. Never was the career of crime made more smooth.

'Why is Hitler striking at Russia . . . making his soldiers suffer this frightful slaughter?'

Now Hitler is striking at Russia with all his might, well knowing the difficulties of geography which stand between Russia and the aid which the Western democracies are trying to bring. We shall strive our utmost to overcome all obstacles and to bring this aid. We have arranged for a conference in Moscow between the United States, British and Russian authorities to settle the whole plan. No barrier must stand in the way. But why is Hitler striking at Russia, and inflicting and suffering himself or, rather, making his soldiers suffer this frightful slaughter? It is with the declared object of turning his whole force upon the British Islands and if he could succeed in beating the life and the strength out of us, which is not so easy, then is the moment when he will settle his account, and it is already a long one, with the people of the United States and generally with the western hemisphere. One by one, there is the process; there is the simple, dismal plan which has served Hitler so well. It needs but one final successful application to make him the master of the world. I am devoutly thankful that some eyes at least are fully opened to it while time remains. I rejoiced to find that the president saw in their true light and proportion the extreme dangers by which the American people as well as the British people are now beset. It was indeed by the mercy of God that he began eight years ago that revival of the strength of the American Navy without which the New World today would have to take its orders from the European dictators, but with which the United States still retains the power to marshal her gigantic strength, and in saving herself to render an incomparable service to mankind.

We had a church parade on the Sunday in our Atlantic bay. The president came on to the quarterdeck of the *Prince of Wales*, where there were mingled together many hundreds of American and British sailors and marines. The sun shone bright and warm while we all sang the old hymns which are our common inheritance and which we learned as children in our homes. We sang the hymn founded on the psalm which John Hampden's soldiers sang when they bore his body to the grave, and in which the brief, precarious span of human life is contrasted with the immutability of Him to whom a thousand ages are but as yesterday, and as a watch in the night. We sang the sailors' hymn 'For those in peril' – and there are very many – 'on the sea'. We sang 'Onward Christian soldiers'. And indeed I felt that this was no vain presumption, but that we had the right to feel that we were serving a cause for the sake of which a trumpet has sounded from on high.

'Back across the ocean waves, uplifted in spirit, fortified in resolve'

When I looked upon that densely-packed congregation of fighting men of the same language, of the same faith, of the same fundamental laws and the same ideals, and now to a large extent of the same interests, and certainly in different degrees facing the same dangers, it swept across me that here was the only hope, but also the sure hope, of saving the world from measureless degradation.

And so we came back across the ocean waves, uplifted in spirit, fortified in resolve. Some American destroyers which were carrying mails to the United States marines in Iceland happened to be going the same way, too, so we made a goodly company at sea together.

And when we were right out in mid-passage one afternoon a noble sight broke on the view. We overtook one of the convoys which carry the munitions and supplies of the New World to sustain the champions of freedom in the Old. The whole broad horizon seemed filled with ships; seventy or eighty ships of all kinds and sizes, arrayed in fourteen lines, each of which could have been drawn with a ruler, hardly a wisp of smoke, not a straggler, but all bristling with cannons and other precautions on which I will not dwell, and all surrounded by their British escorting vessels, while overhead the far-ranging Catalina airboats soared – vigilant, protecting eagles in the sky. Then I felt that – hard and terrible and long drawn-out as this struggle may be – we shall not be denied the strength to do our duty to the end.

'Hitler's madness has infected the Japanese mind'

House of Commons, London, 8 December 1941

On the morning of 7 December 1941, 360 Japanese aircraft launched a devastating attack on the unsuspecting US naval base at Pearl Harbor in Hawaii. The moored fleet was seriously damaged, with eight battleships put out of action and half of all the US airplanes in the Pacific destroyed. A total of 2323 American servicemen were killed. The attack, which President Roosevelt called 'a date which will live in infamy', came before Japan's declaration of war. In one penetrating swoop Tokyo gained mastery of the Pacific Ocean.

Japan's bellicosity was hardly anything new. During the 1930s she had begun appropriating – with colossal barbarity – vast areas of northern China. In 1937 Japan joined Germany and Italy in the Anti-Comintern Pact and, following the fall of France, occupied the French colony of Indo-China (modern Vietnam). Washington responded in July 1941 by freezing Japanese assets in the United States and cutting off oil supplies unless there was to be a withdrawal from Indo-China. The British and exiled Dutch governments took similar action. Without oil, the Japanese could not press ahead with their Chinese ambitions. They would either have to climb down or strike out at those restraining them. In December they made their choice explicit. In doing so, the Japanese were going to war with all their regional enemies simultaneously. At almost the same time as Japan's airmen were targeting the ships in Pearl Harbor, her soldiers were attacking the American garrison in the Philippines and the British colony of Malaya. Thailand and Shanghai were also invaded and the all-important oil wells of the Dutch East Indies – modern Indonesia – came under threat.

ON THIS DAY
8 DECEMBER 1941

• A Japanese invasion of Thailand begins, which will lead to the country surrendering within four days.

• Japanese air attacks strike the RAF base at Kowloon, Hong Kong, and the US Air Force base at Clark Field in the Philippines, while land forces move to seize the European concession areas of Shanghai.

• China prepares to make its official declaration of war on Japan, Germany and Italy.

The following day – 8 December – Washington and London formally declared war on their common aggressor. The US Senate endorsed the president's declaration by 82 votes to none and the House of Representatives by 338 to 1. In the House of Commons, the vote was unanimous. But there was no American declaration of war on Italy or Germany. For Churchill, emotions were therefore mixed. The prospect of having to fight the Axis powers in Europe and North Africa at the same time as the Japanese in the Far East had always hung heavily on his mind. At least he now had assistance with the latter campaign. But what of the war in Europe? The arithmetic looked less promising if the bulk of America's arsenal was redirected to the Pacific and away from the essential supplies she was sending across the Atlantic to bolster Britain's home and European effort.

As soon as I heard, last night, that Japan had attacked the United States, I felt it necessary that Parliament should be immediately summoned. It is indispensable to our system of government that Parliament should play its full part in all the important acts of state and at all the crucial moments of the war; and I am glad to see that so many Members have been able to be in their places, despite the shortness of the notice. With the full approval of the nation, and of the empire, I pledged the word of Great Britain, about a month ago, that should the United States be involved in war with Japan, a British declaration of war would follow within the hour. I therefore spoke to President Roosevelt on the Atlantic telephone last night, with a view to arranging the timing of our respective declarations. The president told me that he would this morning send a message to Congress, which, of course, as is well known, can alone make a declaration of war on behalf of the United States, and I then assured him that we would follow immediately.

'Characteristic Japanese treachery'

However, it soon appeared that British territory in Malaya had also been the object of Japanese attack, and later on it was announced from Tokyo that the Japanese High Command – a curious form; not the Imperial Japanese government – had declared that a state of war existed with Great Britain and the United States. That being so, there was no need to wait for the declaration by Congress. American time is very nearly six hours behind ours. The Cabinet, therefore, which met at 12.30 today, authorized an immediate declaration of war upon Japan.

Churchill read out the instruction to the British Ambassador in Tokyo and welcomed the decision of the Royal Netherlands government to declare war on Japan as well.

… It is worthwhile looking for a moment at the manner in which the Japanese have begun their assault upon the English-speaking world. Every circumstance of calculated and characteristic Japanese treachery was employed against the United States. The Japanese envoys, Nomura and Kurusu, were ordered to prolong their mission in the United States, in order to keep the conversations going while a surprise attack was being prepared, to be made before a declaration of war could be delivered. The president's appeal to the emperor, which I have no doubt many Members will have read – it has been published largely in the papers here – reminding him of their ancient friendship and of the importance of preserving the peace of the Pacific, has received only this base and brutal reply. No one can doubt that every effort to bring about a peaceful solution had been made by the government of the United States, and that immense patience and composure has been shown in face of the growing Japanese menace.

'The heroic people of China'

Now that the issue is joined in the most direct manner, it only remains for the two great democracies to face their task with whatever strength God may give them. We must hold ourselves very fortunate, and I think we may rate our affairs not wholly ill-guided, that we were not attacked alone by Japan in our period of weakness after Dunkirk, or at any time in 1940, before the United States had fully realized the dangers which threatened the whole world and had made much advance in its military preparation. So precarious and narrow was the margin upon which we then lived that we did not dare to express the sympathy which we have all along felt for the heroic people of China. We were even forced for a short time, in the summer of 1940, to agree to closing the Burma Road. But later on, at the beginning of this year, as soon as we could regather our strength, we reversed that policy, and the House will remember that both I and the foreign secretary [Anthony Eden] have felt able to make increasingly outspoken declarations of friendship for the Chinese people and their great leader, General Chiang-Kai-Shek.

'Hitler's madness has infected the Japanese mind'

We have always been friends. Last night I cabled to the generalissimo assuring him that henceforward we would face the common foe together. Although the imperative demands of the war in Europe and in Africa have strained our resources, vast and growing though they are, the House and the empire will notice that some of the finest ships in the Royal Navy have reached their stations in the Far East at a very convenient moment. Every preparation in our power has been made, and I do not doubt that we shall give a good account of ourselves. The closest accord has been established with the powerful American forces, both naval and air, and also with the strong, efficient forces belonging to the Royal Netherlands government in the Netherlands East Indies. We shall all do our best. When we think of the insane ambition and insatiable appetite which have caused this vast and melancholy extension of the war, we can only feel that Hitler's madness has infected the Japanese mind, and that the root of the evil and its branch must be extirpated together.

'We have at least four-fifths of the population of the globe upon our side'

It is of the highest importance that there should be no underrating of the gravity of the new dangers we have to meet, either here or in the United States. The enemy has attacked with an audacity which may spring from recklessness, but which may also spring from a conviction of strength. The ordeal to which the English-speaking world and our heroic Russian allies are being exposed will certainly be hard, especially at the outset, and will probably be long, yet when we look around us over the sombre panorama of the world, we have no reason to doubt the justice of our cause or that our strength and will-power will be sufficient to sustain it. We have at least four-fifths of the population of the globe upon our side.

We are responsible for their safety and for their future. In the past we have had a light which flickered, in the present we have a light which flames, and in the future there will be a light which shines over all the land and sea.

'A long and hard war'

Senate Chamber, Washington, D.C., 26 December 1941

Rallying call to the American people

America was now at war, but only with Japan. However, on 11 December, Germany and Italy declared war on the United States. What prompted Hitler's impulsive action? The most plausible suggestion is that having come to assume American involvement inevitable sooner or later, Hitler calculated it was better to strike at the moment of his own choosing and thereby cement the alliance with Japan while the United States Navy was reeling from Pearl Harbor.

On 12 December Churchill set sail for America, but this time not on HMS *Prince of Wales*, which had been sunk two days previously – together with HMS *Repulse* – by the Japanese off the coast of Malaya. He arrived on 22 December and stayed at the White House for three weeks as a guest of the president. The British and American chiefs of staff also got together and reconfirmed that the European war against Germany, rather than the Pacific war against Japan, should be prioritized. For Churchill, this was perhaps the single most decisive decision taken by his primary ally following its entry into the conflict.

ON THIS DAY
26 DECEMBER 1941

• The British garrison defending Hong Kong enters Japanese captivity, having formally surrendered the previous day. Superior intelligence-gathering and more numerous forces have given the Japanese a speedy and decisive victory.

• Japanese invasion forces advance against British and Indian defenders in Malaya, landing from the sea and coming overland from conquered Thailand.

• In British Burma, the capital Rangoon has been hit by Japanese air attacks.

• The crisis in the Far East and Southeast Asia affects Indian nationalist politics, persuading the Indian Congress Party formally to back the British war effort – though Mohandas 'Mahatma' Gandhi resigns as party leader in protest.

While the prime minister and the president talked, the news from the Pacific continued to darken. The Japanese were driving the Americans out of the Philippines. On Christmas Day, the British garrison at Hong Kong surrendered. The following day, Churchill addressed both Houses of Congress.

Here was a new audience, with no innate love for an ageing British aristocrat with a late Victorian belief in the civilizing mission of his nation's empire. Undaunted, Churchill got the tone right. He reminded them that his mother was an American and that – despite being born amid the opulent baroque splendour of Blenheim Palace – he had early on imbibed from both his mother and his father's examples, the progressive ideals of liberty and democracy.

This was important. Churchill knew that the Grand Alliance would be sustained through difficult times not just through the Atlantic telephone and the combined map plotting of chiefs of staff but by his ability to capture the imagination of the American people. Before war intervened, he had begun writing a great – as it transpired multi-volume – book with the title *A History of the English-Speaking Peoples*. Here, before it was completed, he found himself the instrument through which its lessons about Anglo-Americanism were put into practice.

I feel greatly honoured that you should have invited me to enter the United States Senate Chamber and address the representatives of both branches of Congress. The fact that my American forebears have for so many generations played their part in the life of the United States, and that here I am, an Englishman, welcomed in your midst, makes this experience one of the most moving and thrilling in my life, which is already long and has not been entirely uneventful. I wish indeed that my mother, whose memory I cherish across the vale of years, could have been here to see. By the way, I cannot help reflecting that if my father had been American and my mother British, instead of the other way round, I might have got here on my own. In that case, this would not have been the first time you would have heard my voice. In that case I should not have needed any invitation, but if I had, it is hardly likely it would have been unanimous. So perhaps things are better as they are. I may confess, however, that I do not feel quite like a fish out of water in a legislative assembly where English is spoken.

'Government of the people by the people for the people'

I am a child of the House of Commons. I was brought up in my father's house to believe in democracy. 'Trust the people' – that was his message. I used to see him cheered at meetings and in the streets by crowds of working men way back in those aristocratic Victorian days when, as Disraeli said, the world was for the few, and for the very few. Therefore I have been in full harmony all my life with the tides which have flowed on both sides of the Atlantic against privilege and monopoly, and I have steered confidently towards the Gettysburg ideal of 'government of the people by the people for the people'. I owe my advancement entirely to the House of Commons, whose servant I am. In my country, as in yours, public men are proud to be the servants of the state and would be ashamed to be its masters. On any day, if they thought the people wanted it, the House of Commons could by a simple vote remove me from my office. But I am not worrying about it at all. As a matter of fact, I am sure they will approve very highly of my journey here, for which I obtained the king's permission in order to meet the president of the United States and to arrange with him all that mapping-out of our military plans, and for all those intimate meetings of the high officers of the armed services of both countries, which are indispensable to the successful prosecution of the war.

'I have found an Olympian fortitude'

I should like to say first of all how much I have been impressed and encouraged by the breadth of view and sense of proportion which I have found in all quarters over here to which I have had access. Anyone who did not understand the size and solidarity of the foundations of the United States might easily have expected to find an excited, disturbed, self-centred atmosphere, with all minds fixed upon the novel, startling and painful episodes of sudden war as they hit America. After all, the United States have been attacked and set upon by three most powerfully-armed dictator states. The greatest military power in Europe, the greatest military power in Asia, Germany and Japan, Italy, too, have all declared, and are making, war upon you, and a quarrel is opened, which can only end in their overthrow or yours. But here in Washington, in these memorable days, I have found an Olympian fortitude which, far from being based upon complacency, is only the mask of an inflexible purpose and the proof of a sure and well-grounded confidence in the final outcome. We in Britain had the same feeling in our darkest days. We, too, were sure in the end all would be well. You do not, I am certain, underrate the severity of the ordeal to which you and we have still to be subjected. The forces ranged against us are enormous. They are bitter, they are ruthless. The wicked men and their factions who have launched their peoples on the path of war and conquest know that they will be called to terrible account if they cannot beat down by force of arms the peoples they have assailed. They will stop at nothing. They have a vast accumulation of war weapons of all kinds. They have highly-trained, disciplined armies, navies and air services. They have plans and designs which have long been tried and matured. They will stop at nothing that violence or treachery can suggest.

'We have much to learn in the cruel art of war'

It is quite true that, on our side, our resources in manpower and materials are far greater than theirs. But only a portion of your resources is as yet mobilized and developed, and we both of us have much to learn in the cruel art of war. We have therefore, without doubt, a time of tribulation before us. In this time some ground will be lost which it will be hard and costly to regain. Many disappointments and unpleasant surprises await us. Many of them will afflict us before the full marshalling of our latent and total power can be accomplished. For the best part of twenty years the youth of Britain and America have been taught that war is evil, which is true, and that it would never come again, which has been proved false. For the best part of twenty years the youth of Germany, Japan and Italy have been taught that aggressive war is the noblest duty of the citizen, and that it should be begun as soon as the necessary weapons and organization had been made. We have performed the duties and tasks of peace. They have plotted and planned for war. This, naturally, has placed us in Britain and now places you in the United States at a disadvantage, which only time, courage and strenuous, untiring exertions can correct.

We have indeed to be thankful that so much time has been granted to us. If Germany had tried to invade the British Isles after the French collapse in June 1940, and if Japan had declared war on the British Empire and the United States at about the same date, no one could say what disasters and agonies might not have been our lot. But now at the end of December 1941 our transformation from easy-going peace to total war efficiency has made very great progress. The broad flow of munitions in Great Britain has already begun. Immense strides have been made in the conversion of American industry to military purposes, and now that the United States are at war it is possible for orders to be given every day which a year or eighteen months hence will produce results in war power beyond anything that has yet been seen or foreseen in the dictator states. Provided that every effort is made, that nothing is kept back, that the whole manpower, brain-power, virility, valour, and civic virtue of the English-speaking world with all its galaxy of loyal, friendly, associated communities and states – provided all that is bent unremittingly to the simple and supreme task, I think it would be reasonable to hope that the end of 1942 will see us quite definitely in a better position than we are now, and that the year 1943 will enable us to assume the initiative upon an ample scale.

'I speak of a long and hard war'

Some people may be startled or momentarily depressed when, like your president, I speak of a long and hard war. But our peoples would rather know the truth, sombre though it be. And after all, when we are doing the noblest work in the world, not only defending our hearths and homes but the cause of freedom in other lands, the question of whether deliverance comes in 1942, 1943 or 1944 falls into its proper place in the grand proportions of human history. Sure I am that this day – now – we are the masters of our fate; that the task which has been set us is not above our strength; that its pangs and toils are not beyond our endurance. As long as we have faith in our cause and an unconquerable willpower, salvation will not be denied us. In the words of the Psalmist, 'He shall not be afraid of evil tidings; his heart is fixed, trusting in the Lord.' Not all the tidings will be evil.

'The boastful Mussolini . . . is but a lackey and serf, the merest utensil of his master's will'

On the contrary, mighty strokes of war have already been dealt against the enemy; the glorious defence of their native soil by the Russian armies and people have inflicted wounds upon the Nazi tyranny and system which have bitten deep, and will fester and inflame not only in the Nazi body but in the Nazi mind. The boastful Mussolini has crumbled already. He is now but a lackey and serf, the merest utensil of his master's will. He has inflicted great suffering and wrong upon his own industrious people. He has been stripped of his African empire, Abyssinia has been liberated. Our armies in the East, which were so weak and ill-equipped at the moment of French desertion, now control all the regions from Tehran to Benghazi, and from Aleppo and Cyprus to the sources of the Nile.

For many months we devoted ourselves to preparing to take the offensive in Libya. The very considerable battle, which has been proceeding for the last six weeks in the desert, has been most fiercely fought on both sides. Owing to the difficulties of supply on the desert flanks, we were never able to bring numerically equal forces to bear upon the enemy. Therefore we had to rely upon a superiority in the numbers and quality of tanks and aircraft, British and American. Aided by these, for the first time, we have fought the enemy with equal weapons. For the first time we have made the Hun feel the sharp edge of those tools with which he had enslaved Europe. The armed forces of the enemy in Cyrenaica amounted to about 150,000, of whom about one-third were Germans. General Auchinleck set out to destroy totally that armed force. I have every reason to believe that his aim will be fully accomplished. I am glad to be able to place before you, members of the Senate and of the House of Representatives, at this moment when you are entering the war, proof that with proper weapons and proper organization we are able to beat the life out of the savage Nazi. What Hitler is suffering in Libya is only a sample and foretaste of what we must give him and his accomplices, wherever this war shall lead us, in every quarter of the globe.

'The United States . . . have drawn the sword for freedom and cast away the scabbard'

There are good tidings also from blue water. The life-line of supplies which joins our two nations across the ocean, without which all might fail, is flowing steadily and freely in spite of all the enemy can do. It is a fact that the British Empire, which many thought eighteen months ago was broken and ruined, is now incomparably stronger, and is growing stronger with every month. Lastly, if you will forgive me for saying it, to me the best tidings of all is that the United States, united as never before, have drawn the sword for freedom and cast away the scabbard.

All these tremendous facts have led the subjugated peoples of Europe to lift up their heads again in hope. They have put aside forever the shameful temptation of resigning themselves to the conqueror's will. Hope has returned to the hearts of scores of millions of men and women, and with that hope there burns the flame of anger against the brutal, corrupt invader, and still more fiercely burn the fires of hatred and contempt for the squalid quislings whom he has suborned. In a dozen famous ancient states now prostrate under the Nazi yoke, the masses of the people of all classes and creeds await the hour of liberation, when they too will be able once again to play their part and strike their blows like men. That hour will strike, and its solemn peal will proclaim that the night is past and that the dawn has come.

The onslaught upon us so long and so secretly planned by Japan has presented both our countries with grievous problems for which we could not be fully prepared. If people ask me – as they have a right to ask me in England – why is it that you have not got ample equipment of modern aircraft and army weapons of all kinds in Malaya and in the East Indies, I can only point to the victories General Auchinleck has gained in the Libyan campaign. Had we diverted and dispersed our gradually growing resources between Libya and Malaya, we should have been found wanting in both theatres. If the United States have been found at a disadvantage at various points in the Pacific Ocean, we know well that it is to no small extent because of the aid you have been giving us in munitions for the defence of the British Isles and for the Libyan campaign, and, above all, because of your help in the Battle of the Atlantic, upon which all depends, and which has in consequence been successfully and prosperously maintained. Of course it would have been much better, I freely admit, if we had had enough resources of all kinds to be at full strength at all threatened points; but considering how slowly and reluctantly we brought ourselves to large-scale preparations, and how long such preparations take, we had no right to expect to be in such a fortunate position.

'We are linked in a righteous comradeship of arms'

The choice of how to dispose of our hitherto limited resources had to be made by Britain in time of war and by the United States in time of peace; and I believe that history will pronounce that upon the whole – and it is upon the whole that these matters must be judged – the choice made was right. Now that we are together, now that we are linked in a righteous comradeship of arms, now that our two considerable nations, each in perfect unity, have joined all their life energies in a common resolve, a new scene opens upon which a steady light will glow and brighten.

Many people have been astonished that Japan should in a single day have plunged into war against the United States and the British Empire. We all wonder why, if this dark design, with all its laborious and intricate preparations, had been so long filling their secret minds, they did not choose our moment of weakness eighteen months ago. Viewed quite dispassionately, in spite of the losses we have suffered and the further punishment we shall have to take, it certainly appears to be an irrational act. It is, of course, only prudent to assume that they have made very careful calculations and think they see their way through. Nevertheless, there may be another explanation. We know that for many years past the policy of Japan has been dominated by secret societies of subalterns and junior officers of the army and navy, who have enforced their will upon successive Japanese cabinets and parliaments by the assassination of any Japanese statesman who opposed, or who did not sufficiently further, their aggressive policy. It may be that these societies, dazzled and dizzy with their own schemes of aggression and the prospect of early victories, have forced their country against its better judgment into war. They have certainly embarked upon a very considerable undertaking. For after the outrages they have committed upon us at Pearl Harbor, in the Pacific Islands, in the Philippines, in Malaya and in the Dutch East Indies, they must now know that the stakes for which they have decided to play are mortal.

'What kind of a people do they think we are?'

When we consider the resources of the United States and the British Empire, compared to those of Japan, when we remember those of China, which has so long and valiantly withstood invasion, and when also we observe the Russian menace which hangs over Japan, it becomes still more difficult to reconcile Japanese action with prudence or even with sanity. What kind of a people do they think we are? Is it possible they do not realize that we shall never cease to persevere against them until they have been taught a lesson which they and the world will never forget.

'Twice in our lifetime has the long arm of fate reached across the ocean to bring the United States into the forefront of the battle'

Members of the Senate and members of the House of Representatives, I turn for one moment more from the turmoil and convulsions of the present to the broader basis of the future. Here we are together facing a group of mighty foes who seek our ruin; here we are together defending all that to free men is dear. Twice in a single generation the catastrophe of world war has fallen upon us; twice in our lifetime has the long arm of fate reached across the ocean to bring the United States into the forefront of the battle. If we had kept together after the last war, if we had taken common measures for our safety, this renewal of the curse need never have fallen upon us.

Do we not owe it to ourselves, to our children, to mankind tormented, to make sure that these catastrophes shall not engulf us for the third time? It has been proved that pestilences may break out in the Old World, which carry their destructive ravages into the New World, from which, once they are afoot, the New World cannot by any means escape. Duty and prudence alike command first that the germ-centres of hatred and revenge should be constantly and vigilantly surveyed and treated in good time, and, secondly, that an adequate organization should be set up to make sure that the pestilence can be controlled at its earliest beginnings before it spreads and rages throughout the entire earth.

'The British and American peoples will . . . walk together side by side in majesty, in justice and in peace'

Five or six years ago it would have been easy, without shedding a drop of blood, for the United States and Great Britain to have insisted on fulfilment of the disarmament clauses of the treaties which Germany signed after the Great War; that also would have been the opportunity for assuring to Germany those raw materials which we declared in the Atlantic Charter should not be denied to any nation, victor or vanquished. That chance has passed. It is gone. Prodigious hammer-strokes have been needed to bring us together again, or if you will allow me to use other language, I will say that he must indeed have a blind soul who cannot see that some great purpose and design is being worked out here below, of which we have the honour to be the faithful servants. It is not given to us to peer into the mysteries of the future. Still, I avow my hope and faith, sure and inviolate, that in the days to come the British and American peoples will for their own safety and for the good of all walk together side by side in majesty, in justice and in peace.

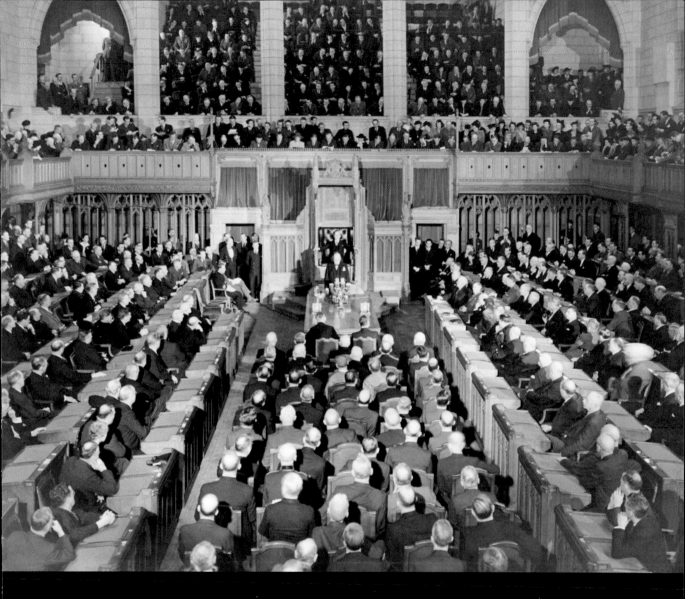

'Some chicken.
Some neck'

Canadian Parliament, Ottawa, 30 December 1941

During the night following his address to Congress on 26 December, Churchill struggled to open the window in his White House bedroom. In the attempt, he suffered a mild heart attack. Rather than advise him to rest and risk the world's press report that the British prime minister was not fit for the fight, Churchill's doctor, Charles Wilson (later Lord Moran), withheld the truth of his condition from his patient and merely told him he had been 'overdoing it'. Refusing to rest, Churchill put to one side the fact he was feeling unwell and got back to work. On 30 December, he arrived in Ottawa to address the Canadian Parliament.

With a population of 12 million, Canada was the senior and highly autonomous Dominion of the British Empire. She began sending reinforcements to help plug Britain's defences shortly after the commencement of the war in Europe. Her financial largesse was equally forthcoming. The United States' Lend-Lease aid was essential to the British war effort, but Canada's $1 billion donation was, as Churchill put it, 'unequalled in its scale in the whole history of the British Empire'. By the war's end, Canada had given $4 billion in money and supplies. Her navy, which grew to 373 warships by 1945, was also critical in providing escort support for the Atlantic convoys.

In the Gothic Revival surroundings of the Parliament in Ottawa, Churchill could feel at home, recognizing there the style and traditions of the mother parliament by the Thames. He was also conscious that he was speaking to a nation whose French-speaking minority needed reassurance after the collapse of their own mother country.

> ## ON THIS DAY
> ### 30 DECEMBER 1941
>
> • Having failed to crack the Soviet Union with the kinds of blitzkrieg tactics used successfully elsewhere, Hitler's forces continue to suffer Russian counter-attacks, today losing control of the city of Kaluga 120 miles (185 km) southwest of Moscow.
>
> • In the Far East, US forces under General MacArthur are on the retreat in the Philippines, while British, Australian and Indian forces are pulling back in Malaya.

Churchill began his speech by describing the 'senior Dominion' as 'a potent magnet'. He cited its huge contribution to the Imperial and Allied war effort. Its soldiers were stationed in Britain, ready to repel invasion. Canadian troops had fought valiantly too in the forlorn defence of Hong Kong. Canada had put its pilot training facilities at the disposal of the RAF. She was building corvettes and merchant ships on a scale almost equal to Britain, as well as turning out vast quantities of other armaments.

We did not make this war, we did not seek it. We did all we could to avoid it. We did too much to avoid it. We went so far at times in trying to avoid it as to be almost destroyed by it when it broke upon us. But that dangerous corner has been turned, and with every month and every year that passes we shall confront the evildoers with weapons as plentiful, as sharp and as destructive as those with which they have sought to establish their hateful domination.

'The peoples of the British Empire may love peace . . . but they are a tough and hardy lot'

I should like to point out to you that we have not at any time asked for any mitigation in the fury or malice of the enemy. The peoples of the British Empire may love peace. They do not seek the lands or wealth of any country, but they are a tough and hardy lot. We have not journeyed all this way across the centuries, across the oceans, across the mountains, across the prairies, because we are made of sugar candy.

'If anybody likes to play rough we can play rough too.'

Look at the Londoners, the Cockneys; look at what they have stood up to. Grim and gay with their cry 'We can take it', and their wartime mood of 'What is good enough for anybody is good enough for us.' We have not asked that the rules of the game should be modified. We shall never descend to the German and Japanese level, but if anybody likes to play rough we can play rough too. Hitler and his Nazi gang have sown the wind; let them reap the whirlwind. Neither the length of the struggle nor any form of severity which it may assume shall make us weary or shall make us quit.

I have been all this week with the president of the United States, that great man whom destiny has marked for this climax of human fortune. We have been concerting the united pacts and resolves of more than thirty states and nations to fight on in unity together and in fidelity one to another, without any thought except the total and final extirpation of the Hitler tyranny, the Japanese frenzy, and the Mussolini flop.

There shall be no halting, or half measures, there shall be no compromise or parley. These gangs of bandits have sought to darken the light of the world; have sought to stand between the common people of all the lands and their march forward into their inheritance. They shall themselves be cast into the pit of death and shame, and only when the earth has been cleansed and purged of their crimes and their villainy shall we turn from the task which they have forced upon us, a task which we were reluctant to undertake, but which we shall now most faithfully and punctiliously discharge.

Churchill then recited the terrible early events in the war – the invasions of Poland, Norway, Denmark, Holland and Belgium.

'Some chicken. Some neck.'

… On top of all this came the great French catastrophe. The French Army collapsed, and the French nation was dashed into utter and, as it has so far proved, irretrievable confusion. The French government had at their own suggestion solemnly bound themselves with us not to make a separate peace. It was their duty and it was also their interest to go to North Africa, where they would have been at the head of the French Empire. In Africa, with our aid, they would have had overwhelming sea power. They would have had the recognition of the United States, and the use of all the gold they had lodged beyond the seas. If they had done this Italy might have been driven out of the war before the end of 1940, and France would have held her place as a nation in the counsels of the Allies and at the conference table of the victors.

But their generals misled them. When I warned them that Britain would fight on alone whatever they did, their generals told their prime minister and his divided Cabinet, 'In three weeks England will have her neck wrung like a chicken.' Some chicken. Some neck.

'We have suffered together and we will conquer together'

What a contrast has been the behaviour of the valiant, stout-hearted Dutch, who still stand forth as a strong living partner in the struggle! Their venerated queen and their government are in England, their princess and her children have found asylum and protection here in your midst. But the Dutch nation are defending their Empire with dogged courage and tenacity by land and sea and in the air. Their submarines are inflicting a heavy daily toll upon the Japanese robbers who have come across the seas to steal the wealth of the East Indies, and to ravage and exploit its fertility and its civilization. The British Empire and the United States are going to the aid of the Dutch. We are going to fight out this new war against Japan together. We have suffered together and we shall conquer together.

Churchill then proceeded to lament the prostration of Vichy France. However, General De Gaulle with his Free French forces refused to 'bow their knees'. Churchill then spoke in French, affirming his confidence that France would rise again and that 'here in Canada, where the French language is honoured and spoken, we are armed and ready to help and to hail this national resurrection'. He ended his speech by returning to English, laying out the next three stages of the conflict, namely 'preparation', 'liberation', and 'assault'.

… the most strenuous exertions must be made by all. As to the form which those exertions take, that is for each partner in the Grand Alliance to judge for himself in consultation with others and in harmony with the general scheme. Let us then address ourselves to our task, not in anyway underrating its tremendous difficulties and perils, but in good heart and sober confidence, resolved that, whatever the cost, whatever the suffering, we shall stand by one another, true and faithful comrades, and do our duty, God helping us, to the end.

'Vote of censure'

House of Commons, London, 2 July 1942

Defending his record following
military defeats

Neither Hitler, Mussolini nor Stalin needed to worry about parliamentary votes. Nor, for that matter, was President Roosevelt – directly elected for a fixed term by the American people – going to have his time in office cut short by a drop in support among the politicians in Congress. No such luxury was afforded Churchill. Alone among the five major war leaders, his political survival depended upon the mood of a parliamentary assembly. As if he needed reminding, the House of Commons had already been truculent enough to engineer the resignation of Neville Chamberlain, his predecessor as prime minister, despite the exigencies of the war situation. There was a limit to how much bad news – however eloquently delivered – it was prepared to tolerate before demanding a fresh sacrifice at the top.

In theory Churchill had little to worry about. At the head of a cross-party coalition spanning the three main parties, he led a broader alliance than had been at Chamberlain's command. Yet, keeping together a body of opinion that ranged from those sympathetic to Marxist ideals (if not Marxist means) at one end to apologists for the more ruthless expressions of diehard British imperialism at the other, undermined the usual party discipline.

During 1942 Churchill faced opposition from various directions. Under the slogan 'Second Front Now', left-wingers (encouraged by the energetic and forceful Lord Beaverbrook, despite his previous right-wing credentials) demanded an invasion of Western Europe within the year as a means of relieving pressure on Stalin's hard-pressed forces. The considered objections by the chiefs of staff that the British Army was not remotely ready for this gamble were brushed aside as further evidence of a lack of fighting spirit among the military leaders. Right-wing libertarians, meanwhile, shuddered at the increases in state control brought about by Churchill's pursuit of 'total war' and the choice of priorities that had left Britain's Asia-Pacific empire to be so easily plundered by Japan. On 15 February the 64,000-strong garrison at Singapore had surrendered to a numerically inferior Japanese force with the result that Britain's hold in the Far East was smashed. It was the greatest humiliation in British military history since the capitulation at Yorktown had brought forward the loss of the American colonies.

Many felt the prime minister – who was also minister of defence – was far too closely involved in war strategy. All were united in utter dismay at the absence of victories. Thus, when Churchill faced a parliamentary vote of no confidence in July 1942 he knew that he had to do more than scrape home with a small majority. He had to win it so comfortably that the vote would silence his critics for months ahead during which time the news might well get even more depressing.

ON THIS DAY
2 JULY 1942

- In the Indian Ocean, the British take possession of the French island of Mayotte, off the coast of the Portuguese colony of Mozambique.

- Alexandria, on Egypt's Mediterranean coast, seems set to fall to the rapid advance of German forces under Erwin Rommel, who have pushed the British and Allied forces into a defensive position at El Alamein. British diplomats in Cairo prepare to evacuate the city.

In the event, he was lucky that many of those MPs who spoke against him made only an incoherent and contradictory case. The motion's Conservative mover, Sir John Wardlaw-Milne, attracted derisive laughter when he suggested appointing the king's brother, the Duke of Gloucester, as the Army's new commander-in-chief. Others showed they had precious little understanding about forces and tactics. It was left to the Welsh socialist and gifted orator, Nye Bevan, to score a rhetorical blow with a memorable jibe: 'The prime minister wins debate after debate and loses battle after battle. The country is beginning to say that he fights debates like a war and the war like a debate.'

Churchill responded with a long, detailed and sober justification of his actions and the necessity of his responsibility in defence matters. Presented with no better alternative, the Commons then voted down the hostile motion of censure by 475 votes to 25. It was a timely declaration of confidence, for even worse news was soon on its way. On the Eastern Front, the Germans had captured Rostov and were pressing on towards Stalingrad, while from the deserts of North Africa, Erwin Rommel was launching his summer offensive against the retreating British Eighth Army.

… I ask no favours either for myself or for His Majesty's government. I undertook the office of prime minister and minister of defence, after defending my predecessor to the best of my ability, in times when the life of the empire hung upon a thread. I am your servant, and you have the right to dismiss me when you please. What you have no right to do is to ask me to bear responsibilities without the power of effective action, to bear the responsibilities of prime minister but clamped on each side by strong men, as the honourable Member said. If today, or at any future time, the House were to exercise its undoubted right, I could walk out with a good conscience and the feeling that I have done my duty according to such light as has been granted to me. There is only one thing I would ask of you in that event. It would be to give my successor the modest powers which would have been denied me.

'It might easily amount to . . . a dictatorship'

But there is a larger issue than the personal one. The mover of this vote of censure has proposed that I should be stripped of my responsibilities for defence in order that some military figure or some other unnamed personage should assume the general conduct of the war, that he should have complete control of the armed forces of the crown, that he should be the chief of the chiefs of the staff, that he should nominate or dismiss the generals or the admirals, that he should always be ready to resign. That is to say, to match himself against his political colleagues, if colleagues they could be considered, if he did not get all he wanted, that he should have under him a royal duke as commander-in-chief of the army, and finally, I presume, though this was not mentioned, that this unnamed personage should find an appendage in the prime minister to make the necessary explanations, excuses and apologies to Parliament when things go wrong, as they often do and often will. That is at any rate a policy. It is a system very different from the parliamentary system under which we live. It might easily amount to or be converted into a dictatorship. I wish to make it perfectly clear that as far as I am concerned I shall take no part in such a system.

'The knell of disappointment will ring in the ears of the tyrants we are striving to overthrow'

... The setting down of this vote of censure by Members of all parties is a considerable event. Do not, I beg you, let the House underrate the gravity of what has been done. It has been trumpeted all around the world to our disparagement, and when every nation, friend or foe, is waiting to see what is the true resolve and conviction of the House of Commons, it must go forward to the end. All over the world, throughout the United States, as I can testify, in Russia, far away in China, and throughout every subjugated country, all our friends are waiting to know whether there is a strong, solid government in Britain and whether its national leadership is to be challenged or not. Every vote counts. If those who have assailed us are reduced to contemptible proportions and their vote of censure on the National government is converted to a vote of censure upon its authors, make no mistake, a cheer will go up from every friend of Britain and every faithful servant of our cause and the knell of disappointment will ring in the ears of the tyrants we are striving to overthrow.

'The end of the
beginning'

In 1941 few newsreels heartened cinema audiences as much as the footage of Italian soldiers – over 100,000 in total – trudging in long lines under the unforgiving North African sun into British custody. Mussolini would not be grabbing the British Empire after all, the accompanying commentary pointed out rather gleefully.

But the tone of superiority was noticeably absent in May 1942 when a heavily reinforced German Afrika Korps, under its inspirational commander Erwin Rommel, launched a major offensive. This was an altogether more formidable opponent, a foe worthy of respect. Despite fierce fighting, British confidence slumped; the victories scored over the Italians in Libya were reversed. In June 1942 came the terrible news that Rommel had captured Tobruk. Its 33,000 defenders – so recently fêted for their heroism – had laid down their weapons and begun their own journey into captivity.

From Tobruk, Rommel pushed the British Eighth Army into Egypt. There, they fell back on a small settlement significant only because it had a railway station – El Alamein. It was hardly a renowned citadel from which to save the Middle East. 150 miles away in Cairo, the British authorities weighed the odds and began burning classified documents. Their lack of confidence was understandable. Alamein could easily prove to be the last stand. If Rommel could force his way through, his route was clear to reach the Suez Canal. From there he could cut Britain's direct supply line with Asia and Australasia and move up into the Middle East, seizing the oilfields.

Famous though it was not, Alamein was nonetheless a well chosen spot. Here was a 30-mile stretch of sand, the flanks of which were protected to the north by the Mediterranean coast and to the south by the impassable Qattara depression. And, at Rommel's first attempt in July, his offensive was contained. An impulsive soldier might have taken this opportunity to seize the initiative. But Bernard Montgomery, the Eighth Army's popular new commander, was a man of ascetic tastes and not given to rash reflexes when so much was at stake. In preparing his counter-attack, he knew that the defensive advantages offered by the site could now benefit Rommel, whose positions were protected by a minefield five miles deep. The terrain prevented going around it. Montgomery's men would have to go through this 'Devil's Garden'. To stand any chance at all they would need considerable

---

ON THIS DAY
10 NOVEMBER 1942

- Following the morale-boosting defeat of Rommel's forces at El Alamein, Lieutenant-General Bernard Montgomery and his Eighth Army are heroes of the hour. Montgomery is knighted and promoted to the rank of full general.

- Operation Torch, the Allied invasion of French-speaking North Africa, begins, with the hope that the Vichy colonial regimes in Morocco and Algeria will come over to the Allied side without resistance. It is not to be the case, but nevertherless within a day Algiers and Casablanca are under Allied control.

- Spurred on by Operation Torch, German forces prepare to march into Vichy France the following day, ostensibly to 'save' it from Allied invasion. Within two days most of Vichy's home territory, except the naval base at Toulon, is under German control.

superiority of men and arms. 'Monty' would have to wait and choose his moment. Intercepting and decrypting German communications certainly helped in this respect.

Building up a force of 195,000 troops gave Montgomery a two-to-one advantage in manpower, supplemented in firepower by the same margin – 1000 tanks against Rommel's 500. During the night of 23 October the first wave was sent in. This was Operation Lightfoot, with infantry advancing across the 'Devil's Garden' while those behind them tried to clear narrow mine-free paths for the tanks to follow – a precarious endeavour under fierce fire. It was a tactical success but the wider strategic victory was far from assured. However, this duly came in the early hours of 2 November, when Operation Supercharge was launched in a fusillade of devastating power with the tanks pushing through the Axis lines. Two days later, Rommel signalled the Afrika Korps to retreat. In England, Churchill issued his own order – that the church bells be rung. It was the first time bells were permitted to peal since war had begun.

The events of Alamein were almost immediately followed by the news that Anglo-American forces under General Eisenhower had landed at Casablanca, Oran and Algiers in French North Africa. The Germans responded by occupying Vichy France, ending the last pretence of independent government on the French mainland.

El Alamein was one of the British Empire's finest hours with large contingents of Australian, New Zealand, South African and Indian soldiers fighting alongside their British comrades. Little wonder that Churchill took this moment to announce that he had not 'become the king's First Minister in order to preside over the liquidation of the British Empire'. Ironically, the rest of the war would see British imperial forces under the wider allied command. It was certainly, as Churchill suggested, the 'end of the beginning'. It would soon be more than that. Marshal Zhukov's Soviet forces captured the Kalach bridge over the River Don. Over a quarter of a million soldiers of the German Sixth Army were now trapped at Stalingrad. The war, in fact, was reaching its turning point.

I notice, my Lord Mayor, by your speech that you had reached the conclusion that the news from the various fronts has been somewhat better lately. In our wars the episodes are largely adverse, but the final results have hitherto been satisfactory. Away we dash over the currents that may swirl around us, but the tide bears us forward on its broad, resistless flood. In the last war the way was uphill almost to the end. We met with continual disappointments, and with disasters far more bloody than anything we have experienced so far in this one. But in the end all the oppositions fell together, and all our foes submitted themselves to our will.

'Now, however, we have a new experience. We have victory'

We have not so far in this war taken as many German prisoners as they have taken British, but these German prisoners will no doubt come in in droves at the end just as they did last time. I have never promised anything but blood, tears, toil, and sweat. Now, however, we have a new experience. We have victory – a remarkable and definite victory. The bright gleam has caught the helmets of our soldiers, and warmed and cheered all our hearts.

The late Monsieur Venizelos observed that in all her wars England – he should have said Britain, of course – always wins one battle – the last. It would seem to have begun rather earlier this time. General Alexander, with his brilliant comrade and lieutenant, General Montgomery, has gained a glorious and decisive victory in what I think should be called the Battle of Egypt. Rommel's army has been defeated. It has been routed. It has been very largely destroyed as a fighting force.

This battle was not fought for the sake of gaining positions or so many square miles of desert territory. General Alexander and General Montgomery fought it with one single idea. They meant to destroy the armed force of the enemy, and to destroy it at the place where the disaster would be most far-reaching and irrecoverable.

'The fight between the British and the Germans was intense and fierce in the extreme.'

All the various elements in our line of battle played their parts – Indian troops, fighting French, the Greeks, the representatives of Czechoslovakia and the others who took part. The Americans rendered powerful and invaluable service in the air. But as it happened – as the course of the battle turned – it has been fought throughout almost entirely by men of British blood from home and from the Dominions on the one hand, and by Germans on the other. The Italians were left to perish in the waterless desert or surrender as they are doing.

The fight between the British and the Germans was intense and fierce in the extreme. It was a deadly grapple. The Germans have been outmatched and outfought with the very kind of weapons with which they had beaten down so many small peoples, and also large unprepared peoples. They have been beaten by the very technical apparatus on which they counted to gain them the domination of the world. Especially is this true of the air and of the tanks and of the artillery, which has come back into its own on the battlefield. The Germans have received back again that measure of fire and steel which they have so often meted out to others.

'Now this is not the end. It is not even the beginning of the end. But it is, perhaps, the end of the beginning'

Now this is not the end. It is not even the beginning of the end. But it is, perhaps, the end of the beginning. Henceforth Hitler's Nazis will meet equally well-armed, and perhaps better-armed troops. Henceforth they will have to face in many theatres of war that superiority in the air which they have so often used without mercy against others, of which they boasted all round the world, and which they intended to use as an instrument for convincing all other peoples that all resistance to them was hopeless. When I read of the coastal road crammed with fleeing German vehicles under the blasting attacks of the Royal Air Force, I could not but remember those roads of France and Flanders, crowded, not with fighting men, but with helpless refugees – women and children – fleeing with their pitiful barrows and household goods, upon whom such merciless havoc was wreaked. I have, I trust, a humane disposition, but I must say I could not help feeling that what was happening, however grievous, was only justice grimly reclaiming her rights.

It will be my duty in the near future to give to Parliament a full and particular account of these operations. All I will say of them at present is that the victory which has already been gained gives good prospect of becoming decisive and final so far as the defence of Egypt is concerned.

But this Battle of Egypt, in itself so important, was designed and timed as a prelude and counterpart of the momentous enterprise undertaken by the United States at the western end of the Mediterranean – an enterprise under United States command in which our Army, Air Force, and, above all, our Navy, are bearing an honourable and important share. Very full accounts have been published of all that is happening in Morocco, Algeria, and Tunis. The president of the United States, who is commander-in-chief of the armed forces of America, is the author of this mighty undertaking, and in all of it I have been his active and ardent lieutenant.

You have no doubt read the declaration of President Roosevelt, solemnly endorsed by His Majesty's government, of the strict respect which will be paid to the rights and interests of Spain and Portugal, both by America and Great Britain. Towards those countries our only policy is that they shall be independent and free, prosperous and at peace. Britain and the United States will do all that they can to enrich the economic life of the Iberian Peninsula. The Spaniards especially, after all their troubles, require and deserve peace and recuperation.

'I declare to you my faith that France will rise again'

At this time our thoughts turn towards France, groaning in bondage under the German heel. Many ask themselves the question: Is France finished? Is that long and famous history, adorned by so many manifestations of genius and valour, bearing with it so much that is precious to culture and civilization, and above all to the liberties of mankind – is all that now to sink forever into the ocean of the past, or will France rise again and resume her rightful place in the structure of what may one day be again the family of Europe. I declare to you here, on this considerable occasion, even now when misguided or suborned Frenchmen are firing upon their rescuers, I declare to you my faith that France will rise again. While there are men like General de Gaulle and all those who follow him – and they are legion throughout France – and men like General Giraud, that gallant warrior whom no prison can hold, while there are men like those to stand forward in the name and in the cause of France, my confidence in the future of France is sure.

'Let me make this clear . . . we mean to hold our own'

For ourselves we have no wish but to see France free and strong, with her empire gathered around her and with Alsace-Lorraine restored. We covet no French possession; we have no acquisitive appetites or ambitions in North Africa or any other part of the world. We have not entered this war for profit or expansion, but only for honour and to do our duty in defending the right.

Let me, however, make this clear, in case there should by any mistake about it in any quarter.

We mean to hold our own. I have not become the king's First Minister in order to preside over the liquidation of the British Empire. For that task, if ever it were prescribed, someone else would have to be found, and, under democracy, I suppose the nation would have to be consulted. I am proud to be a member of that vast commonwealth and society of nations and communities gathered in and around the ancient British monarchy, without which the good cause might well have perished from the face of the earth. Here we are, and here we stand, a veritable rock of salvation in this drifting world.

There was a time, not long ago, when for a whole year we stood all alone. Those days, thank God, have gone. We now move forward in a great and gallant company. For our record we have nothing to fear, we have no need to make excuses or apologies. Our record pleads for us, and will gain gratitude in the breasts of free men and women in every part of the world.

'To cleanse the shores of Africa from the stain of Nazi and fascist tyranny'

As I have said, in this war we desire no territorial gains and no commercial favours; we wish to alter no sovereignty or frontier for our own benefit or profit. We have come into North Africa shoulder to shoulder with our American friends and allies for one purpose, and one purpose only – namely, to gain a vantage ground from which to open a new front against Hitler and Hitlerism, to cleanse the shores of Africa from the stain of Nazi and fascist tyranny, to open the Mediterranean to Allied sea-power and air-power, and thus effect the liberation of the peoples of Europe from the pit of misery into which they have been cast by their own improvidence and by the brutal violence of the enemy.

These two African undertakings, in the east and in the west, were part of a single strategic and political conception which we have laboured long to bring to fruition, and about which we are now justified in entertaining good and reasonable confidence. Thus, taken together, they were two aspects of a grand design, vast in its scope, honourable in its motive, noble in its aim. The British and American affairs continue to prosper in the Mediterranean, and the whole event will be a new bond between the English-speaking peoples and a new hope for the whole world.

'Their children's lips shall echo them'

I recall to you some lines of Byron, which seem to me to fit the event, the hour, and the theme:

> Millions of tongues record thee, and anew
> Their children's lips shall echo them, and say –
> 'Here, where the sword united nations drew,
> Our countrymen were warring on that day!'
> And this is much, and all which will not pass away.

'Not a seat but a springboard'

World broadcast, London, 29 November 1942

On the European repercussions of the North African campaign

In the weeks following the British Eighth Army's victory at El Alamein, the Allies found themselves dealing with something new in the struggle – a constant flow of good news. The most important events of all were unfolding around Stalingrad, where the tide was turning dramatically against the Wehrmacht. When Churchill came to the microphone to deliver a world broadcast on 29 November, his task was to pay fulsome tribute to the endeavours of the Red Army and also to explain the relevance of British and American operations in North Africa.

Certainly, the news from the desert represented a remarkable turnaround. The Eighth Army retook Tobruk on 13 November and Benghazi the following week. Rommel's depleted and disorientated forces were pushed further and further west into what remained of Axis-occupied Libya. Meanwhile, the success of Operation Torch had transformed the situation in France's North African colonies. Finding himself in Algiers when the Anglo-American landings began, Admiral Darlan, Vichy's military commander-in-chief, had acted sufficiently promptly in switching to the Allies for General Eisenhower to accept him as High Commissioner. Thus began a power struggle for the Free French leadership in which the competing claims of Darlan, Charles de Gaulle and General Henri Giraud (who had made a daring escape from German captivity and was Roosevelt's preference) were tested. The assassination of Darlan on Christmas Eve by a local member of the French Resistance removed him from the equation and eventually de Gaulle's force of personality and obvious claims upon his countrymen's loyalty proved irresistible.

The immediate consequence of Operation Torch was the German decision to occupy Vichy France, thereby bringing all of mainland France directly under Nazi control. Churchill, having struggled to share Roosevelt's hope that Vichy politicians might yet prove pliable to Allied aims, saw the obvious advantage in Germany's decision to cast aside the figleaf of French national dignity that Vichy's non-occupied zone had contrived to offer. Previously divided in their loyalties, French citizens could now unite in a common patriotic cause.

For the campaigns in North Africa to be accorded their proper prominence, Churchill needed to emphasize their relevance to the European theatre of war. This he achieved in his metaphor of a 'springboard' rather than a 'seat'. Securing the Mediterranean was the next task. A priority was relieving the pressure on the strategically important island of Malta, which – close to starvation – had been nobly holding out against almost unremitting Axis air attacks since June 1940. An Allied invasion of Sicily was also in the offing. In discussions with

---

ON THIS DAY
29 NOVEMBER 1942

• The RAF bombs Turin for the twelfth time, on this occasion using 8000-pound bombs.

• In Tunisia, the Allies continue their effort to wrest the colony from the German forces which have recently reinforced it. The Battle of Tebourba begins, but it will result in defeat for the Allies in early December.

• On the Eastern Front, the tables have turned in the titanic struggle for the city of Stalingrad, with the besieging German Sixth Army under General Paulus itself now caught in a pincer movement by Soviet advances from the southwest and the northwest.

his chiefs of staff, Churchill became much more bullish about the prospects for an invasion of southern France and the Italian mainland. The industrial Italian cities were already receiving a sustained pounding from the air. Hours before Churchill made his world broadcast, Turin had been subjected to the RAF's new 8000-pound bombs. Mussolini's dreams of imperial glory were bringing misery to his people and the implication in the British prime minister's rhetoric was clear – the time had come for Italians to overthrow Il Duce.

'It is not a seat but a springboard'

… I have been speaking about Africa, about the 2000 miles of coastline fronting the underside of subjugated Europe. From all this we intend, and I will go so far as to say we expect, to expel the enemy before long. But Africa is no halting-place: it is not a seat but a springboard. We shall use Africa only to come to closer grips. Anyone can see the importance to us of reopening the Mediterranean to military traffic and saving the long voyage around the Cape. Perhaps by this shortcut and the economy of shipping resulting from it, we may strike as heavy a blow at the U-boats as has happened in the whole war; but there is another advantage to be gained by the mastery of the North African shore: we open the air battle upon a new front … our operations in French North Africa should enable us to bring the weight of the war home to the Italian Fascist State, in a manner not hitherto dreamed of by its guilty leaders, or still less by the unfortunate Italian people Mussolini has led, exploited and disgraced. Already the centres of war industry in northern Italy are being subjected to harder treatment than any of our cities experienced in the winter of 1940. But if the enemy should in due course be blasted from the Tunisian tip, which is our aim, the whole of the south of Italy – all the naval bases, all the munition establishments and other military objectives wherever situated – will be brought under prolonged, scientific, and shattering air attack.

'The hyena in his nature broke all bounds of decency'

It is for the Italian people, forty millions of them, to say whether they want this terrible thing to happen to their country or not. One man, and one man alone, has brought them to this pass. There was no need for them to go to war: no one was going to attack them. We tried our best to induce them to remain neutral, to enjoy peace and prosperity and exceptional profits in a world of storm. But Mussolini could not resist the temptation of stabbing prostrate France, and what he thought was helpless Britain, in the back. Mad dreams of imperial glory, the lust of conquest and of booty, the arrogance of long unbridled tyranny, led him to his fatal, shameful act. In vain I warned him: he would not hearken. On deaf ears and a stony heart fell the wise, far-seeing appeals of the American president. The hyena in his nature broke all bounds of decency and even common sense. Today his Empire is gone. We have over a hundred Italian generals and nearly three hundred thousand of his soldiers in our hands as prisoners-of-war. Agony grips the fair land of Italy. This is only the beginning, and what have the Italians to show for it? A brief promenade by German permission along the Riviera; a flying visit to Corsica; a bloody struggle with the heroic patriots of Yugoslavia; a deed of undying shame in Greece; the ruins of Genoa, Turin, Milan; and this is only a foretaste. One man and the regime he has created have brought these measureless calamities upon the hard-working, gifted, and once happy Italian people, with whom, until the days of Mussolini, the English-speaking world had so many sympathies and never a quarrel. How long must this endure?

'Agony grips the fair land of Italy'

Churchill then spoke admiringly of 'the prodigious blows which Russia is striking on the Eastern Front', before continuing:

... I must conduct you back to the West – to France, where another vivid scene of this strange melancholy drama has been unfolded. It was foreseen when we were planning the descent upon North Africa that this would bring about immediate reactions in France. I never had the slightest doubt myself that Hitler would break the armistice, overrun all France, and try to capture the French fleet at Toulon; such developments were to be welcomed by the United Nations, because they entailed the extinction for all practical purposes of the sorry farce and fraud of the Vichy government. This was a necessary prelude to that reunion of France without which French resurrection is impossible. We have taken a long step towards that unity. The artificial division between occupied and unoccupied territory has been swept away. In France all Frenchmen are equally under the German yoke, and will learn to hate it with equal intensity. Abroad all Frenchmen will fire at the common foe. We may be sure that after what has happened, the ideals and the spirit of what we have called Fighting France, will exercise a dominating influence upon the whole French nation. I agree with General de Gaulle that the last scales of deception have now fallen from the eyes of the French people; indeed, it was time.

'For a people that makes a voluntary surrender saps its own character'

'A clever conqueror', wrote Hitler in Mein Kampf, 'will always, if possible, impose his demands on the conquered by instalments. For a people that makes a voluntary surrender saps its own character, and with such a people you can calculate that none of those oppressions in detail will supply quite enough reason for it to resort once more to arms.' How carefully, how punctiliously he lives up to his own devilish doctrines! The perfidy by which the French fleet was ensnared is the latest and most complete example. That fleet, brought by folly and by worse than folly to its melancholy end, redeemed its honour by an act of self-immolation, and from the flame and smoke of the explosions at Toulon, France will rise again.

'I promise nothing. I predict nothing'

The ceaseless flow of good news from every theatre of war, which has filled the whole month of November, confronts the British people with a new test. They have proved that they can stand defeat; they have proved that they can bear with fortitude and confidence long periods of unsatisfactory and unexplained inaction. I see no reason at all why we should not show ourselves equally resolute and active in the face of victory. I promise nothing. I predict nothing. I cannot even guarantee that more successes are not on the way. I commend to all the immortal lines of Kipling:

> If you can dream – and not make dreams your master;
> If you can think – and not make thoughts your aim;
> If you can meet with Triumph and Disaster
> And treat those two impostors just the same –

there is my text for this Sunday's sermon, though I have no licence to preach one. Do not let us be led away by any fair-seeming appearances of fortune; let us rather put our trust in those deep, slow-moving tides that have borne us thus far already, and will surely bear us forward, if we know how to use them, until we reach the harbour where we would be.

'Before the leaves of autumn fall'

Guildhall, London, on receiving the Freedom of the City of London, 30 June 1943

In anticipation of fighting in the Mediterranean

Churchill and Roosevelt had met at Casablanca in January 1943, where they agreed to prioritize the Mediterranean theatre of war (starting with an invasion of Sicily) ahead of sending an armada across the English Channel to liberate France. While the British and American leaders conversed under the Moroccan sun, to the east the Axis soldiers were putting up tenacious resistance in Tunisia. A North African campaign that at one point seemed winnable by Christmas was dragging on alarmingly and the delay this caused had to be factored into the plans for the Sicily landings. This irritated Churchill, who as early as February was complaining to Harry Hopkins, the president's closest adviser, about how awful it was 'that in April, May and June, not a single American or British soldier will be killing a single German or Italian soldier, while the Russians are chasing 185 divisions around'.

The magnitude of the turnaround on the Eastern Front fully justified Churchill's determination to show that the Western Allies were pulling their weight. The Battle of Stalingrad came to its dramatic conclusion when Friedrich Paulus surrendered what was left of his German Sixth Army on 31 January. The previous day, Hitler had elevated Paulus to the rank of field marshal believing he would not dishonour the distinction, but surrounded and running out of vital supplies the shivering Wehrmacht soldiers had no alternative survivable option. By the time their remnants were herded into captivity, the Germans constituted many of the 1.5 million bodies from both sides who lay amid the rubble of the city on the Volga. Apart from the cruelty and the cold the reality was that the bloodiest siege in history had ended with a crushing blow to the German aspiration of seizing the Caucasian oil fields.

Nothing happening in the warmer North African climate could compare in magnitude, but the fighting performance there of the German and Italian troops, coming after their 2000-mile retreat from Alamein, bolstered Hitler's confidence. The troops had prevented a swift Allied seizure of Tunis and their reward came in the form of reinforcements – ultimately a mixed blessing because it meant deploying more men in a cause that looked as if it would eventually be lost. Rommel recognized the reality of the situation and in March he flew to see Mussolini and Hitler to assure them that fighting on in Tunisia was only delaying an inevitable defeat at the additional cost of the loss of thousands of battle-hardened troops who would be better deployed defending the southern European flank from attack. His appeals fell on deaf ears and he found himself relieved of active command in Africa.

ON THIS DAY
30 JUNE 1943

- Allied bombers continue to pound cities in Sicily and the Italian mainland.

- In the Far East, General MacArthur lands forces on the northern coast of New Guinea, as other US and Australian units launch attacks in the Solomon Islands. The principal target will be the large Japanese centre of power at Rabaul, on the island of New Britain.

- In an indication that the danger of imminent invasion has passed, the British government announces the removal of some anti-tank precautions at home and the restoration of signposts in the countryside, which had been removed to confuse any German invaders.

It fell to Rommel's successor to prove his fears well grounded. Nonetheless, the Allies gained absolute control of the coast only on 12 May following Tunis's capture and the capitulation of all Axis forces in North Africa. This was a reversal not just for German arms; it also represented the final demise of the best part of the Italian Army and its mechanized units. Consequently, Italy was now highly vulnerable. With the capture of the islands of Lampedusa and Linosa in June, the first step – landings on Sicily – could be attempted.

Meanwhile, the bomber offensive over Germany was pursued with merciless tenacity. In February, Cologne was subjected to heavy raids. The following month, the RAF stepped up its bombing of Berlin. The industrial belt of the Ruhr received a terrible pounding and in May bouncing bombs dropped by Lancaster bombers burst the Mohne and Eder dams, flooding the surrounding area. When Churchill watched film footage of the devastation of the German city of Wuppertal which had been engulfed in a firestorm, he found himself asking aloud, 'Are we beasts? Are we taking this too far?' The raids continued, nonetheless.

… Wars come with great suddenness, and many of the deep, slow courses which lead to the explosion are often hidden from or only dimly comprehensive by the masses of the people, even in the region most directly affected. Time, distance, the decorum of diplomacy, and the legitimate desire to preserve peace – all impose their restraints upon public discussion and upon prior arrangements.

Alone in history, the British people, taught by the lessons they had learned in the past, have found the means to attach to the motherland vast self-governing Dominions upon whom there rests no obligation, other than that of sentiment and tradition, to plunge into war at the side of the motherland.

'None of these Dominions . . . has ever failed to respond . . . to the trumpet-call of a supreme crisis'

None of these Dominions, except Southern Ireland, which does not under its present dispensation fully accept Dominion status, has ever failed to respond, with all the vigour of democratic institutions, to the trumpet-call of a supreme crisis to the overpowering influences and impulses that make Canada, that make Australia – and we have here in Dr Evatt a distinguished Australian – that make New Zealand and South Africa send their manhood across the ocean to fight and die.

In each one of these countries, with their long and varied history behind them, this extraordinary spectacle is an outstanding example of the triumph of mind over matter, of the human heart over fear and short-sighted self-interest.

In the vast sub-continent of India, which we trust will presently find full satisfaction within the British Commonwealth of Nations, the martial races and many others have thronged to the imperial standards. More than 2,000,000 have joined the armed forces, and have distinguished themselves in many cases during the fiercest conflicts with Germans, Italians and Japanese.

All the great countries engaged in this war count their armies by millions, but the Indian Army has a peculiar characteristic not found in the armies of Britain or the United States or Russia or France or in the armies of our foes, in that it is entirely composed of volunteers. No one has been conscripted or compelled. The same thing is broadly true throughout our great colonial empire.

… But now I must speak of the great republic of the United States whose power arouses no fear and whose pre-eminence excites no jealousy in British bosoms. Upon the fraternal association and intimate alignment of policy of the United States and the British Commonwealth and Empire depends, more than on any other factor, the immediate future of the world. If they walk, or if need be march, together in harmony and in accordance with the moral and political conceptions to which the English-speaking peoples have given birth, and which are frequently referred to in the Atlantic Charter, all will be well. If they fall apart and wander astray from the commanding beacon-light of their destiny, there is no end or measure to the miseries and confusion which await modern civilization.

'Those who sowed the wind are reaping the whirlwind'

… Three years ago Hitler boasted that he would 'rub out' – that was the term – the cities of Britain, and certainly in the nine months before he abandoned his attack we suffered very heavy damage to our buildings and grievous hindrance to our life and work, and more than 40,000 of our people were killed and more than 120,000 wounded. But now those who sowed the wind are reaping the whirlwind. In the first half of this year, which ends today, the Royal Air Force alone has cast upon Germany alone thirty-five times the tonnage of bombs which in the same six months of this year has been discharged upon this island. Not only has the weight of our offensive bombing grown and its accuracy multiplied, but our measures of defence, tactical and scientific, have improved beyond all compare. In one single night, nay, mainly in one single hour, we cast upon Düsseldorf, to take an example, 2000 tons of terrible explosive and incendiary bombs for a loss of 38 aircraft, while in the first half of this same year the enemy has discharged upon us no more than 1500 tons of bombs at a cost to him of 245 aircraft.

… I cannot go farther today than to say that it is very probable there will be heavy fighting in the Mediterranean and elsewhere before the leaves of autumn fall.

For the rest, we must leave the unhappy Italians and their German tempters and taskmasters to anxieties which will aggravate from week to week and from month to month.

'We, the United Nations, demand from the Nazi, Fascist, and Japanese tyrannies unconditional surrender'

This, however, I will add before I sit down. We, the United Nations, demand from the Nazi, Fascist, and Japanese tyrannies unconditional surrender. By this we mean that their willpower to resist must be completely broken, and that they must yield themselves absolutely to our justice and mercy. It also means that we must take all those farsighted measures which are necessary to prevent the world from being again convulsed, wrecked and blackened by their calculated plots and ferocious aggressions. It does not mean, and it never can mean, that we are to stain our victorious arms by inhumanity or by mere lust of vengeance, or that we did not plan a world in which all branches of the human family may look forward to what the American Constitution finely calls 'life, liberty, and the pursuit of happiness'.

'The keystone of the Fascist arch has crumbled'

Having squandered his finest troops and almost all of his available tanks in North Africa, Mussolini presided over a problem of his own making: how was Italy to be defended without the necessity for a massive deployment of German troops in Italy? Despite all the rhetoric of a 'Pact of Steel', the ties that bound the two Axis leaders were not sufficiently close that Europe's first Fascist dictator wanted to become a mere puppet of the Führer. Mussolini was sufficiently concerned that he insisted that the offer of German reinforcements should come under Italian command.

Although neither Hitler nor Mussolini could be absolutely sure where the first strike would happen, the Allies had decided to land on Sicily. This island had the additional advantage that its occupation would assist the opening up of the Mediterranean's sea lanes (up to this point, most supplies for Egypt and India still had to take the long route around the South African Cape). Had the Allies considered themselves ready to attack Sicily immediately after the surrender of the Axis forces in Tunisia on 13 May they would have found the island very lightly defended. Instead, a delay until July gave German Panzer divisions time to cross the Straits of Messina and take up position.

Nonetheless, the Allied planners could be forgiven their reluctance to attack before every precaution had been thought through. The scale of the operation and the importance of getting right the first seaborne assault on Fortress Europe militated against swift and potentially risky activity. Initially both the British Joint Planning Committee and Eisenhower were wary of proceeding on account of the two German divisions that had joined the six Italian divisions on the island. Churchill was astonished by such 'pusillanimous and defeatist doctrines', angrily postulating 'what Stalin would think of this when he has 185 German divisions on his front, I cannot imagine'. Churchill's will prevailed. On 10 July – in the middle of a storm – the first of the 250,000 British and 228,000 American soldiers landed. The Italian defenders were caught off guard, having assumed that a storm was not the sort of weather for invasion, and they were quickly overwhelmed.

ON THIS DAY
27 JULY 1943

- With Mussolini under arrest, and with intelligence that Italy is to take itself out of the war, Hitler begins moves to occupy Italy and to restore Il Duce to power.

- In the Solomon Islands, American forces fight for control of Horseshoe Hill in New Georgia.

- On the Eastern Front, having failed to destroy the Soviet salient at Kursk earlier in July in the biggest tank battle in history, the German armies in the front line further north at Orel are also having to retreat.

- The RAF and US Air Force is midway through Operation Gomorrah, several days of firebombing over Hamburg, which will turn the city into a disaster zone and cause more casualties than the Blitz.

All went well as the troops pushed inland from their initial bridgeheads in the southeast of the island. Within little more than a fortnight, western Sicily was conquered. Palermo fell on 23 July. The one great missed opportunity was that by making their gains in the northwest rather than northeast the Allies failed to cut off the retreating German divisions. These divisions managed to escape back to the Italian mainland, where they would later prove a formidable obstacle to Allied aspirations for an easy advance upon Rome in 1944.

For the first time – on 19 July 1943 – the 'eternal city'· was bombed and Naples was already being subjected to sustained air assault. These attacks, together with the reversals in Sicily, prompted those in the highest echelons of Italian power to act before events overwhelmed them. On 24 July, a majority of the Fascist Grand Council passed a vote of no confidence in Mussolini. Even his own son-in-law and foreign minister, Count Ciano, voted for his removal. The following day, King Victor Emmanuel III dismissed Mussolini from office. As the fallen leader left the royal palace he was arrested – the most high-level victim yet of the Axis's war of aggression.

As Churchill prophesied, without Mussolini the entire totalitarian state edifice duly collapsed. The Fascist Grand Council was abolished and the Fascist Party suppressed. It was the end of 21 years of rule, at that time the fascist ideology's longest experiment in power. Moving swiftly, Victor Emmanuel appointed the disaffected soldier, Marshal Badoglio, as the new prime minister. Badaglio immediately declared in a broadcast that 'the war continues at the side of our Germanic ally'. This was a bluff. Secretly, he was entering into negotiations with the Allies.

For the Allies, the question was how to deal with this new government in Italy, staffed as it was with those who had served the Fascist state when it had promised them reward. Churchill's response was pragmatic. The day after Mussolini's fall, he telegraphed Roosevelt, 'I should deal with any non-Fascist government which can deliver the goods'; by this he meant whoever had the authority to allow the Allies to use Italy as a base from which to wage war against the Germans.

'The keystone of the Fascist arch has crumbled'

The House will have heard with satisfaction of the downfall of one of the principal criminals of this desolating war. The end of Mussolini's long and severe reign over the Italian people undoubtedly marks the close of an epoch in the life of Italy. The keystone of the Fascist arch has crumbled, and, without attempting to prophesy, it does not seem unlikely that the entire Fascist edifice will fall to the ground in ruins, if it has not already so fallen. The totalitarian system of a single party, armed with secret police, engrossing to itself practically all the offices, even the humblest, under the government, with magistrates and courts under the control of the executive, with its whole network of domestic spies and neighbourly informants – that system, when applied over a long period of time, leaves the broad masses without any influence upon their country's destinies and without any independent figures apart from the official classes. That, I think, is a defence for the people of Italy – one defence – although there can be no really valid defence for any country or any people which allows its freedom and inherent rights to pass out of its own hands.

The external shock of war has broken the spell which in Italy held all these masses for so long, in fact for more than twenty years, in physical and even more in moral subjection. We may, therefore, reasonably expect that very great changes will take place in Italy. What their form will be, or how they will impinge upon the forces of German occupation and control, it is too early to forecast. The guilt and folly of Mussolini have cost the Italian people dear. It looked so safe and easy in May 1940 to stab falling France in the back and advance to appropriate the Mediterranean interests and possessions of what Mussolini no doubt sincerely believed was a decadent and ruined Britain. It looked so safe and easy to fall upon the much smaller state of Greece. However, there have been undeceptions. Events have taken a different course. By many hazardous turns of fortunes and by the long marches of destiny, the British and United States armies, having occupied the Italian African Empire, the North of Africa, and the bulk of Sicily, now stand at the portals of the Italian mainland armed with the powers of the sea and the air, and with a very large land and amphibious force equipped with every modern weapon and device.

'The main wish of the Italian people is to be quit of their German taskmasters'

What is it that these masterful forces bring to Italy? They bring, if the Italian people so decide, relief from the war, freedom from servitude, and, after an interval, a respectable place in the new and rescued Europe. When I learn of the scenes enacted in the streets of the fine city of Palermo on the entry of the United States armies, and review a mass of detailed information with which I have been furnished, I cannot doubt that the main wish of the Italian people is to be quit of their German taskmasters, to be spared a further and perfectly futile ordeal of destruction, and to revive their former democratic and parliamentary institutions. These they can have. The choice is in their hands. As an alternative the Germans naturally desire that Italy shall become a battleground, a preliminary battleground, and that by Italian sufferings the ravages of war shall be kept as far away as possible for as long as possible from the German fatherland. If the Italian government and people choose that the Germans shall have their way, no choice is left open to us. We shall continue to make war upon Italy from every quarter; from north and south, from the sea and from the air, and by amphibious descents, we shall endeavour to bring the utmost rigour of war increasingly upon her. Orders to this effect have been given to all the Allied commanders concerned.

'Italy will be seared and scarred and blackened from one end to the other'

A decision by the Italian government and people to continue under the German yoke will not affect seriously the general course of the war. Still less will it alter its ultimate result. The only consequence will be that in the next few months Italy will be seared and scarred and blackened from one end to the other. I know little or nothing of the new government. I express no opinion, but it is obvious that so far as their own people are concerned they have a very important decision to take. Meanwhile I am anxious that the various processes by which this decision is reached should be allowed to run their course under no other pressure than that of relentless war. This operation may well take some time. There may be several stages of transition. Past experiences shows that when great changes of heart and character take place in the government of a nation, very often one stage is rapidly succeeded by another. I cannot tell. So far, we have had no approaches from the Italian government, and therefore no new decisions are called upon from us, except those which are connected with the bringing of the maximum avalanche of fire and steel upon all targets of military significance throughout the length and breadth of Italy.

'We certainly do not seek to reduce Italian life to a condition of chaos and anarchy'

However, I must utter a word of caution. We do not know what is going to happen in Italy, and now that Mussolini has gone, and once the Fascist power is certainly and irretrievably broken, we should be foolish to deprive ourselves of any means of coming to general conclusions with the Italian nation. It would be a grave mistake, when Italian affairs are in this flexible, fluid, formative condition, for the rescuing powers, Britain and the United States, so to act as to break down the whole structure and expression of the Italian state. We certainly do not seek to reduce Italian life to a condition of chaos and anarchy, and to find ourselves without any authorities with whom to deal. By so doing, we should lay upon our armies and upon our war effort the burden of occupying, mile by mile, the entire country, and of forcing the individual surrender of every armed or coherent force in every district into which our troops may enter. An immense task of garrisoning, policing and administering would be thrown upon us, involving a grievous expenditure of power, and still more of time.

We must be careful not to get ourselves into the kind of position into which the Germans have blundered in so many countries – that of having to hold down and administer in detail, from day to day, by a system of gauleiters, the entire life of very large populations, thereby becoming responsible under the hard conditions of this present period for the whole of their upkeep and well-being. Such a course night well, in practice, turn the sense of liberation, which it may soon be in our power to bestow upon the Italian people, into a sullen discontent against us and all our works. The rescuers might soon, indeed, be regarded as tyrants; they might even be hated by the Italian people as much or almost as much as their German allies. I certainly do not wish, in the case of Italy, to tread a path which might lead to execution squads and concentration camps, and above all to have to carry on our shoulders a lot of people who ought to be made to carry themselves …

'This Nazi war machine is the hateful incubus upon Europe'

The German national strength is still massive. The German armies, though seriously mauled by the three Russian campaigns, are still intact and quite unbroken. Hitler has under his orders over 300 German divisions, excluding the satellites. Three-quarters are mobile and most of them continue to be well equipped. We are fighting some of these divisions in Sicily at this moment, and, as we see, they offer a stubborn resistance in positions well adapted to defence. The authority of the central government in Germany grips and pervades every form of German life. The resources of a dozen lands are in their hands for exploitation. The harvest prospects are reported to be fairly good. This Nazi war machine is the hateful incubus upon Europe which we are resolved utterly to destroy, and the affairs of Italy must be handled with this supreme object constantly in view. Both our strategy and our policy, I venture to claim, have been vindicated by events, and I look forward to offering to Parliament, as the months unfold, further convincing proof of this assertion; but we cannot afford to make any large mistake which we can by careful forefought avoid, nor can we afford to prolong by any avoidable mismanagement the sombre journey in which we shall persevere to the end.

'The price of greatness is responsibility'

Harvard University, Massachusetts, on receiving an honorary degree,
6 September 1943

On a future world security based on
Anglo-American unity

The conquest of Sicily was completed on 17 August, 38 days after the first landings. When confirmation was received, Churchill was in Quebec, discussing strategy with Roosevelt. They agreed that the priority for 1944 was a cross-Channel invasion of France. To accommodate this, the occupation of Italy should not advance beyond a line between Pisa and Ancona.

ON THIS DAY
6 SEPTEMBER 1943

• The Allies send 157 B-17 bombers against the German city of Stuttgart.

• As the Allied–Japanese struggle continues in the strategically important Solomon Islands, the Japanese strike back at Arundel Island. By 21 September, though, the Japanese have effectively given up the islands.

• The status of Italy remains publicly uncertain today. In fact, by the terms of a secret treaty signed with the Allies in Sicily on 3 September, Italy is already out of the war, but the announcement is delayed so as not to compromise imminent Allied landings at Salerno or alert the Germans.

The Quebec Conference ended on 24 August. After it, Churchill went to Washington and from there to Boston and to Cambridge, Massachusetts, where Harvard University bestowed upon him an honorary degree. In the speech he delivered before the country's oldest university, he laid out his belief that America could never retreat back into isolationism. The United States' decision not to join the League of Nations was widely acknowledged as the main reason the international body, set up after the First World War, had proved weak and toothless. Churchill was convinced that the League's successor (which would become the United Nations) should not be similarly handicapped from the beginning. He used the occasion to warn that whatever form the postwar international institutions for global security would take, they would not work effectively without the active participation of the two greatest English-speaking nations sharing a common vision.

Churchill recognized that Germany's defeat would inevitably ensure the Soviet Union's place in the front rank of world powers. A strong Anglo-American front was thus necessary, as he informed the South African Field Marshal Smuts on the eve of his speech at Harvard, in order to 'put us on good terms and in a friendly balance with Russia at least for the period of rebuilding. Further than that I cannot see with mortal eye, and I am not as yet fully informed about the celestial telescope.'

'Twice in my lifetime the long arm of destiny has searched across the oceans'

… Twice in my lifetime the long arm of destiny has searched across the oceans and involved the entire life and manhood of the United States in a deadly struggle. There was no use in saying 'We don't want it; we won't have it; our forebears left Europe to avoid these quarrels; we have founded a New World which has no contact with the Old.' There was no use in that. The long arm reaches out remorselessly, and everyone's existence, environment, and outlook undergo a swift and irresistible change. What is the explanation, Mr President, of these strange facts, and what are the deep laws to which they respond? I will offer you one explanation – there are others, but one will suffice. The price of greatness is responsibility. If the people of the United States had continued in a mediocre station, struggling with the wilderness, absorbed in their own affairs, and a factor of no consequence in the movement of the world, they might have remained forgotten and undisturbed beyond their protecting oceans: but one cannot rise to be in many ways the leading community in the civilized world without being involved in its problems, without being convulsed by its agonies and inspired by its causes.

'The price of greatness is responsibility'

… We have learned from hard experience that stronger, more efficient, more rigorous world institutions must be created to preserve peace and to forestall the causes of future wars. In this task the strongest victorious nations must be combined, and also those who have borne the burden and heat of the day and suffered under the flail of adversity; and, in this task, this creative task, there are some who say: 'Let us have a world council and under it regional or continental councils', and there are others who prefer a somewhat different organization.

All these matters weigh with us now in spite of the war, which none can say has reached its climax, which is perhaps entering for us, British and Americans, upon its most severe and costly phase. But I am here to tell you that, whatever form your system of world security may take, however the nations are grouped and ranged, whatever derogations are made from national sovereignty for the sake of the large synthesis, nothing will work soundly or for long without the united effort of the British and American peoples.

'If we are together, nothing is impossible. If we are divided, all will fail'

If we are together, nothing is impossible. If we are divided, all will fail. I therefore preach continually the doctrine of the fraternal association of our two peoples, not for any purpose of gaining invidious material advantages for either of them, not for territorial aggrandisement or the vain pomp of earthly domination, but for the sake of service to mankind and for the honour that comes to those who faithfully serve great causes.

Here let me say how proud we ought to be, young and old alike, to live in this tremendous, thrilling, formative epoch in the human story, and how fortunate it was for the world that when these great trials came upon it there was a generation that terror could not conquer and brutal violence could not enslave. Let all who are here remember, as the words of the hymn we have just sung suggest, let all of us who are here remember that we are on the stage of history, and that whatever our station may be, and whatever part we have to play, great or small, our conduct is liable to be scrutinized not only by history but by our own descendants.

Let us rise to the full level of our duty and of our opportunity, and let us thank God for the spiritual rewards he has granted for all forms of valiant and faithful service.

'Preparation, effort and resolve'

The House of Commons, London, 22 February 1944

On the Italian campaign, the Balkans and Poland

On 3 September 1943, the Italian government – having hidden Mussolini from the Germans – secretly accepted the Allies' surrender terms. The same day, British and Canadian troops crossed the Straits of Messina and marched onto the European mainland. Five days later, Italy announced it was switching sides. At that very moment, the American Fifth Army and British forces were sailing for the Gulf of Salerno, south of Naples. However, the immediate result of Italy's surrender was not a bloodless occupation by the Allies. Before the Allies could capitalize on their seemingly easy victory, German troops poured into Italy, occupying Rome and preparing to repel the Allied incursion, to which they were initially numerically superior. In a daring expedition, German paratroopers even liberated Mussolini from his mountain incarceration. His reward was a new lease of life as the nominal ruler of northern Italy. In practice, this meant he was his rescuers' lackey.

For the Allies, all did not go according to plan. The Salerno beachhead came under intense pressure from the German counter-attack and at one point appeared close to being lost. Consequently, it was not until 1 October that the Fifth Army reached Naples, by which time it had already suffered 12,000 casualties. Soon afterwards, a new enemy arrived to confound plans – bad weather. The narrow boot of Italy, with the spine of the Apennine Mountains down the centre, offered better terrain for the defender than for the attacker. Waterlogged conditions and demolished bridges further slowed the pace of advance, giving the German commander, Field Marshal Kesselring, time to establish a succession of defensive lines with which to stall both the Fifth Army under the US general Mark Clark on the Mediterranean side of the country and Montgomery's Eighth Army, which was moving up on the Adriatic side.

By early January 1944, four months after landing at Salerno, the Fifth Army had advanced only 70 miles and had suffered 40,000 casualties. Churchill, who had always been keener on the Italian campaign than the Americans, became increasingly impatient, citing the failure to make better use of amphibious assault. 'There are few instances, even in this war', he telegrammed the British chiefs of staff, 'of such valuable forces being so completely wasted'.

> ## ON THIS DAY
> ### 22 FEBRUARY 1944
>
> • With the war going badly for Japan, General Tojo, already prime minister and holder of other cabinet positions, fires the heads of the army and navy and assumes command of the army.
>
> • In the Pacific, US forces take territory in the Marshall Islands.
>
> • Finland's government is considering terms for surrender to the Soviet Union, a matter sharpened by a bombing raid against Helsinki three days later.

Such was the strength of Kesselring's Gustav Line that making an amphibious landing behind it made more sense than relying upon a costly frontal assault alone. This attempt to turn the German flank came on 22 January, south of Rome, with landings at Anzio. Not for the first time, the Allies' obsession with consolidating their position rather than advancing gave the Germans an opportunity to reinforce. Again, it took much bitter fighting to stop the German troops driving the landing party back into the sea.

So effective was Kesselring at holding the Allies' advance at bay – it took them four assaults over four months and 54,000 casualties just to capture the strategic mountain abbey of Monte Cassino – that the Anglo-American campaign aim degenerated into one of maximizing the number of German divisions tied down in Italy. There, at least, they could not be used to greet the all-important planned summer invasion on the shores of northern France. This was possibly a contribution to the latter's initial success, but it was an expensive means of distracting the enemy considering that at one stage the Italian campaign involved twice as many Allied troops as German ones. Rome finally fell to the Fifth Army on 4 June. Only two days later, D-Day arrived in Normandy.

The overriding necessity of winning the war and keeping at bay Stalin's suspicions that the British and Americans were leaving the Soviet Union to do all the hard fighting were the driving forces for Churchill and Roosevelt as they prepared for what they hoped would be the decisive phase of the war. It meant supporting unflinching action: whether maintaining the bombing offensive that devastated Germany's cities or, in Yugoslavia, ending support for the royalist but increasingly ineffective and divided Chetniks under Draža Mihailović in favour of their communist partisan enemies under the ruthless leadership of Marshal Tito. Among the British liaison officers establishing links with Tito was Churchill's son, Randolph.

Switching horses in Yugoslavia was but one of the difficult decisions to be made when Churchill and Roosevelt met Stalin for the Tehran Conference in November 1943. Roosevelt did his best to win Stalin's approval, even at the cost of occasionally distancing himself from Churchill. One area of disagreement that remained was the British enthusiasm for the Italian campaign, with Stalin suspicious of anything that looked like postponing the main opening of a second front in northern France. Neither he nor Roosevelt were prepared to let the date for the cross-Channel invasion slip beyond May. The other major issue for discussion concerned the postwar boundaries of Poland. Stalin was determined to keep the eastern part of the country he had annexed with Hitler's connivance back in 1939. Churchill did not feel Britain was in any position to prevent this, knowing that the security of the Russian western frontier was important to Stalin. However, determined that the future Polish state needed to be a strong one, he supported the idea of allowing Poland to gain compensatory German land so that it would remain of viable size, albeit shifted geographically westwards. Seemingly able to break and shape nations and boundaries, it was little wonder that he mused that those gathered together at Tehran represented the 'greatest concentration of world power that had ever been seen in the history of mankind'. But the uniformed millions under their command had still to win the war first.

'It is a time for preparation, effort and resolve'

This is no time for sorrow or rejoicing. It is a time for preparation, effort and resolve. The war is still going on. I have never taken the view that the end of the war in Europe is at hand, or that Hitler is about to collapse, and I have certainly given no guarantees, or even held out any expectations, that the year 1944 will see the end of the European war. Nor have I given any guarantees the other way. On the whole, my information – and I have a good deal – goes to show that Hitler and his police are still in full control, and that the Nazi party and the generals have decided to hang together. The strength of the German Army is about 300 divisions, though many of these are substantially reduced in numbers. The fighting quality of the troops is high. The German General Staff system, which we failed to liquidate after the last war, represents an order comprising many thousands of highly trained officers and a school of doctrine of long, unbroken continuity. It possesses great skill, both in the handling of troops in action and in their rapid movement from place to place. The recent fighting in Italy should leave no doubt on these points.

'We intend to make war production . . . impossible in all German cities, towns and factory centres'

… Turning to the air, the honour of bombing Berlin has fallen almost entirely to us. Up to the present we have delivered the main attack upon Germany. Excluding Dominion and Allied squadrons working with the Royal Air Force, the British islanders have lost 38,300 pilots and air crews killed and 10,400 missing, and over 10,000 aircraft since the beginning of the war – and they have made nearly 900,000 sorties into the North European theatre. As for the army, the British Army was little more than a police force in 1939, yet they have fought in every part of the world – in Norway, France, Holland, Belgium, Egypt, Eritrea, Abyssinia, Somaliland, Madagascar, Syria, North Africa, Persia, Sicily, Italy, Greece, Crete, Burma, Malaya, Hong Kong. I cannot now in this speech attempt to describe these many campaigns, so infinitely varied in their characteristics, but history will record how much the contribution of our soldiers has been beyond all proportion to the available manpower of these islands. The Anglo-American air attack upon Germany must be regarded as our chief offensive effort at the present time. Till the middle of 1943 we had by far the larger forces in action. As the result of the enormous transportations across the Atlantic which have been made during 1943 the United States bomber force in this island now begins to surpass our own, and will soon be substantially greater still, I rejoice to say.

'The Germans, bit by bit, have been drawn down into Italy'

… The spring and summer will see a vast increase in the force of the attacks directed upon all military targets in Germany and in German-occupied countries. Long-range bombing from Italy will penetrate effectively the southern parts of Germany. We look for very great restriction and dislocation of the entire German munitions supply, no matter how far the factories have been withdrawn. In addition, the precision of the American daylight attack produces exceptional results upon particular points, not only in clear daylight, but now, thanks to the development of navigational aids, through cloud. The whole of this air offensive constitutes the foundation upon which our plans for overseas invasion stand. Scales and degrees of attack will be reached far beyond the dimensions of anything which has yet been employed or, indeed, imagined. The idea that we should fetter or further restrict the use of this prime instrument for shortening the war will not be accepted by the governments of the Allies. The proper course for German civilians and non-combatants is to quit the centres of munition production and take refuge in the countryside. We intend to make war production in its widest sense impossible in all German cities, towns and factory centres.

… Our other great joint Anglo-American offensive is in Italy. Many people have been disappointed with the progress there since the capture of Naples in October. This has been due to the extremely bad weather which marks the winter in those supposedly sunshine lands, and which this year has been worse than usual. Secondly, and far more, it is because the Germans, bit by bit, have been drawn down into Italy and have decided to make extreme exertions for the retention of the city of Rome. In October, they began to move a number of divisions southwards from the Valley of the Po and to construct a winter line south of Rome in order to confront and delay the advance of the Fifth and Eighth Armies under General Alexander. We were, therefore, committed to a frontal advance in extremely mountainous country which gave every advantage to the defence. All the rivers flow at right angles to our march, and the violent rains, this year above the normal, often turned these rivers into raging torrents, sweeping away all military bridges which had been thrown across them, and sometimes leaving part of the assaulting force already committed to the attack on the far side and beyond the reach of immediate reinforcements or support.

'We have, of course, the complete command of the seas'

In addition to the difficulties I have mentioned, there has been the need to build up a very large supply of stores and vehicles of all kinds in Italy. Also, the strategic air force which is being developed for the attack on Southern Germany has made extremely large priority inroads upon our transportation, especially upon those forms of transportation which are most in demand. An immense amount of work has, however, been done, and the results will become apparent later on. Among the Allies we have, of course, much the largest army in Italy. The American air force in the Mediterranean, on the other hand, is larger than the British, and the two together possess an enormous superiority, quantitative and also, we believe, qualitative, over the enemy. We have also, of course, the complete command of the seas, where an American squadron is actively working with the British fleet. Such being the position, many people wondered why it was not possible to make a large amphibious turning movement, either on the eastern or western side of Italy, to facilitate the forward advance of the Army.

'Hitler has apparently resolved to defend Rome with the same obstinacy which he showed at Stalingrad'

The need for this was, of course, obvious to all the commanders, British and American, but the practicability of carrying it into effect depended upon this effort being properly fitted-in with the general Allied programme for the year. This programme comprises larger issues and forces than those with which we are concerned in Italy. The difficulties which had hitherto obstructed action were, I am glad to say, removed at the conferences which were held at Carthage at Christmas and at Marrakesh in January. The conclusions were approved, step by step, by the president of the United States and the combined chiefs of staff. All that the Supreme War Direction could do was done by the first week in January. Preparations had already been begun in anticipation of the final surmounting of difficulties, and January 22 was fixed as the zero day by General Alexander, on whom rests the responsibility for fighting the battle. It was certainly no light matter to launch this considerable army – 40,000 or 50,000 men – in the first instance with all the uncertainty of winter weather and all the unknowable strength of enemy fortifications – to launch it out upon the seas.

The operation itself was a model of combined work. The landing was virtually unopposed. Subsequent events did not, however, take the course which had been hoped or planned. In the upshot, we got a great army ashore, equipped with masses of artillery, tanks and very many thousands of vehicles, and our troops moving inland came into contact with the enemy. The German reactions to this descent have been remarkable. Hitler has apparently resolved to defend Rome with the same obstinacy which he showed at Stalingrad, in Tunisia, and, recently, in the Dnieper Bend. No fewer than seven extra German divisions were brought rapidly down from France, Northern Italy and Yugoslavia, and a determined attempt has been made to destroy the bridgehead and drive us into the sea. Battles of prolonged and intense fierceness and fury have been fought. At the same time, the American and British Fifth Army to the southward is pressing forward with all its strength. Another battle is raging there.

'On the southern front, the Cassino front, British, American, Dominion, Indian, French and Polish troops are fighting side by side in a noble comradeship'

On both fronts there has been in the last week a most severe and continuous engagement, very full accounts of which have been given every day in the press and in the official communiqués. Up to the present moment the enemy has sustained very heavy losses, but has not shaken the resistance of the bridgehead army. The forces are well matched, though we are definitely the stronger in artillery and armour, and, of course, when the weather is favourable our air-power plays an immense part. General Alexander, who has probably seen more fighting against the Germans than any living British commander – unless it be General Freyberg, who is also in the fray – says that the bitterness and fierceness of the fighting now going on both in the bridgehead and at the Cassino front surpass all his previous experience. He even used in one message to me the word 'terrific'. On the southern front, the Cassino front, British, American, Dominion, Indian, French and Polish troops are fighting side by side in a noble comradeship. Their leaders are confident of final success. I can say no more than what I have said, for I would not attempt to venture on a more sanguine prediction, but their leaders are confident; and the troops are in the highest spirit of offensive vigour.

'Greece, Yugoslavia, Italy – all will be perfectly free to settle what form their governments shall take'

On broad grounds of strategy, Hitler's decision to send into the south of Italy as many as eighteen divisions involving, with their maintenance troops, probably something like a half a million Germans, and to make a large secondary front in Italy, is not unwelcome to the Allies. We must fight the Germans somewhere, unless we are to stand still and watch the Russians. This wearing battle in Italy occupies troops who could not be employed in other greater operations, and it is an effective prelude to them. We have sufficient forces at our disposal in Africa to nourish the struggle as fast as they can be transported across the Mediterranean. The weather is likely to improve as the spring approaches, and as the skies clear, the Allied air power will reach its fullest manifestation.

Churchill went on to summarize the situation in Yugoslavia and Britain's increasing conviction that Marshal Tito's partisans – rather than General Mihailović's royalist forces – represented the better bet for defeating the German occupation

… What, then is the position of King Peter and the royal Yugoslav government in Cairo? King Peter, as a boy of seventeen, escaped from the clutches of the regent, and, with the new royal Yugoslav government, found shelter in this country. We cannot dissociate ourselves in any way from him. He has undoubtedly suffered in the eyes of the partisans by the association of his government with General Mihailović and his subordinate commanders. Here, in these islands, we are attached to the monarchical principle, and we have experienced the many blessings of constitutional monarchy, but we have no intention of obtruding our ideas upon the people of any country. Greece, Yugoslavia, Italy – all will be perfectly free to settle what form their governments shall take, so far as we are concerned, once the will of the people can be ascertained under conditions of comparative tranquility. In the meantime, the position is a somewhat complicated one, and I hope to have the confidence of the House in working with my right honourable friend the foreign secretary to unravel it, as far as possible, in concert with our Russian and United States allies, who both, I am glad to say, are now sending missions to Marshal Tito. Our feelings here, as everywhere else, I should like the House to see, follow the principle of keeping good faith with those who have kept good faith with us, and of striving, without prejudice or regard for political affections, to aid those who strike for freedom against the Nazi rule and thus inflict the greatest injury upon the enemy.

'I heard from Marshal Stalin that he, too, was resolved upon the creation and maintenance of a strong integral independent Poland'

… I took occasion to raise personally with Marshal Stalin the question of the future of Poland. I pointed out that it was in fulfilment of our guarantee to Poland that Great Britain declared war upon Nazi Germany; that we had never weakened in our resolve even in the period when we were all alone; and that the fate of the Polish nation holds a prime place in the thought and policies of His Majesty's government and of the British Parliament. It was with great pleasure that I heard from Marshal Stalin that he, too, was resolved upon the creation and maintenance of a strong integral independent Poland as one of the leading powers in Europe. He has several times repeated these declarations in public, and I am convinced that they represent the settled policy of the Soviet Union.

Churchill went on to make clear that, nonetheless, because of Russia's need for security, the exact boundaries of a future independent Poland remained a matter for negotiation and that she would probably make territorial gains from Germany but lose eastern territory to the Soviet Union.

'Smite the Hun by land, sea and air'

… There is one thing that we agreed at Tehran, above all others, to which we are all bound in solemn compact, and that is to fall upon and smite the Hun by land, sea and air with all the strength that is in us during the coming spring and summer. It is to this task that we must vow ourselves every day anew. It is to this ordeal that we must address our minds with all the moral fortitude we possess. The task is heavy, the toil is long, and the trials will be severe. Let us all try our best to do our duty. Victory may not be so far away, and will certainly not be denied us in the end.

'An immense armada'

House of Commons, London, 6 June 1944

On the Normandy landings and the
liberation of Rome

Operation Overlord – the liberation of Western Europe – was the fruit of months of planning, training and subterfuge. Under the overall command of General Eisenhower, 73,000 American and 83,000 British and Canadian troops were to be sent across the English Channel in the first wave of the assault on the heavily defended coastline of Hitler's Fortress Europe. The Normandy beaches were their destination, and accompanying their voyage were over 1200 warships and 5725 other vessels. Supported in the air by over 10,000 aircraft, it was the largest seaborne invasion the world would ever see. The logistical feat of assembling such a force – and keeping its movements secret – was a triumph in itself.

Yet, for all this awesome display of men and arms, the success of D-Day was far from assured. The Allies' experiences at Salerno and Anzio vividly demonstrated the risky nature of launching seaborne invasions. Although ultimately successful, these attempts to establish beachheads on the Italian mainland had come perilously close to being repelled.

Churchill had particular cause to worry. As First Lord of the Admiralty during the First World War, he had advocated the landings against the Turks in the Dardanelles. Misconceived and badly executed, the campaign had been a calamitous failure. Ever since then, Churchill's critics had cited the fighting and ultimate evacuation from Gallipoli as evidence of his poor judgment. He knew how great were the stakes involved.

Surprise was crucial. Even if this was achieved, the first wave had all the problems of navigating mines and fortified positions. Indeed, just breaking though the inevitable congestion on the beach was difficult enough. Unless this vanguard could achieve its objectives and press beyond the cramped landing grounds quickly, the cream of the fifty-eight Wehrmacht divisions at Hitler's disposal in Western Europe would quickly bear down upon them – with disastrous consequences.

However, the Germans did not hold all the cards. True, Hitler suspected the landings might come in Normandy and Rommel was feverishly engaged strengthening the region's coastal defences. But the commander-in-chief in the west, Field Marshal von Rundstedt, expected the assault to come near Calais where the invading armada would be exposed to a far shorter voyage across the English Channel. Therefore, while code breakers at Bletchley

ON THIS DAY
6 JUNE 1944

• The US amphibious forces of Operation Overlord find completely contrasting levels of hazard awaiting their assaults on Utah and Omaha beaches, suffering fewer than 170 casualties at Utah while struggling through the bloodbath that is Omaha Beach.

• Almost 24,000 British and US paratroopers land behind enemy lines, transported during the night by gliders. The high winds have caused havoc with the landings, but nevertheless commanders on the ground manage to regroup sufficiently to attack most of their designated targets.

• News of the D-Day landings finally reaches Hitler's HQ at his retreat in Berchtesgaden, but it is 9 am before he is awake and responding to the situation.

• Erwin Rommel arrives back at the HQ of Army Group B at La Roche Guyon at 4 pm. He has been taking leave in Ulm, Germany, to celebrate his wife's birthday.

Park in Buckinghamshire were reading Wehrmacht encrypts indicating the location of their forces, the Germans were unsure where or when the strike would come.

The Allies also had other advantages: they enjoyed air superiority. This not only diverted the attention of the Luftwaffe away from the streams of men and munitions disembarking, it also allowed for the routes along which German reinforcements would arrive to be bombed. Furthermore, British ingenuity had overcome what would otherwise be a major handicap. Floating 'Mulberry' harbours were devised, allowing supplies to be offloaded speedily. This was vital given that it would be days – perhaps weeks – before the Allies took control of any major ports.

Churchill recognized that the landings – given the codename Operation Overlord – represented one of history's great gambles. It took a direct intervention from King George VI to dissuade him from sailing with the invasion. When D-Day struck, the weather conditions were far from ideal for crossing the Channel. The decision to proceed fooled several of the key German commanders in the region who, like Rommel, assumed the rough conditions mitigated against the armada putting to sea. Their absence from the battlefront during the critical first hours of the assault hampered the Wehrmacht's response.

On D-Day the landing parties faced only one Panzer division. Four days later, this had risen to ten. Had several of those been there on the first day, the operation would probably have ended catastrophically. However, Hitler feared the consequences of leaving the area north of Paris under-defended should there be a follow-up landing on the Pas de Calais. In creating a shadow army seemingly camped and ready for this second invasion, the Allies underlined the importance of deception in warfare.

Planning, resolve and good fortune ensured that the Allies clung on to their beachheads. Nonetheless, their objective of taking Caen by the end of the first day was not met. It took more than a month of bloody fighting for the cathedral city to fall. The great breakout spearheaded by General Patton's Third Army did not come until 56 days after D-Day, much slower than Montgomery and Eisenhower had planned. But for all the desperate slog ahead, the Allies' ability to hold on to their Normandy foothold and not be driven back into the sea was one of the most remarkable achievements in the history of warfare.

'An immense armada of upwards of 4000 ships, together with several thousand smaller craft, crossed the Channel'

The House should, I think, take formal cognizance of the liberation of Rome by the Allied armies under the command of General Alexander, with General Clark of the United States Service and General Oliver Leese in command of the Fifth and Eighth Armies respectively. This is a memorable and glorious event, which rewards the intense fighting of the last five months in Italy. The original landing, made on January 22 at Anzio, has, in the end, borne good fruit.

… I have also to announce to the House that during the night and the early hours of this morning the first of the series of landings in force upon the European continent has taken place. In this case the liberating assault fell upon the coast of France. An immense armada of upwards of 4000 ships, together with several thousand smaller craft, crossed the Channel. Massed airborne landings have been successfully effected behind the enemy lines, and landings on the beaches are proceeding at various points at the present time. The fire of the shore batteries has been largely quelled. The obstacles that were constructed in the sea have not proved so difficult as was apprehended. The Anglo-American allies are sustained by about 11,000 first-line aircraft, which can be drawn upon as may be needed for the purposes of the battle. I cannot, of course, commit myself to any particular details. Reports are coming in in rapid succession. So far the commanders who are engaged report that everything is proceeding according to plan. And what a plan! This vast operation is undoubtedly the most complicated and difficult that has ever taken place. It involves tides, wind, waves, visibility, both from the air and the sea standpoint, and the combined employment of land, air and sea forces in the highest degree of intimacy and in contact with conditions which could not and cannot be fully foreseen.

'The ardour and spirit of the troops . . . embarking in these last few days was splendid to witness'

There are already hopes that actual tactical surprise has been attained, and we hope to furnish the enemy with a succession of surprises during the course of the fighting. The battle that has now begun will grow constantly in scale and in intensity for many weeks to come, and I shall not attempt to speculate upon its course. This I may say, however. Complete unity prevails throughout the Allied armies. There is a brotherhood in arms between us and our friends of the United States. There is complete confidence in the supreme commander, General Eisenhower, and his lieutenants, and also in the commander of the Expeditionary Force, General Montgomery. The ardour and spirit of the troops, as I saw myself, embarking in these last few days was splendid to witness. Nothing that equipment, science or forethought could do has been neglected, and the whole process of opening this great new front will be pursued with the utmost resolution both by the commanders and by the United States and British governments whom they serve.

'The passage of the sea has been made with far less loss than we apprehended'

Churchill returned later the same day to update the House of Commons on developments:

I have been at the centres where the latest information is received, and I can state to the House that this operation is proceeding in a thoroughly satisfactory manner. Many dangers and difficulties which at this time last night appeared extremely formidable are behind us. The passage of the sea has been made with far less loss than we apprehended. The resistance of the batteries has been greatly weakened by the bombing of the Air Force, and the superior bombardment of our ships quickly reduced their fire to dimensions which did not affect the problem. The landings of the troops on a broad front, both British and American – Allied troops, I will not give lists of all the different nationalities they represent – but the landings along the whole front have been effective, and our troops have penetrated in some cases several miles inland. Lodgments exist on a broad front.

The outstanding feature has been the landings of the airborne troops, which were on a scale far larger than anything that has been seen so far in the world. These landings took place with extremely little loss and with great accuracy. Particular anxiety attached to them, because the conditions of light prevailing in the very limited period of the dawn – just before the dawn – the conditions of visibility made all the difference. Indeed, there might have been something happening at the last minute which would have prevented airborne troops from playing their part. A very great degree of risk had to be taken in respect of the weather.

'General Eisenhower's courage is equal to all the necessary decisions that have to be taken'

But General Eisenhower's courage is equal to all the necessary decisions that have to be taken in these extremely difficult and uncontrollable matters. The airborne troops are well established, and the landings and the follow-ups are all proceeding with much less loss – very much less – than we expected. Fighting is in progress at various points. We have captured various bridges which were of importance, and which were not blown up. There is even fighting proceeding in the town of Caen, inland. But all this, although a very valuable first step – a vital and essential first step – gives no indication of what may be the course of the battle in the next days and weeks, because the enemy will now probably endeavour to concentrate on this area, and in that event heavy fighting will soon begin and will continue without end, as we can push troops in and he can bring other troops up. It is, therefore, a most serious time that we enter upon. Thank God, we enter upon it with our great allies all in good heart and all in good friendship.

'For the liberation of the soil of France'

House of Commons, London, 28 September 1944

On the seven dramatic weeks since D-Day

The capture of Cherbourg at the end of June finally provided the Allies with a deep-water port from which they could speed-up the unloading of supplies. Nonetheless, it was not until 31 July, when the Americans captured Avranches, that the great breakout from the congested Normandy pocket in which they had been cooped up for almost seven weeks was achieved. The American Fifth Army under George S. Patton then swung southeast of Paris.

Narrowly surviving an assassination attempt plotted by senior German officers, Hitler committed the bulk of his forces in the west to trying to contain the breakout rather than have his forces retreat to a strong defensive position along the Seine. It was little wonder that Churchill joked that the survival of 'Corporal Schickelgruber' (as he dubbed the Führer) was indeed 'providential'. The result of Hitler's strategy was that when his divisions were overwhelmed after hard fighting in the Bocage, the Allies' path was clear for a rapid advance eastwards.

Paris was liberated on 25 August, 55 days ahead of schedule. The following day, Charles de Gaulle led his Free French forces down the Champs-Elysées amid scenes of unrestrained joy and periodic bursts of badly aimed gunfire. But there was no let up. While the Americans advanced east towards Alsace, the British raced north across Belgium, taking Brussels on 3 September and, the next day, Antwerp. Meanwhile, observed by Churchill through binoculars from on board HMS *Kimberley*, successful landings were also made along the Riviera: the start of the liberation of southern France.

ON THIS DAY
28 SEPTEMBER 1944

• Over 6500 British and Polish troops enter German captivity as a result of the failed attempt to secure the bridge across the Rhine at Arnhem.

• In Normandy, Canadians attacking the important defensive gun battery at Cap Gris-Nez prepare for their final, successful assault.

• Feuding Greek partisan factions negotiate under British authority about forming a united front to ward off potential civil war, as the German occupiers attempt to retreat northwards.

• Allied foreign ministers prepare for the Dumbarton Oaks conference, beginning the next day, which will move towards the creation of the United Nations.

In the first fortnight of September, the Allies had the opportunity to cross the last great natural barrier in their way: the Rhine. Beyond – and with minimal military opposition in the way – the Ruhr, the Reich's industrial heartland, was there for the taking. The statistics had never looked more favourable. Across the western theatre of operations, the Allies outnumbered the Germans by 20:1 in tanks and 25:1 in airplanes. A decision to press ahead might have ended the war by the month's end.

But the Allies were victims of their own success. After breaking out from Normandy, the pace of advance had been so rapid that supply lines had become over-extended. With the Germans still in control of the Channel ports (Calais fell only on 1 October), most of the supplies were having to be unloaded at Cherbourg and then conveyed by truck. Use of the great docks at Antwerp was restricted by the presence along the Scheldt of German forces, which were not removed until the end of November.

With Patton's Third Army running out of fuel and temporarily stuck at Metz, Montgomery masterminded a daring attempt to use paratroopers in the largest airborne assault in history to secure for the British Second Army a northerly passage across the Rhine. Commencing on 17 September, Operation Market Garden succeeded in taking the Waal bridge at Nijmegen. However, despite intense fighting and extraordinary heroism after virtually landing on top of a Panzer division, the British First Airborne Division lost the all-important battle to seize the bridge across the Rhine at Arnhem. In his speech, Churchill lauded their efforts which he insisted were 'not in vain'.

But the truth was that Arnhem had proved 'a bridge too far' and the tough German resistance had helped postpone defeat for the Third Reich. Consequently, the Allies did not manage to cross the Rhine until March the following year. The cost of the Wehrmacht's success at Arnhem was ultimately paid in several more million lives, the further destruction of Germany's great cities and the Soviet Army occupying the heart of Europe.

Little more than seven weeks have passed since we rose for the summer vacation, but this short period has completely changed the face of the war in Europe. When we separated, the Anglo-American armies were still penned in the narrow bridgehead and strip of coast from the base of the Cherbourg peninsula to the approaches to Caen, which they had wrested from the enemy several weeks before. The Brest peninsula was untaken, the German Army in the west was still hopeful of preventing us from striking out into the fields of France, the Battle of Normandy, which had been raging bloodily from the date of the landing, had not reached any decisive conclusion. What a transformation now meets our eyes! Not only Paris, but practically the whole of France, has been liberated as if by enchantment. Belgium has been rescued, part of Holland is already free, and the foul enemy who for four years inflicted his cruelties and oppression upon these countries, has fled, losing perhaps 400,000 in killed and wounded, and leaving in our hands nearly half a million prisoners. Besides this, there may well be 200,000 cut off in the coastal fortresses or in Holland, whose destruction or capture may now be deemed highly probable. The Allied armies have reached and in some places crossed the German frontier and the Siegfried Line.

'The world-famous Battle of Normandy, the greatest and most decisive single battle of the entire war'

All these operations have been conducted under the supreme command of General Eisenhower, and were the fruit of the world-famous Battle of Normandy, the greatest and most decisive single battle of the entire war. Never has the exploitation of victory been carried to a higher perfection. The chaos and destruction wrought by the Allied air forces behind the battle front have been indescribable in narrative, and a factor of the utmost potency in the actual struggle. They have far surpassed, and reduce to petty dimensions, all that our army had to suffer from the German Air Force in 1940. Nevertheless, when we reflect upon the tremendous fire-power of modern weapons and the opportunity which they give for defensive and delaying action, we must feel astounded at the extraordinary speed with which the Allied armies have advanced. The vast and brilliant encircling movement of the American armies will ever be a model of military art, and an example of the propriety of running risks not only in the fighting – because most of the armies are ready to do that – but even more on the Q side, or, as the Americans put it, the logistical side. It was with great pleasure that all of us saw the British and Canadian armies, who have so long fought against heavy resistance by the enemy along the hinge of the Allied movement, show themselves also capable of lightning advances which have certainly not been surpassed anywhere.

'Our first Airborne Division . . . will, in succeeding generations, inspire our youth with the highest ideals of duty and of daring'

Finally, by the largest airborne operation ever conceived or executed, a further all-important forward bound in the north has been achieved. Here I must pay a tribute, which the House will consider due, to the superb feat of arms performed by our First Airborne Division. Full and deeply-moving accounts have already been given to the country and to the world of this glorious and fruitful operation, which will take a lasting place in our military annals, and will, in succeeding generations, inspire our youth with the highest ideals of duty and of daring. The cost has been heavy; the casualties in a single division have been grievous; but for those who mourn there is at least the consolation that the sacrifice was not needlessly demanded nor given without results. The delay caused to the enemy's advance upon Nijmegen enabled their British and American comrades in the other two airborne divisions, and the British Second Army, to secure intact the vitally important bridges, and to form a strong bridgehead over the main stream of the Rhine at Nijmegen. 'Not in vain' may be the pride of those who have survived and the epitaph of those who fell.

'"Not in vain" may be the pride of those who have survived and the epitaph of those who fell'

To return to the main theme, Brest, Havre, Dieppe, Boulogne and Antwerp are already in our hands. All the Atlantic and Channel ports, from the Spanish frontier to the Hook of Holland, will presently be in our possession, yielding fine harbours and substantial masses of prisoners-of-war. All this has been accomplished by the joint exertions of the British and American armies, assisted by the vehement and widespread uprising and fighting efforts of the French Maquis.

While this great operation has been taking its course, an American and French landing on the Riviera coast, actively assisted by a British airborne brigade, a British air force, and the Royal Navy, has led with inconceivable rapidity to the capture of Toulon and Marseilles, to the freeing of the great strip of the Riviera coast, and to the successful advance of General Patch's army up the Rhône Valley. This army, after taking over 80,000 prisoners, joined hands with General Eisenhower, and has passed under his command. When I had the opportunity on August 15 of watching – alas, from afar – the landing at Saint Tropez, it would have seemed audacious to hope for such swift and important results. They have, however, under the spell of the victories in the north, already been gained in superabundance, and in less than half the time prescribed and expected in the plans which were prepared beforehand. So much for the fighting in France.

'The price in blood . . . for the liberation of the soil of France'

… I am now going to give a few facts and figures about the operations in Europe. These have been very carefully chosen to give as much information as possible to the House and to the public, while not telling the enemy anything he does not already know, or only telling him too late for it to be of any service to him. The speed with which the mighty British and American armies in France were built up is almost incredible. In the first twenty-four hours a quarter of a million men were landed, in the teeth of fortified and violent opposition. By the twentieth day a million men were ashore. There are now between two and three million men in France … Some time ago, a statement was made by a senator to the effect that the American public would be shocked to learn that they would have to provide eighty per cent of the forces to invade the Continent. I then said that at the outset of the invasion of France the British and American forces would be practically equal, but that thereafter the American build-up would give them steadily the lead. I am glad to say that after 120 days of fighting we still bear, in the cross-Channel troops, a proportion of two to three in personnel and of four to five-and-a-half in fighting divisions in France. Casualties have followed very closely the proportions of the numbers. In fact, these troops fight so level that the casualties almost exactly follow the numbers engaged. We have, I regret to say, lost upwards of 90,000 men, killed, wounded and missing, and the United States, including General Patch's army, over 145,000. Such is the price in blood paid by the English-speaking democracies for the actual liberation of the soil of France.

'Hitler . . . a squalid caucus boss and butcher'

… But we must not forget that we owe a great debt to the blunders – the extraordinary blunders – of the Germans. I always hate to compare Napoleon with Hitler, as it seems an insult to the great Emperor and warrior to connect him in any way with a squalid caucus boss and butcher. But there is one respect in which I must draw a parallel. Both these men were temperamentally unable to give up the tiniest scrap of any territory to which the high watermark of their hectic fortunes had carried them. Thus, after Leipzig in 1813, Napoleon left all his garrisons on the Rhine, and 40,000 men in Hamburg. He refused to withdraw many other vitally important elements of his armies, and he had to begin the campaign of 1814 with raw levies and a few seasoned troops brought in a hurry from Spain. Similarly, Hitler has successfully scattered the German armies all over Europe, and by obstination at every point from Stalingrad and Tunis down to the present moment, he has stripped himself of the power to concentrate in main strength for the final struggle.

He has lost, or will lose when the tally is complete, nearly a million men in France and the Low Countries. Other large armies may well be cut off in the Baltic states, in Finland and in Norway. Less than a year ago, when the relative weakness of Germany was already becoming apparent, he was ordering further aggressive action in the Aegean, and the reoccupation of the islands which the Italians had surrendered, or wished to surrender. He has scattered and squandered a very large army in the Balkan peninsula, whose escape will be very difficult; twenty-seven divisions, many of them battered, are fighting General Alexander in Northern

Italy. Many of these will not be able to re-cross the Alps to defend the German fatherland. Such a vast frittering-away and dispersal of forces has never been seen, and is, of course, a prime cause of the impending ruin of Germany.

'Corporal Schickelgruber has so notably contributed to our victory'

When Herr Hitler escaped his bomb on July 20 he described his survival as providential; I think that from a purely military point of view we can all agree with him, for certainly it would be most unfortunate if the Allies were to be deprived, in the closing phases of the struggle, of that form of warlike genius by which Corporal Schickelgruber has so notably contributed to our victory.

'It would be a miserable disaster if the Italian people . . . were to emerge from the European struggle only to fall into violent internal feuds'

... What impressed and touched me most in my journey through Italy was the extraordinary good will to the British and American troops everywhere displayed by the Italian people. As I drove through the small towns and villages behind the line of the armies day after day the friendliness and even enthusiasm of the peasants, workmen and shopkeepers, indeed of all classes, was spontaneous and convincing, I cannot feel – I make my confession – any sentiments of hostility towards the mass of the misled or coerced Italian people. Obviously, no final settlement can be made with them or with their government until the north of Italy and its great cities have been liberated and the basis on which the present government stands has been broadened and strengthened. There are good hopes that this will be achieved, I might say soon, but it would be safer to say in due course. Indeed, it would be a miserable disaster if the Italian people, after all their maltreatment by their former allies and by the Fascist remnants still gathered around Mussolini, were to emerge from the European struggle only to fall into violent internal feuds. It was for that reason, on leaving Rome, that I tried to set before the Italian nation some of those broad simple, liberal safeguards and conceptions which are the breath of our nostrils in this country – so much so that we scarcely notice them – and which sustain the rights and freedoms of the individual against all forms of tyranny, no matter what liveries they wear or what slogans they mouth.

'The Maquis have shown . . . free men may strike a blow for the honour and life of their country'

... It will be remembered that we told the French government that we would not reproach them for making a separate peace in the fearful circumstances of June 1940, provided they sent their fleet out of the reach and power of the Germans. The terms of the Cabinet offer to France in this tragical hour are also on record. I, therefore, have never felt anything but compassion for the French people as a whole who found themselves deprived of all power of resistance and could not share the good fortune of those who, from our shores or in the French Empire, had the honour and opportunity to continue the armed struggle. What could a humble, ordinary man do? He might be on the watch for opportunity, but he might be rendered almost powerless. The Maquis have shown one way in which at the end, and after much suffering, and having overcome all the difficulties of getting weapons, free men may strike a blow for the honour and life of their country; but that is given to the few, to the young and active, those who can obtain weapons.

For my part, I have always felt that the heart of the French nation was sound and true, and that they would rise again in greatness and power, and that we should be proud to have taken a part in aiding them to recover their place in the van of the nations and at the summit of the cultural life of the world …

'I never felt so grave a sense of responsibility'

The House of Commons, London, 27 February 1945

On the conference at Yalta

Churchill had long believed that Hitler's great hope was that there would be an irreparable fallout between the Allies. The future of liberated nations was an obvious issue for those separated by very different interests and ideologies to disagree about. As a British Conservative, Churchill had to balance his instinctive repugnance for left-wing totalitarianism with a pragmatic recognition of what could not realistically be refused to Stalin as he already had the whip hand over nations his troops were occupying. In this form of diplomacy, possession was likely to prove nine-tenths of the law. Unfortunately for those wanting to see a free and democratic Eastern Europe, the British and American forces had still not crossed the Rhine when Churchill and Roosevelt met Stalin at Yalta, on the Crimea, to determine the postwar world.

A nasty foretaste of what might be in store was proffered throughout August and September 1944. Believing Warsaw's deliverance was close at hand from the fast approaching Soviet Army, a mere 15 miles away, the city's underground 'Polish Home Army' rose-up to overthrow their German masters. Instead of helping, Stalin not only ordered his forces to stand aside and watch the uprising's ruthless suppression but even frustrated Churchill's efforts to have nearby airfields put temporarily at the RAF's disposal so that they could more easily drop supplies to the Polish insurgents – who held out against desperate odds for 63 days. Ultimately, the Soviet dictator wanted to install his own puppet government in the ruins of Poland's capital and was not upset to see a rival leadership fall victim to Nazi barbarism. The Germans were left to raze Warsaw to the ground and slaughter nearly a quarter of a million of its inhabitants.

Churchill flew to Moscow in October. He hoped to broker a compromise whereby the Free Polish government exiled in London would accept Soviet annexation of eastern Poland in return for Stalin agreeing to significant representation for them in Warsaw's postwar government. However, neither Stalin nor the Free Poles were prepared to bend sufficiently, a result that ensured the total marginalization of the latter in the future running of their country. In an unofficial scribbling of rough percentage interests, Churchill and Stalin contemplated quantifying their respective nations' say in determining the future of the other freed nations. The Soviet Union would have minimal input determining Greece's future, there would be equality with Britain and America over Yugoslavia and Hungary's and a majority influence in Bulgaria and Romania. This was,

ON THIS DAY
27 FEBRUARY 1945

• As the end of the war is now forseeable, other nations rush to declare war on Germany and Japan to secure a voice in discussions over the new world order and the United Nations. Yesterday it was Syria, today it is Lebanon, and tomorrow it will be Saudia Arabia.

• The US Air Force mounts its biggest daytime bombing raid over Berlin, involving over 1100 bombers. Earlier in the month, Dresden suffered devastating firestorms as a result of Allied air power.

• Soviet forces continue to push into East Prussia with a ruthlessness matched by numerous atrocities including mass rape and murder of civilians. At the same time, the Western Allies prepare to launch Operations Lumberjack and Undertone to drive their German opponents back across the Rhine.

according to opinion, either a cynical attempt at a carve-up or a desperate effort by Churchill to make the western democracies more than spectators when Kremlin-backed communists took over throughout Eastern Europe and the Balkans.

Stalin's insistence that the great conference of the 'Big Three' should be at Yalta – which forced the American president and British prime minister, both in frail health, to make arduous journeys – prompted Churchill to joke with the US emissary Harry Hopkins, 'If we had spent ten years on research, we could not have found a worse place in the world.' When Roosevelt arrived, gaunt and quiet, it was clear he was dying. He was in no state for the poker game involved.

With his troops moving to within 40 miles of Berlin, Stalin appeared to hold the best cards. Churchill sought to modify Stalin's insistence that Germany should be dissolved into several separate states or that she be squeezed for a great reparations bill. But he hardly felt able to refuse Soviet demands that their advance be aided with the carpet bombing of Berlin, Dresden and Leipzig. Churchill did insist that Poland should have 'full and free elections'. With unabashed cynicism, Stalin agreed to this request. As he well knew, the democrats would struggle to find means of keeping him to his word. On Greece and Yugoslavia, Stalin also made reassuring noises. A secret pledge was made for Soviet entry into the war against Japan as soon as Germany was defeated. There was also agreement that the Great Powers should be equally represented on the Security Council of what would become the United Nations.

Faced with such apparent reasonableness, Churchill agreed that Soviet nationals captured fighting for the Germans should be repatriated. It was a further sign of Stalin's duplicity that he specifically asked that the British should not mistreat these PoWs before returning them to his care. Perhaps it should have been foreseen, but it could not be taken as a certainty, that he was preparing a worse fate for them. The conference ended in agreement. The 'Big Three' of Stalin, Churchill and Roosevelt posed for photographs and signed a Declaration on Liberated Europe in which they agreed to uphold 'the right of all peoples to choose the form of government under which they will live'.

But not everyone in the House of Commons Smoking Room took Stalin at his word. However, given that he had rather more armed divisions at his command than were at the disposal of a few backbench grumblers in the Tory Party, the options for opposing him were limited. In defending his diplomacy at Yalta, Churchill could point to the written guarantees committing Stalin to supporting democracy in the lands his forces were occupying. And so the ageing prime minister found himself waving pieces of paper as proof of a dictator's good faith. It was inescapably reminiscent of Neville Chamberlain returning from Munich in 1938.

… It is on the Great Powers that the chief burden of maintaining peace and security will fall. The new world organization must take into account this special responsibility of the Great Powers, and must be so framed as not to compromise their unity, or their capacity for effective action if it is called for at short notice. At the same time, the world organization cannot be based upon a dictatorship of the Great Powers. It is their duty to serve the world and not to rule it. We trust the voting procedure on which we agreed at Yalta meets these two essential points, and provides a system which is fair and acceptable, having regard to the evident difficulties which will meet anyone who gives prolonged thought to the subject.

'It is to this strongly-armed body that we look to prevent wars of aggression'

The conference at San Francisco will bring together, upon the invitation of the United States, Great Britain, the British Commonwealth, the Union of Soviet Socialist Republics, the provisional government of the French Republic, and the Republic of China, all those members of the United Nations who have declared war on Germany or Japan by March 1, 1945, and who have signed the United Nations conference declaration. Many are declaring war or have done so since Yalta, and their action should be treated with respect and satisfaction by those who have borne the burden and heat of the day. Our future will be consolidated and enriched by the participation of these Powers, who, together with the founder members, will take the opening steps to form the world organization to which it is hoped that ultimately and in due course all states will belong. It is to this strongly-armed body that we look to prevent wars of aggression, or the preparation for such wars, and to enable disputes between states, both great and small, to be adjusted by peaceful and lawful means, by persuasion, by the pressure of public opinion, by legal method, and eventually by another category of method which constitutes the principle of this new organization.

'It will not shrink from establishing its will against the evil-doer, or evil-planner'

The former League of Nations, so hardly used and found to be inadequate for the tasks it attempted, will be replaced by a far stronger body in which the United States will play a vitally important part. It will embody much of the structure and characteristics of its predecessor. All the work that was done in the past, all the experience that has been gathered by the working of the League of Nations, will not be cast away; but the new body will differ from it in the essential point that it will not shrink from establishing its will against the evil-doer, or evil-planner, in good time and by force of arms. This organization, which is capable of continuous progress and development, is at any rate appropriate to the phase upon which the world will enter after our present enemies have been beaten down, and we may have good hopes, and, more than hopes, a resolute determination that it shall shield humanity from a third renewal of its agonies. We have all been made aware in the interval between the two world wars of the weaknesses of international bodies, whose work is seriously complicated by the misfortune which occurred in the building of the Tower of Babel. Taught by bitter experience, we hope now to make the world conscious of the strength of the new instrument, and of the protection which it will be able to afford to all who wish to dwell in peace within their habitations.

… I now come to the most difficult and agitating part of the statement which I have to make to the House – the question of Poland. For more than a year past, and since the tide of war has turned so strongly against Germany, the Polish problem has been divided into two main issues – the frontiers of Poland and the freedom of Poland.

'To establish a free Polish nation with a good home to live in has always far outweighed, in my mind, the actual tracing of the frontier line'

The House is well aware from the speeches I have made to them that the freedom, independence, integrity and sovereignty of Poland have always seemed to His Majesty's government more important than the actual frontiers. To establish a free Polish nation with a good home to live in has always far outweighed, in my mind, the actual tracing of the frontier line, or whether these boundaries should be shifted on both sides of Poland farther to the west. The Russian claim, first advanced at Tehran in November 1943, has always been unchanged for the Curzon Line in the east, and the Russian offer has always been that ample compensation should be gained for Poland at the expense of Germany in the north and in the west. All these matters are tolerably well known now. The foreign secretary explained in detail last December the story of the Curzon Line. I have never concealed from the House that, personally, I think the Russian claim is just and right. If I champion this frontier for Russia, it is not because I bow to force. It is because I believe it is the fairest division of territory that can, in all the circumstances, be made between the two countries whose history has been so chequered and intermingled.

'The Curzon Line was drawn . . . when Russia had few friends among the Allies'

The Curzon Line was drawn in 1919 by an expert commission, of which one of our most distinguished foreign office representatives of those days, Sir Eyre Crowe, was a member. It was drawn at a time when Russia had few friends among the Allies. In fact, I may say that she was extremely unpopular. One cannot feel that either the circumstances or the personalities concerned would have given undue favour to Soviet Russia. They just tried to find out what was the right and proper line to draw. The British government in those days approved this line, including, of course, the exclusion of Lvov from Poland. Apart from all that has happened since, I cannot conceive that we should not regard it as a well-informed and fair proposal.

There are two things to be remembered in justice to our great ally. I can look back to August 1914, when Germany first declared war against Russia under the Tsar. In those days, the Russian frontiers on the west were far more spacious than those for which Russia is now asking after all her sufferings and victories. The Tsarist frontiers included all Finland and the whole of the vast Warsaw salient stretching to within 60 miles of Breslau. Russia is, in fact, accepting a frontier which over immense distances is 200 or 300 miles farther to the east than what was Russian territory and had been Russian territory for many generations under the Tsarist regime.

'The most horrifying act of cruelty, which has ever darkened the passage of man on the earth'

... There is a second reason which appeals to me, apart from this sense of continuity which I personally feel. But for the prodigious exertions and sacrifices of Russia, Poland was doomed to utter destruction at the hands of the Germans. Not only Poland as a state and as a nation, but the Poles as a race were doomed by Hitler to be destroyed or reduced to a servile station. Three and a half million Polish Jews are said to have been actually slaughtered. It is certain that enormous numbers have perished in one of the most horrifying acts of cruelty, probably the most horrifying act of cruelty, which has ever darkened the passage of man on the earth. When the Germans had clearly avowed their intention of making the Poles a subject and inferior race under the Herrenvolk, suddenly, by a superb effort of military force and skill, the Russian armies, in little more than three weeks, since, in fact, we spoke on these matters here, have advanced from the Vistula to the Oder, driving the Germans in ruin before them and freeing the whole of Poland from the awful cruelty and oppression under which the Poles were writhing.

In supporting the Russian claim to the Curzon Line, I repudiate and repulse any suggestion that we are making a questionable compromise or yielding to force or fear, and I assert with the utmost conviction the broad justice of the policy upon which for the first time, all the three great Allies have now taken their stand. Moreover, the three Powers have now agreed that Poland shall receive substantial accessions of territory both in the north and in the west. In the north she will certainly receive, in the place of a precarious corridor, the great city of Danzig, the greater part of East Prussia west and south of Koenigsberg, and a long, wide sea front on the Baltic. In the west she will receive the important industrial province of Upper Silesia and, in addition, such other territories to the east of the Oder as it may be decided at the peace settlement to detach from Germany after the views of a broadly based Polish government have been ascertained.

'The vital interest, which Poland has in having complete agreement with her powerful neighbour to the east'

... I have now dealt with the frontiers of Poland. I must say I think it is a case which I can outline with great confidence to the House. An impartial line traced long ago by a British commission in which Britain took a leading part; the moderation with which the Russians have strictly confined themselves to that line; the enormous sacrifices they have made and the sufferings they have undergone; the contributions they have made to our present victory; the great interest, the vital interest, which Poland has in having complete agreement with her powerful neighbour to the east – when you consider all those matters and the way they have been put forward, the temperate, patient manner in which they have been put forward and discussed, I say that I have rarely seen a case in this House which I could commend with more confidence to the good sense of Members of all sides.

'The home of the Poles is settled. Are they to be masters in their own house?'

But even more important than the frontiers of Poland, within the limits now disclosed, is the freedom of Poland. The home of the Poles is settled. Are they to be masters in their own house? Are they to be free, as we in Britain and the United States or France are free? Is their sovereignty and their independence to be untrammelled, or are they to become a mere projection of the Soviet state, forced against their will, by an armed minority, to adopt a communist or totalitarian system. Well, I am putting the case in all its bluntness. It is a touchstone far more sensitive and vital than the drawing of frontier lines. Where does Poland stand? Where do we all stand on this?

Most solemn declarations have been made by Marshal Stalin and the Soviet Union that the sovereign independence of Poland is to be maintained, and this decision is now joined in both by Great Britain and the United States. Here also, the world organization will in due course assume a measure of responsibility. The Poles will have their future in their own hands, with the single limitation that they must honestly follow, in harmony with their allies, a policy friendly to Russia. That is surely reasonable.

… Our two guiding principles in dealing with all these problems of the Continent and of liberated countries have been clear: while the war is on, we give help to anyone who can kill a Hun; when the war is over, we look to the solution of a free, unfettered, democratic election. Those are the two principles which this coalition government have applied, to the best of their ability, to the circumstances and situations in this entangled and infinitely varied development.

'What are democratic parties?'

… The House should read carefully again and again – those Members who have doubts – the words and the terms of the declaration, every word of which was the subject of the most profound and searching attention by the heads of the three governments, and by the foreign secretaries and all their experts. How will this declaration be carried out? How will phrases like 'Free and unfettered elections on the basis of universal suffrage and secret ballot' be interpreted? Will the 'new' government be 'properly' constituted within a fair representation of the Polish people, as far as can be made practicable at the moment, and as soon as possible? Will the elections be free and unfettered? Will the candidates of all democratic parties be able to present themselves to the electors, and to conduct their campaigns? What are democratic parties? People always take different views. Even in our own country there has been from time to time an effort by one party or the other to claim that they are the true democratic party, and the rest are either Bolsheviks or Tory landlords. What are democratic parties? Obviously this is capable of being settled. Will the election be what we should say was fair and free in this country, making some allowance for the great confusion and disorder which prevails? There are a great number of parties in Poland. We have agreed that all those that are democratic parties – not Nazi or Fascist parties or parties of collaborators with the enemy – all these will be able to take their part.

'Sombre indeed would be the fortunes of mankind if some awful schism arose between the western democracies and the Russian Soviet Union'

These are questions upon which we have the clearest views, in accordance with the principles of the declaration on liberated Europe, to which all three governments have duly subscribed. It is on that basis that the Moscow commission of three was intended to work, and on that basis it has already begun to work.

The impression I brought back from the Crimea, and from all my other contacts, is that Marshal Stalin and the Soviet leaders wish to live in honourable friendship and equality with the western democracies. I feel also that their word is their bond. I know of no government which stands to its obligations, even in its own despite, more solidly than the Russian Soviet government. I decline absolutely to embark here on a discussion about Russian good faith. It is quite evident that these matters touch the whole future of the world. Sombre indeed would be the fortunes of mankind if some awful schism arose between the western democracies and the Russian Soviet Union, if the future world organization were rent asunder, and if new cataclysms of inconceivable violence destroyed all that is left of the treasures and liberties of mankind.

Finally, on this subject, His Majesty's government recognize that the large forces of Polish troops, soldiers, sailors and airmen, now fighting gallantly, as they have fought during the whole war, under British command, owe allegiance to the Polish government in London. We have every confidence that once the new government, more fully representative of the will of the Polish people than either the present government in London or the provisional adminis-tration in Poland, has been established, and recognized by the Great Powers, means will be found of overcoming these formal difficulties in the wider interest of Poland. Above all, His Majesty's government are resolved that as many as possible of the Polish troops shall be enabled to return in due course to Poland, of their own free will, and under every safeguard, to play their part in the future life of their country.

'His Majesty's government will never forget the debt they owe to the Polish troops'

In any event, His Majesty's government will never forget the debt they owe to the Polish troops who have served them so valiantly, and to all those who have fought under our command I earnestly hope it may be possible to offer the citizenship and freedom of the British Empire, if they so desire. I am not able to make a declaration on that subject today, because all matters affecting citizenship require to be discussed between this country and the Dominions, and that takes time. But so far as we are concerned we should think it an honour to have such faithful and valiant warriors dwelling among us as if they were men of our own blood.

'Peace reigned over the beautiful, immortal city'

... On the way back from the Crimea to say goodbye to the president at Alexandria, the foreign secretary and I stopped in Athens. I must say that from my point of view this was the high spot of the whole journey. I could not help recalling the grim conditions of our visit only seven weeks before, when the cannon were firing close at hand, and bullets continually struck the walls and people were killed and wounded in the streets not far away. The contrast between those violent scenes and the really rapturous welcome we received from vast crowds of delighted citizens was one of the most vivid, impressive and agreeable experiences of my life. Peace reigned over the beautiful, immortal city. Its citizens were wild with joy. His Beatitude the Archbishop was seated in the Regency, firmly grasping the reins of power. Together we drove through the crowded streets, lined by the first instalment of the new national Greek Army, until I found myself called upon to address what was, incomparably, the largest and most enthusiastic gathering that in a very long experience of such demonstrations I have ever seen. There is no subject in my recollection on which the policy of His Majesty's government has received more complete vindication than in regard to Greece, nor has there been any on which greater prejudice and misrepresentation has been poured out against them in the United States – not without some assistance from these shores. All this was done with a gay, and, as I said, a wanton disregard of the ill-effects produced on the spot, and the encouragement given to the resistance of the terrorists in Greece. I am sure we rescued Athens from a horrible fate. I believe that the Greek people will long acclaim our action, both military and political. Peace without vengeance has been achieved. A great mass of arms has been surrendered. Most of the prisoners and hostages have been restored. The great work of bringing in food supplies has resumed its former activity. Public order and security are so established that UNRRA [United Nations Relief and Rehabilitation Administration] is about to resume its functions. The popularity of British troops and of those who have guided the course of policy, such as Mr Leeper and General Scobie, is unbounded in these regions, and their conduct continues to receive the approbation of His Majesty's coalition government.

'In all this war I never felt so grave a sense of responsibility as I did at Yalta'

… I suppose that during these last three winter months the human race all the world over has undergone more physical agony and misery than at any other period through which this planet has passed. In the Stone Age the numbers were fewer, and the primitive creatures, little removed from their animal origin, knew no better. We suffer more, and we feel more. I must admit that in all this war I never felt so grave a sense of responsibility as I did at Yalta. In 1940 and 1941, when we in this island were all alone, and invasion was so near, the actual steps one ought to take and our attitude towards them seemed plain and simple. If a man is coming across the sea to kill you, you do everything in your power to make sure he dies before finishing his journey. That may be difficult, it may be painful, but at least it is simple. Now we are entering a world of imponderables, and at every stage occasions for self-questioning arise. It is a mistake to look too far ahead. Only one link in the chain of destiny can he handled at a time.

'The lights burn brighter and shine more broadly than before. Let us walk forward together'

I trust the House will feel that hope has been powerfully strengthened by our meeting in the Crimea. The ties that bind the three Great Powers together, and their mutual comprehension of each other, have grown. The United States has entered deeply and constructively into the life and salvation of Europe. We have all three set our hands to far-reaching engagements at once practical and solemn. United, we have the unchallengeable power to lead the world to prosperity, freedom and happiness. The Great Powers must seek to serve and not to rule. Joined with other states, both large and small, we may found a world organization which, armed with ample power, will guard the rights of all states, great or small, from aggression, or from the gathering of the means of aggression. I am sure that a fairer choice is open to mankind than they have known in recorded ages. The lights burn brighter and shine more broadly than before. Let us walk forward together.

'The greatest American friend we have ever known'

House of Commons, London, 17 April 1945

On the death of President Roosevelt

On 18 March 1945, shortly before flying out to watch Montgomery's assault across the Rhine, Churchill confided to Roosevelt, 'Our friendship is the rock on which I build for the future of the world so long as I am one of the builders.'

There was certainly need of a strong ally in Washington. Churchill was greatly alarmed at reports coming in from Poland and Romania that the Soviets were arresting independent politicians and anti-communists rather than adhering to Stalin's commitments at Yalta to plurality and democracy. Drawing the appropriate conclusions, Churchill was eager for the British and American forces to press on to capture Berlin before the Soviets reached it. This put him at loggerheads with Eisenhower who was content to wait at the River Elbe, 70 miles from the Reich's capital, thereby allowing the great prize to be taken by Stalin.

This was the situation when Churchill received the news of Roosevelt's death. It was a huge personal blow and, in other circumstances, might have proved a political setback too. The British prime minister had not even met the president's successor, Harry S Truman, although he would soon find him of like mind. Yet, as it transpired, the pace of events was already overtaking the incumbents of Downing Street and Pennsylvania Avenue. Within days, American and Soviet troops were shaking hands on the Elbe and the Russians were fighting their way through the ruins of Berlin. The great enterprise was hurtling towards its destination.

ON THIS DAY
17 APRIL 1945

- The former SS guards at the Bergen-Belsen concentration camp are forced by their British captors to bury the bodies of thousands of their Jewish, Gypsy (Roma) and other victims. Two weeks later, enraged American troops liberating Dachau exact vengeance on SS guards there, executing over a hundred of them. The sheer horror of the Holocaust begins to reveal itself.

- The Red Army, having already pushed on over the River Oder, begins the second day of the final assault on Berlin.

- In Berlin, Eva Braun, Hitler's mistress, has arrived the previous day from Berchtesgaden, to join him in the underground bunker.

'His accustomed clear vision and vigour upon perplexing and complicated matters'

My friendship with the great man to whose work and fame we pay our tribute today began and ripened during this war. I had met him, but only for a few minutes, after the close of the last war, and as soon as I went to the Admiralty in September 1939, he telegraphed inviting me to correspond with him direct on naval or other matters if at any time I felt inclined. Having obtained the permission of the prime minister, I did so. Knowing President Roosevelt's keen interest in sea warfare, I furnished him with a stream of information about our naval affairs, and about the various actions, including especially the action of the Plate River [the cornering of the pocket battleship *Admiral Graf Spee*], which lighted the first gloomy winter of the war.

When I became prime minister, and the war broke out in all its hideous fury, when our own life and survival hung in the balance, I was already in a position to telegraph to the president on terms of an association which had become most intimate and, to me, most agreeable. This continued through all the ups and downs of the world struggle until Thursday last, when I received my last messages from him. These messages showed no falling-off in his accustomed clear vision and vigour upon perplexing and complicated matters. I may mention that this correspondence which, of course, was greatly increased after the United States entry into the war, comprises to and fro between us, over 1700 messages. Many of these were lengthy messages, and the majority dealt with those more difficult points which come to be discussed upon the level of heads of governments only after official solutions have not been reached at other stages. To this correspondence there must be added our nine meetings – at Argentia, three in Washington, at Casablanca, at Tehran, two at Quebec and, last of all, at Yalta, comprising in all about 120 days of close personal contact, during a great part of which I stayed with him at the White House or at his home at Hyde Park or in his retreat in the Blue Mountains, which he called Shangri-la.

'It is, indeed, a loss, a bitter loss to humanity that those heart-beats are stilled forever'

I conceived an admiration for him as a statesman, a man of affairs, and a war leader. I felt the utmost confidence in his upright, inspiring character and outlook, and a personal regard – affection I must say – for him beyond my power to express today. His love of his own country, his respect for its constitution, his power of gauging the tides and currents of its mobile public opinion, were always evident, but added to these were the beatings of that generous heart which was always stirred to anger and to action by spectacles of aggression and oppression by the strong against the weak. It is, indeed, a loss, a bitter loss to humanity that those heart-beats are stilled forever.

President Roosevelt's physical affliction lay heavily upon him. It was a marvel that he bore up against it through all the many years of tumult and storm. Not one man in ten millions, stricken and crippled as he was, would have attempted to plunge into a life of physical and mental exertion and of hard, ceaseless political controversy. Not one in ten millions would have tried, not one in a generation would have succeeded, not only in entering this sphere, not only in acting vehemently in it, but in becoming indisputable master of the scene. In this extraordinary effort of the spirit over the flesh, of willpower over physical infirmity, he was inspired and sustained by that noble woman his devoted wife, whose high ideals marched with his own, and to whom the deep and respectful sympathy of the House of Commons flows out today in all fullness.

'Imagination is often more torturing than reality'

There is no doubt that the president foresaw the great dangers closing in upon the pre-war world with far more prescience than most well-informed people on either side of the Atlantic, and that he urged forward with all his power such precautionary military preparations as peacetime opinion in the United States could be brought to accept. There never was a moment's doubt, as the quarrel opened, upon which side his sympathies lay. The fall of France, and what seemed to most people outside this island, the impending destruction of

Great Britain, were to him an agony, although he never lost faith in us. They were an agony to him not only on account of Europe, but because of the serious perils to which the United States herself would have been exposed had we been overwhelmed or the survivors cast down under the German yoke. The bearing of the British nation at that time of stress, when we were all alone, filled him and vast numbers of his countrymen with the warmest sentiments towards our people. He and they felt the Blitz of the stern winter of 1940–1, when Hitler set himself to rub out the cities of our country, as much as any of us did, and perhaps more indeed, for imagination is often more torturing than reality. There is no doubt that the bearing of the British and, above all, of the Londoners, kindled fires in American bosoms far harder to quench than the conflagrations from which we were suffering. There was also at that time, in spite of General Wavell's victories – all the more, indeed, because of the reinforcements which were sent from this country to him – the apprehension widespread in the United States that we should be invaded by Germany after the fullest preparation in the spring of 1941. It was in February that the president sent to England the late Mr Wendell Willkie, who, although a political rival and an opposing [presidential] candidate, felt as he did on many important points. Mr Willkie brought a letter from Mr Roosevelt, which the president had written in his own hand, and this letter contained the famous lines of Longfellow:

'Sail on, O ship of State!
Sail on, O Union, strong and great!
Humanity with all its fears,
With all the hopes of future years,
Is hanging breathless on thy fate!'

'Lend-Lease will stand forth as the most unselfish and unsordid financial act of any country in all history'

At about that same time he devised the extraordinary measure of assistance called Lend-Lease, which will stand forth as the most unselfish and unsordid financial act of any country in all history. The effect of this was greatly to increase British fighting power, and for all the purpose of the war effort to make us, as it were, a much more numerous community. In that autumn I met the president for the first time during the war at Argentia in Newfoundland, and together we drew up the declaration which has since been called the Atlantic Charter, and which will, I trust, long remain a guide for both our peoples and for other people of the world.

All this time in deep and dark and deadly secrecy, the Japanese were preparing their act of treachery and greed. When next we met in Washington, Japan, Germany and Italy had declared war upon the United States, and both our countries were in arms, shoulder to shoulder. Since then we have advanced over the land and over the sea through many difficulties and disappointments, but always with a broadening measure of success. I need not dwell upon the series of great operations which have taken place in the western hemisphere, to say nothing of that other immense war proceeding on the other side of the world. Nor need I speak of the plans which we made with our great ally, Russia, at Tehran, for these have now been carried out for all the world to see.

'His captivating smile, his gay and charming manner, had not deserted him'

But at Yalta I noticed that the president was ailing. His captivating smile, his gay and charming manner, had not deserted him, but his face had a transparency, an air of purification, and often there was a faraway look in his eyes. When I took my leave of him in Alexandria harbour I must confess that I had an indefinable sense of fear that his health and his strength were on the ebb. But nothing altered his inflexible sense of duty. To the end he faced his innumerable tasks unflinching. One of the tasks of the president is to sign maybe a hundred or two state papers with his own hand every day, commissions and so forth. All this he continued to carry out with the utmost strictness. When death came suddenly upon him 'he had finished his mail'. That portion of his day's work was done. As the saying goes, he died in harness, and we may well say in battle harness, like his soldiers, sailors, and airmen, who side by side with ours are carrying on their task to the end all over the world. What an enviable death was his! He had brought his country through the worst of its perils and the heaviest of its toils. Victory had cast its sure and steady beam upon him.

'In war he had raised the strength, might and glory of the great republic to a height never attained by any nation in history'

In the days of peace he had broadened and stabilized the foundations of American life and union. In war he had raised the strength, might and glory of the great republic to a height never attained by any nation in history. With her left hand she was leading the advance of the conquering Allied armies into the heart of Germany, and with her right, on the other side of the globe, she was irresistibly and swiftly breaking up the power of Japan. And all the time ships, munitions, supplies, and food of every kind were aiding on a gigantic scale her allies, great and small, in the course of the long struggle.

'In Franklin Roosevelt there died the greatest American friend we have ever known'

But all this was no more than worldly power and grandeur, had it not been that the causes of human freedom and of social justice, to which so much of his life had been given, added a lustre to this power and pomp and warlike might, a lustre which will long be discernible among men. He has left behind him a band of resolute and able men handling the numerous interrelated parts of the vast American war machine. He has left a successor who comes forward with firm step and sure conviction to carry on the task to its appointed end. For us, it remains only to say that in Franklin Roosevelt there died the greatest American friend we have ever known, and the greatest champion of freedom who has ever brought help and comfort from the New World to the Old.

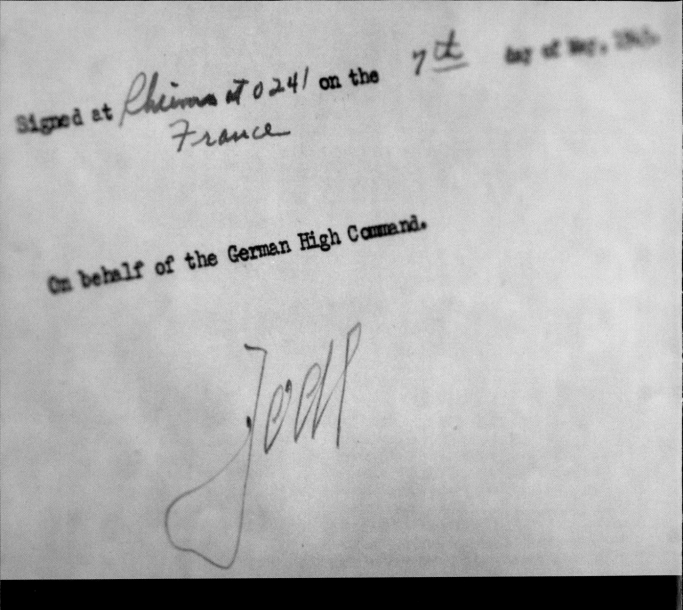

'This is your victory!'

On 28 April, Mussolini was captured and shot by Italian partisans. His corpse was strung up alongside that of his mistress, Clara Petacci, for a crowd to kick and spit upon. The man who had promised Italian greatness ended up trying to evade detection disguised in a German soldier's greatcoat.

Shortly before dictating a rambling polemic blaming the Jews for his country's misfortunes, Hitler broke off his relationship with the German nation and settled instead for a hurried marriage to his mistress Eva Braun. The dream of a thousand-year Reich lay in ruins above the Berlin bunker that had become the limits of their world. Rather than face reality, on 30 April they committed suicide together. The Hitler regime had lasted 12 years, Germany reduced to the misery she had previously been content to mete out to any who stood in her way. On 8 May, the war in Europe ended.

The conflict had extinguished more than 50 million lives. The continent was devastated. Millions of civilians, now refugees, were on the move, a few miserable possessions under their arm or piled in carts. Many had cause to fear retribution. For some, the worst days were ahead with indiscriminate vengeance accompanying justice. And as shocked Allied forces discovered as they pressed on, crimes of matchless depravity had been perpetrated behind the barbed wire and guard towers of the concentration camps where a 'final solution' had been applied to exterminate the Jews.

London on Victory in Europe Day also bore the scars of war. Large areas were in rubble, not just from the Blitz of 1940–1 but from the missile attacks the city had been subjected to in more recent times. But its streets were filled with a laughing, cheering, singing tide of humanity. Across the country and in other places where the airwaves brought news of victory rather than defeat, the scenes in the British capital were repeated in varying degrees of restraint or abandon. It was, as Churchill had prophesied in darker times, 'victory in spite of all terror'.

The war in the Pacific still raged and would continue to do so until August when Japan surrendered following the dropping of the atom bombs that foreshadowed a new age in

ON THIS DAY
8 MAY 1945

• Churchill's broadcast, formally announcing the end of hostilities in Europe, takes place at 3pm, from Downing Street. He later speaks to the House of Commons before going to Buckingham Palace, where he appears with King George VI on the balcony, to the rapturous welcome of the crowds below. They sing 'Land of Hope and Glory'.

• American soldiers arrest Hermann Goering, the once proud head of the Luftwaffe.

• In Prague, where fighting continues between the Czech resistance and hardcore German SS units, the Red Army prepares to enter the city in strength. By tomorrow this last European capital will be free of Nazi control.

• In Washington, D.C., President Truman reminds the American people amid their jubilation that the war against Japan continues.

• In San Francisco, the various Allied nations meeting to draft a charter for the United Nations Organization continue their deliberations, but the fate of Poland continues to be a bone of contention.

which the world itself might be destroyed. Nonetheless, the torment of the last few years had begun with Hitler. His downfall and Germany's defeat were reasons enough for rejoicing. Churchill's long, unbending resolve had finally been vindicated. Wherever he went, he was cheered to the echo. When he assured the crowds 'This is your victory' a chorus answered, 'No – it is yours'.

Yesterday morning at 2.41am at headquarters, General Jodl, the representative of the German High Command, and Grand Admiral Doenitz, the designated head of the German state, signed the act of unconditional surrender of all German land, sea, and air forces in Europe to the Allied Expeditionary Force, and simultaneously to the Soviet High Command.

General Bedell Smith, chief of staff of the Allied Expeditionary Force, and General François Sevez signed the document on behalf of the supreme commander of the Allied Expeditionary Force, and General Susloparov signed on behalf of the Russian High Command.

Today this agreement will be ratified and confirmed at Berlin where Air-Chief-Marshal Tedder, deputy supreme commander of the Allied Expeditionary Force, and General de Lattre de Tassigny will sign on behalf of General Eisenhower. Marshal Zhukov will sign on behalf of the Soviet High Command. The German representatives will be Field-Marshal Keitel, chief of the High Command, and the commanders-in-chief of the German Army, Navy, and Air Forces.

'Hostilities will end officially at one minute after midnight tonight'

Hostilities will end officially at one minute after midnight tonight (Tuesday, 8 May), but in the interests of saving lives the 'Cease fire' began yesterday to be sounded all along the front, and our dear Channel Islands are also to be freed today.

The Germans are still in places resisting the Russian troops, but should they continue to do so after midnight they will, of course, deprive themselves of the protection of the laws of war, and will be attacked from all quarters by the Allied troops. It is not surprising that on such long fronts and in the existing disorder of the enemy the orders of the German High Command should not in every case be obeyed immediately. This does not, in our opinion, with the best military advice at our disposal, constitute any reason for withholding from the nation the facts communicated to us by General Eisenhower of the unconditional surrender already signed at Rheims, nor should it prevent us from celebrating today and tomorrow (Wednesday) as Victory-in-Europe days.

'The German war is therefore at an end'

Today, perhaps we shall think mostly of ourselves. Tomorrow we shall pay a particular tribute to our Russian comrades, whose prowess in the field has been one of the grand contributions to the general victory.

The German war is therefore at an end. After years of intense preparation, Germany hurled herself on Poland at the beginning of September 1939; and, in pursuance of our guarantee to Poland and in agreement with the French Republic, Great Britain, the British Empire and Commonwealth of Nations, declared war upon this foul aggression. After gallant France had been struck down we, from this island and from our united Empire, maintained the struggle single-handed for a whole year until we were joined by the military might of Soviet Russia, and later by the overwhelming power and resources of the United States of America.

Finally almost the whole world was combined against the evildoers, who are now prostrate before us. Our gratitude to our splendid allies goes forth from all our hearts in this island and throughout the British Empire.

'Our gratitude to our splendid allies goes forth from all our hearts in this island and throughout the British Empire'

We may allow ourselves a brief period of rejoicing; but let us not forget for a moment the toil and efforts that lie ahead. Japan, with all her treachery and greed, remains unsubdued. The injury she has inflicted on Great Britain, the United States, and other countries, and her detestable cruelties, call for justice and retribution. We must now devote all our strength and resources to the completion of our task, both at home and abroad. Advance, Britannia! Long live the cause of freedom. God save the King.

To huge cheers, Churchill then addressed the swelling crowds in Whitehall from the balcony of the Ministry of Health building.

'This is your victory!'

God bless you all. This is your victory! It is the victory of the cause of freedom in every land. In all our long history we have never seen a greater day than this. Everyone, man or woman, has done their best. Everyone has tried. Neither the long years, nor the dangers, nor the fierce attacks of the enemy, have in any way weakened the independent resolve of the British nation. God bless you all.

Eleven weeks later, on 26 July, the results of the general election were announced. The Conservative Party suffered a landslide defeat. Churchill was relieved of office.

'An iron curtain has descended'

Westminster College, Fulton, Missouri, 5 March 1946

On the new dangers to world peace

In the last days of the Second World War – 29 April 1945 – with Vienna falling to Soviet forces and Berlin about to follow suit, Churchill became so disturbed by reports that Stalin was crushing all non-communist opinion in the countries he was occupying that he decided to appeal to him in blunt and desperate terms. 'Do not, I beg you, my friend Stalin, underrate the divergencies which are opening about matters which you may think are small to us, but which are symbolic of the way the English-speaking democracies look at life' he warned. 'There is not much comfort' Churchill made clear, 'in looking into a future where you and the countries you dominate, plus the Communist parties in many other states, are all drawn up on one side, and those who rally to the English-speaking nations and their associates or Dominions are on the other. It is quite obvious that their quarrel would tear the world to pieces, and that all of us leading men on either side who had anything to do with that would be shamed before history.'

Roosevelt had envisaged American troops staying in Europe for no more than two years after Germany's defeat. But Churchill now began to perceive that Stalin had deceived the western democracies at Yalta as comprehensively as Britain and France had been tricked by Hitler at the Munich conference that averted war in 1938. No longer in office, but still leader of the Conservative Party and of the Opposition, Churchill again assumed the mantle of a prophet warning of the new danger to world peace. The devastating power of nuclear annihilation had been demonstrated upon Hiroshima and Nagasaki. It might consume the world. A lasting settlement had to be found and Churchill surmised that Stalin would not take Britain and the United States seriously unless they demonstrated their firmness. When President Harry Truman invited him to his home state of Missouri, Churchill chose a degree ceremony at Westminster College in Fulton to speak what, for the moment, were once again unpalatable truths to all those who did not yet wish to hear them.

> ## ON THIS DAY
> ### 5 MARCH 1946
>
> • At the trials for War Crimes, now taking place in Nuremberg, attention focuses on the case of Julius Streicher, the virulently anti-Semitic newspaper owner, whose *Der Stürmer* had been a propaganda tool of the Nazi regime. He will later be sentenced to death and hanged.
>
> • As the imperial powers of Britain and France struggle with the emerging realities of the postwar world, the French government prepares to recognize Vietnam as a free republic within a wider Indo-Chinese federation.

A shadow has fallen upon the scenes so lately lighted by the Allied victory. Nobody knows what Soviet Russia and its Communist international organization intends to do in the immediate future, or what are the limits, if any, to their expansive and proselytising tendencies. I have a strong admiration and regard for the valiant Russian people and for my wartime comrade, Marshal Stalin. There is deep sympathy and goodwill in Britain – and I doubt not here also – towards the peoples of all the Russias and a resolve to persevere through many differences and rebuffs in establishing lasting friendships. We understand the Russian need to be secure on her western frontiers by the removal of all possibility of German aggression. We welcome Russia to her rightful place among the leading nations of the world. We welcome her flag upon the seas. Above all, we welcome constant, frequent and growing contacts between the Russian people and our own people on both sides of the Atlantic. It is my duty, however, for I am sure you would wish me to state the facts as I see them to you, to place before you certain facts about the present position in Europe.

'From Stettin in the Baltic to Trieste in the Adriatic, an iron curtain has descended'

From Stettin in the Baltic to Trieste in the Adriatic, an iron curtain has descended across the Continent. Behind that line lie all the capitals of the ancient states of Central and Eastern Europe. Warsaw, Berlin, Prague, Vienna, Budapest, Belgrade, Bucharest and Sofia, all these famous cities and the populations around them lie in what I must call the Soviet sphere, and all are subject in one form or another, not only to Soviet influence but to a very high and, in many cases, increasing measure of control from Moscow. Athens alone – Greece with its immortal glories – is free to decide its future at an election under British, American and French observation. The Russian-dominated Polish government has been encouraged to make enormous and wrongful inroads upon Germany, and mass expulsions of millions of Germans on a scale grievous and undreamed-of are now taking place. The Communist parties, which were very small in all these Eastern states of Europe, have been raised to pre-eminence and power far beyond their numbers and are seeking everywhere to obtain totalitarian control. Police governments are prevailing in nearly every case, and so far, except in Czechoslovakia, there is no true democracy.

Turkey and Persia are both profoundly alarmed and disturbed at the claims which are being made upon them and at the pressure being exerted by the Moscow government. An attempt is being made by the Russians in Berlin to build up a quasi-Communist party in their zone of occupied Germany by showing special favours to groups of left-wing German leaders. At the end of the fighting last June, the American and British armies withdrew westwards, in accordance with an earlier agreement, to a depth at some points of 150 miles upon a front of nearly 400 miles, in order to allow our Russian allies to occupy this vast expanse of territory which the western democracies had conquered.

'This is certainly not the liberated Europe we fought to build up. Nor is it one which contains the essentials of permanent peace'

If now the Soviet government tries, by separate action, to build up a pro-Communist Germany in their areas, this will cause new serious difficulties in the British and American zones, and will give the defeated Germans the power of putting themselves up to auction between the Soviets and the western democracies. Whatever conclusions may be drawn from these facts – and facts they are – this is certainly not the liberated Europe we fought to build up. Nor is it one which contains the essentials of permanent peace.

The safety of the world requires a new unity in Europe, from which no nations should be permanently outcast. It is from the quarrels of the strong parent races in Europe that the world wars we have witnessed, or which occurred in former times, have sprung. Twice in our own lifetime we have seen the United States, against their wishes and their traditions, against arguments, the force of which it is impossible not to comprehend, drawn by irresistible forces, into these wars in time to secure the victory of the good cause, but only after frightful slaughter and devastation had occurred. Twice the United States has had to send several millions of its young men across the Atlantic to find the war; but now war can find any nation, wherever it may dwell between dusk and dawn. Surely we should work with conscious purpose for a grand pacification of Europe, within the structure of the United Nations and in accordance with its Charter. That I feel is an open cause of policy of very great importance.

'The Communist parties or fifth columns constitute a growing challenge and peril to Christian civilization'

In front of the iron curtain which lies across Europe are other causes for anxiety. In Italy the Communist Party is seriously hampered by having to support the communist-trained Marshal Tito's claims to former Italian territory at the head of the Adriatic. Nevertheless the future of Italy hangs in the balance. Again one cannot imagine a regenerated Europe without a strong France. All my public life I have worked for a strong France and I never lost faith in her destiny, even in the darkest hours. I will not lose faith now. However, in a great number of countries, far from the Russian frontiers and throughout the world, communist fifth columnists are established and work in complete unity and absolute obedience to the directions they receive from the communist centre. Except in the British Commonwealth and in the United States where communism is in its infancy, the communist parties or fifth columns constitute a growing challenge and peril to Christian civilization. These are sombre facts for anyone to have to recite on the morrow of a victory gained by so much splendid comradeship in arms and in the cause of freedom and democracy; but we should be most unwise not to face them squarely while time remains.

The outlook is also anxious in the Far East and especially in Manchuria. The agreement which was made at Yalta, to which I was a party, was extremely favourable to Soviet Russia, but it was made at a time when no one could say that the German war might not extend all through the summer and autumn of 1945 and when the Japanese war was expected to last for a further 18 months from the end of the German war. In this country you are all so well-informed about the Far East, and such devoted friends of China, that I do not need to expatiate on the situation there.

'I do not see or feel that same confidence or even the same hopes in the haggard world at the present time'

I have felt bound to portray the shadow which, alike in the west and in the east, falls upon the world. I was a high minister at the time of the Versailles Treaty and a close friend of Mr Lloyd George, who was the head of the British delegation at Versailles. I did not myself agree with many things that were done, but I have a very strong impression in my mind of that situation, and I find it painful to contrast it with that which prevails now. In those days there were high hopes and unbounded confidence that the wars were over, and that the League of Nations would become all-powerful. I do not see or feel that same confidence or even the same hopes in the haggard world at the present time.

'Our difficulties and dangers will not be removed by closing our eyes to them'

On the other hand I repulse the idea that a new war is inevitable; still more that it is imminent. It is because I am sure that our fortunes are still in our own hands and that we hold the power to save the future, that I feel the duty to speak out now that I have the occasion and the opportunity to do so. I do not believe that Soviet Russia desires war. What they desire is the fruits of war and the indefinite expansion of their power and doctrines. But what we have to consider here today while time remains, is the permanent prevention of war and the establishment of conditions of freedom and democracy as rapidly as possible in all countries. Our difficulties and dangers will not be removed by closing our eyes to them. They will not be removed by mere waiting to see what happens; nor will they be removed by a policy of appeasement. What is needed is a settlement, and the longer this is delayed, the more difficult it will be and the greater our dangers will become.

From what I have seen of our Russian friends and Allies during the war, I am convinced that there is nothing they admire so much as strength, and there is nothing for which they have less respect than weakness, especially military weakness. For that reason the old doctrine of a balance of power is unsound. We cannot afford, if we can help it, to work on narrow margins, offering temptations to a trial of strength. If the western democracies stand together in strict adherence to the principles of the United Nations Charter, their influence for furthering those principles will be immense and no one is likely to molest them. If however they become divided or falter in their duty and if these all-important years are allowed to slip away then indeed catastrophe may overwhelm us all.

'There never was a war in all history easier to prevent by timely action than the one which has just desolated such great areas of the globe'

Last time I saw it all coming and cried aloud to my own fellow-countrymen and to the world, but no one paid any attention. Up till the year 1933 or even 1935, Germany might have been saved form the awful fate which has overtaken her and we might all have been spared the miseries Hitler let loose upon mankind. There never was a war in all history easier to prevent by timely action than the one which has just desolated such great areas of the globe. It could have been prevented in my belief without the firing of a single shot, and Germany might be powerful, prosperous and honoured today; but no one would listen and one by one we were all sucked into the awful whirlpool. We surely must not let that happen again. This can only be achieved by reaching now, in 1946, a good understanding on all points with Russia under the general authority of the United Nations Organization and by the maintenance of that good understanding through many peaceful years, by the world instrument, supported by the whole strength of the English-speaking word and all its connections. There is the solution which I respectfully offer to you in this Address to which I have the given the title 'The Sinews of Peace'.

'**If all British moral and material forces and convictions are joined with your own in fraternal association, the high-roads of the future will be clear**'

Let no man underrate the abiding power of the British Empire and Commonwealth. Because you see the 46 millions in our island harassed about their food supply, of which they only grow one half, even in wartime, or because we have difficulty in restarting our industries and export trade after six years of passionate war effort, do not suppose that we shall not come through these dark years of privation as we have come through the glorious years of agony, or that half a century from now, you will not see 70 or 80 millions of Britons spread about the world and united in defence of our traditions, our way of life, and of the world causes which you and we espouse. If the population of the English-speaking Commonwealths be added to that of the United States with all that such cooperation implies in the air, on the sea, all over the globe and in science and in industry, and in moral force, there will be no quivering, precarious balance of power to offer its temptation to ambition or adventure. On the contrary, there will be an overwhelming assurance of security. If we adhere faithfully to the Charter of the United Nations and walk forward in sedate and sober strength seeking no one's land or treasure, seeking to lay no arbitrary control upon the thoughts of men; if all British moral and material forces and convictions are joined with your own in fraternal association, the high-roads of the future will be clear, not only for us but for all, not only for our time, but for a century to come.

Index of Notable Lines

A miracle of deliverance, achieved by valour, by perseverance, by perfect discipline, by faultless service, by resource, by skill, by unconquerable fidelity, is manifest to us all. (p. 49)

And now it has come to us to stand alone in the breach, and face the worst that the tyrant's might and enmity can do. (p. 67)

'Arm yourselves, and be ye men of valour' (p. 45)

As they look out tonight from their blatant, panoplied, clattering Nazi Germany, they cannot find one single friendly eye in the whole circumference of the globe. (p. 26)

But in Germany, on a mountain peak, there sits one man, who in a single day can release the world from the fear which now oppresses it; or, in a single day can plunge all that we have and are into a volcano of smoke and flame. (p. 14)

'But westward look, the land is bright' (p. 100)

Death and ruin have become small things compared with the shame of defeat or failure in duty. (p. 74)

From Stettin in the Baltic to Trieste in the Adriatic, an iron curtain has descended across the Continent. (p. 198)

Herr Hitler protests with frantic words and gestures that he has only desired peace. What do these ravings and outpourings count before the silence of Neville Chamberlain's tomb? (p. 89)

History with its flickering lamp stumbles along the trail of the past, trying to reconstruct its scenes, to revive its echoes, and kindle with pale gleams the passion of former days. (p. 89)

Hitler and his Nazi gang have sown the wind; let them reap the whirlwind. (p. 129)

I always hate to compare Napoleon with Hitler, as it seems an insult to the great emperor and warrior to connect him in any way with a squalid caucus boss and butcher. (p. 175)

I am a child of the House of Commons. (p. 121)

I cannot forecast to you the action of Russia. It is a riddle wrapped in a mystery inside an enigma … (p. 20)

I have nothing to offer but blood, toil, tears and sweat. (p. 39)

I must admit that in all this war I never felt so grave a sense of responsibility as I did at Yalta. (p. 186)

If we are together, nothing is impossible. If we are divided, all will fail. (p. 158)

If we can stand up to him, all Europe may be free and the life of the world may move forward into broad, sunlit uplands. But if we fail, then the whole world, including the United States, including all that we have known and cared for, will sink into the abyss of a new dark age … (p. 59)

… in Franklin Roosevelt there died the greatest American friend we have ever known, and the greatest champion of freedom who has ever brought help and comfort from the New World to the Old. (p. 191)

In the past we have had a light which flickered, in the present we have a light which flames, and in the future there will be a light which shines over all the land and sea. (p. 118)

… let all of us who are here remember that we are on the stage of history, and that whatever our station may be, and whatever part we have to play, great or small, our conduct is liable to be scrutinized not only by history but by our own descendants. (p. 158)

Let us therefore brace ourselves to our duties, and so bear ourselves that, if the British Empire and its Commonwealth last for a thousand years, men will still say, 'This was their finest hour.' (p. 59)

Like the Mississippi, it just keeps rolling along. Let it roll. Let it roll on full flood, inexorable, irresistible, benignant, to broader lands and better days. (p. 77)

Military defeat or miscalculation can be redeemed. The fortunes of war are fickle and changing. But an act of shame would deprive us of the respect which we now enjoy throughout the world, and this would sap the vitals of our strength. (p. 98)

Never in the field of human conflict was so much owed by so many to so few. (p. 76)

Now that we are together, now that we are linked in a righteous comradeship of arms, now that our two considerable nations, each in perfect unity, have joined all their life energies in a common resolve, a new scene opens upon which a steady light will glow and brighten. (p. 124)

Now this is not the end. It is not even the beginning of the end. But it is, perhaps, the end of the beginning. (p. 138)

Outside, the storms of war may blow and the lands may be lashed with the fury of its gales, but in our own hearts this Sunday morning there is peace. (p. 13)

Peaceful parliamentary countries, which aim at freedom for the individual and abundance for the mass, start with a heavy handicap against a dictatorship whose sole theme has been war, the preparation for war, and the grinding up of everything and everybody into its military machine. (p. 25)

... the best tidings of all is that the United States, united as never before, have drawn the sword for freedom and cast away the scabbard. (p. 123)

The British nation is stirred and moved as it has never been at any time in its long, eventful, famous history, and it is no hackneyed trope of speech to say that they mean to conquer or to die. (p. 97)

... the fact that the British Empire stands invincible, and that Nazidom is still being resisted, will kindle again the spark of hope in the breasts of hundreds of millions of downtrodden or despairing men and women throughout Europe, and far beyond its bounds, and that from these sparks there will presently come cleansing and devouring flame. (p. 75)

There has never been, I suppose, in all the world, in all the history of war, such an opportunity for youth (p. 50)

There is a brotherhood in arms between us and our friends of the United States. (p. 169)

There is a hush over all Europe, nay, over all the world, broken only by the dull thud of Japanese bombs falling on Chinese cities ... (p. 13)

This is a war of the unknown warriors; but let all strive without failing in faith or in duty, and the dark curse of Hitler will be lifted from our age. (p. 69)

This is not a question of fighting for Danzig or fighting for Poland. We are fighting to save the whole world from the pestilence of Nazi tyranny and in defence of all that is most sacred to man. (p. 17)

This is your victory! It is the victory of the cause of freedom in every land. (p. 195)

Three and a half million Polish Jews are said to have been actually slaughtered. It is certain that enormous numbers have perished in one of the most horrifying acts of cruelty, probably the most horrifying act of cruelty, which has ever darkened the passage of man on the earth. (p. 183)

Twice in my lifetime the long arm of destiny has searched across the oceans and involved the entire life and manhood of the United States in a deadly struggle. (p. 157)

We mean to hold our own. I have not become the king's First Minister in order to preside over the liquidation of the British Empire. (p. 139)

... we have not only fortified our hearts but our island. (p. 74)

... we shall fight on the beaches, we shall fight on the landing grounds, we shall fight in the fields and in the streets, we shall fight in the hills; we shall never surrender ... (p. 52)

We shall not fail or falter; we shall not weaken or tire. Neither the sudden shock of battle, nor the long-drawn trials of vigilance and exertion will wear us down. Give us the tools, and we will finish the job. (p. 94)

What a frightful fate has overtaken Poland! ... ground beneath the heel of two rival forms of withering and blasting tyranny. (p. 31)

What General Weygand called the Battle of France is over. I expect that the Battle of Britain is about to begin. Upon this battle depends the survival of Christian civilization. (p. 59)

What is this New Order which they seek to fasten first upon Europe and if possible – for their ambitions are boundless – upon all the continents of the globe? It is the rule of the Herrenvolk – the master-race – who are to put an end to democracy, to parliaments, to the fundamental freedoms and decencies of ordinary men and women, to the historic rights of nations; and give them in exchange the iron rule of Prussia, the universal goose-step ... (p. 111)

What kind of a people do they think we are? Is it possible they do not realize that we shall never cease to persevere against them until they have been taught a lesson which they and the world will never forget. (p. 125)

When Herr Hitler escaped his bomb on July 20 he described his survival as providential; I think that from a purely military point of view we can all agree with him, for certainly it would be most unfortunate if the Allies were to be deprived, in the closing phases of the struggle, of that form of warlike genius by which Corporal Schickelgruber has so notably contributed to our victory. (p. 176)

When I warned them that Britain would fight on alone whatever they did, their generals told their prime minister and his divided Cabinet, 'In three weeks England will have her neck wrung like a chicken.' Some chicken. Some neck. (p. 129)

You ask what is our policy? I will say: It is to wage war, by sea, land and air, with all our might and with all the strength that God can give us ... You ask, what is our aim? I can answer in one word: Victory – victory at all costs, victory in spite of all terror, victory, however long and hard the road may be; for without victory, there is no survival. (p. 40)

Index

Picture credits
2 Getty Images; 9 Bettmann/Corbis;
10 & 15 Getty Images; 18 Corbis;
23 Hulton-Deutsch Collection/
Corbis; 28, 33 & 37 Getty Images;
41 & 46 Hulton-Deutsch
Collection/Corbis; 53 Bettmann/
Corbis; 60 Getty Images; 65 Corbis;
70 Bettmann/Corbis; 78 Getty
Images; 83 & 87 Hulton-Deutsch
Collection/Corbis; 90 Hulton-
Deutsch-Collection/Corbis;
95 Getty Images; 101 Corbis; 107,
115, 119, 127 & 131 Bettmann/
Corbis; 135 Time & Life Pictures/
Getty Images; 141 Getty Images;
146 Bettmann/Corbis; 151 Corbis;
156 & 159 Time & Life Pictures/
Getty Images; 166 Hulton-Deutsch
Collection/Corbis; 171 dpa/Corbis;
178 Hulton-Deutsch Collection/
Corbis; 187 Bettmann/Corbis; 192
Jonathan Ernst/Reuters/Corbis; 196
Time & Life Pictures/Getty Images

Project manager
Mark Hawkins-Dady

Editor
Rosie Anderson

Design
Jane McKenna

Picture research
Su Alexander

Proofreader
Gordon Lee

Indexer
Patricia Hymans

First published in Great Britain in 2007 by

Quercus
21 Bloomsbury Square
London
WC1A 2NS

Introductions © Graham Stewart 2007
Speeches © Crown copyright / Estate of Winston S. Churchill

A CIP catalogue reference for this book is available from the
British Library

Cloth case edition
ISBN 10: 1 84724 201 4
ISBN 13: 978 1 84724 201 3

Printed case edition
ISBN 10: 1 84724 193 X
ISBN 13: 978 1 84724 193 1

Printed and bound in China

10 9 8 7 6 5 4 3 2 1